HANDFULS ON PURPOSE

SERIES VI

BY

Pastor JAMES SMITH

Author of "A Survey of the Wondrous Cross,"
"Spiritual Patterns" etc.

WM. B. EERDMANS PUBLISHING COMPANY

Grand Rapids   Michigan

American Edition

————

Published in 1947, by

WM. B. EERDMANS PUBLISHING CO.
by
Special Arrangement with

PICKERING & INGLIS, LTD.
14 Paternoster Row, London, E.C.4
229 Bothwell St., Glasgow, C.2
Manchester—Newcastle—Liverpool—Edinburgh

PHOTOLITHOPRINTED BY GRAND RAPIDS BOOK MANUFACTURERS, INC.
GRAND RAPIDS, MICHIGAN
PRINTED IN THE UNITED STATES OF AMERICA

Guide to Series 1 to 12

OLD TESTAMENT

NEW TESTAMENT

SERIES 1 to 10 .. By Pastor JAMES SMITH
SERIES 11 and 12, .. By ROBERT LEE
SERIES 13, COMPLETE INDEX TO SERIES

ORIGINAL PREFACE

THESE *Handfuls* do not claim to have any literary or critical value. They have been sent out after much prayerful study of the Word in the hope that they might be helpful to some busy workers for the Master who may not have much leisure for study.

In these days when there is so much to tempt us away from the simplicity of the truth it is needful for us to have our own minds and hearts well fortified with the deep and powerful thoughts of God. Other facts and things may interest and amuse, but we must have the "sincere milk of the Word" if we are to GROW. Everything that awakens and increases our appreciation of the Word of God is of immense value to our spiritual life, but our love for and delight in the Word will only be in proportion as we go on to *experience* its mighty power in our lives. We are convinced that the way to stir up and deepen the desires of others after Christ and the Scriptures is to present those God-given truths which meet the needs of an individual soul in all its various states and conditions. No book in all the world comes within a thousand miles of the Bible in this great and glorious mission, "PREACH THE WORD."

JAMES SMITH.

PREFACE TO SIXTH SERIES

THIS Sixth Volume will, we trust, be found quite as fresh and helpful as any of its companions. As our readers are aware, their aim is more to be spiritual than critical or historical. We can lay no claim to the critical faculty, but such as we have we desire to give. There are abundance of other books, easily accessible, where a careful criticism of the text can be had. What we are concerned about is to encourage the reader to dig deeper down into those rich veins of spiritual thought that abound beneath the surface of this wonderful Book, that stimulate and enrich the inner man. After all that we can say, we feel that we have just slightly scratched the surface of the field. But so rich is the soil here, that even a scratch reveals some sparkling gems beneath. The treasures hid in this field are not meant to be discovered by chance; they yield themselves plentifully to the hand of the diligent seeker. "SEEK AND YE SHALL FIND."

J. S.

GENERAL INDEX OF SUBJECTS

BIBLE READINGS.

SEED THOUGHTS.

ILLUSTRATIONS.

INDEX OF TEXTS

Handfuls on Purpose

Expositions, Bible Readings, and Illustrations

ELIJAH, THE MAN OF GOD
2 KINGS 1. 1-16

"A king sang once
Long years ago: 'My soul is athirst for God,
Yea, for the living God '—thy thirst and his
Are one. . . . Life is not enough,
Nor love, nor learning—Death is not enough,
Give us now, now!—to live in the life of God;
Give us now, now!—to be at one with HIM."—*Ingelow.*

AHAZIAH, the son of a wicked father, meets with an accident, and is sick, then he desires to inquire of the god of Ekron. His fall might have been a great blessing to him as it made him feel the need of divine assistance; but, instead of calling upon the God of Heaven, he chose to inquire of the god of flies, and thus ignore the Lord God ot Israel. But God is not mocked; He thrusts His servant Elijah right in front of the king's messengers with the sentence of death. The prophet appears before us here as a "man of God," and as such let us consider him.

I. **He was Commissioned.** "The angel of the Lord said unto Elijah, Arise, go...and say unto them, Is it

because there is no God in Israel that ye go to inquire of
Baal-zebub?" (v. 3, R.V.). As a man of God, he was called
upon to speak on God's behalf. Is there not a great need
for definite testimony along this line to-day, when multitudes are forsaking God, the Fountain of Living Water,
and hewing out for themselves broken cisterns that can
hold no water (Jer. 2. 11-13). Is it because Christ has
failed that men seek after the pleasures of sin? Is it
because the Gospel of God has lost its power that men go
after another gospel? Oh, man of God, be true to thy
calling, and preach Christ.

II. **He was Believed.** The turning back of the
messengers proved that they were convinced that this man
spoke with more than human authority, then, after describ-
ing his appearance to the king, he said, "It is Elijah the
Tishbite" (v. 8). The manner of the "man of God"
cannot be the same as ordinary mortals. If Elijah had
addressed them in the fashion in which many preach the
Gospel, they would have smiled and went on after their
"lying vanities" to the forsaking of their own mercy.
(Jonah 2.8). Although they knew not the name of the man,
they felt that there was a supernatural ring about his
message. "It is Elijah!" It is just like that man who is
constantly doing wonders in the name of his God, in turning
sinners from the error of their ways.

III. **He was Mocked.** Ahaziah did not blame his
servants from turning back, but that man for predicting his
death. So a captain with his fifty men were ordered to
apprehend him. They found Elijah on the top of a hill
(perhaps Carmel), and, in a tone of contempt and insolence,
they said: "Thou man of God, the king hath said, Come
down" (v. 9), as if the saying of the king was of greater
weight than the message of God. He demanded him to
come down. The captain of the second fifty was even

more insolent in saying, "Come down quickly." They seemed utterly helpless of themselves to bring him down. There is a hill-top from which no power on earth can bring down a "man of God"—that is the hill-top of peaceful communion in the divine presence. It is the delight of the enemy to get a man of God down. (See Neh. 6. 2, 3).

IV. He was Vindicated. "Elijah said, If I be a man of God, then let fire come down from Heaven," etc. (vv. 10-12). There are those who labour to justify Elijah here, as if Elijah had manufactured the avenging fire, or had prevailed on God to do something derogatory to his holy character. It was the Holy Name of God these captains were sneering at when they spoke so contemptuously of the man of God. The devouring fire was God's vindication of His own Name as represented by His servant Elijah. Our God is a consuming fire, and He will not hold them guiltless who taketh His Name in vain. Elijah did not need to vindicate himself, but His God, who is ever jealous of His Holy Name, did it in a most convincing and overwhelming fashion. It is God that justifieth. "Take heed, that ye despise not one of these little (humble) ones which believe in ME" (Matt. 18. 10).

V. He was Feared. The third captain, who came with his fifty, came in a different spirit. He had learned, through the terrible doom of his predecessors, that this seemingly meek and helpless "man of God" was not to be spoken against with impunity. He was a man for whom the Almighty fought, and who had all the forces of Heaven on his side. "He came and fell on his knees before Elijah, and besought him for his life and the life of the fifty." He had discovered that it was not only with the man he had to do, but with the God who was for the man.

VI. He was Obedient. "The angel of the Lord said unto Elijah, Go down with him, and he arose and went"

(v. 15). The third captain prevailed, not by commanding
the man of God to "come down," but by casting himself
down at the prophet's feet. God had respect unto this
man's prayer. It was just like a man of God to be ready
to render immediate obedience to the Lord whenever His
will is made known, whether the call is to go up or go
down. "Anywhere with Jesus," says the Christian heart.

VII. He was Faithful. He went down to Samaria,
not as a prisoner, but as a prince surrounded with his body-
guard, and fearlessly delivered his unwelcome message to
the guilty king (v. 16). He would surely die, because
he had sought help from the dead god of Ekron, and had
despised the living God of Israel. Every soul that so sins
shall surely die. Oh, man, fallen by thy sin, and sick unto
death, hear His voice of mercy saying, "Look unto ME, and
be ye saved,...for I am God, and there is none else"·-who
can deliver. "There is none other Name under Heaven,
given among men, whereby we must be saved." (Acts 6. 12).

ELISHA;

OR, EQUIPPED FOR SERVICE.

2 KINGS 2. 1-15.

"Only work that is for God alone
　Hath an increasing guerdon of delight;
A guerdon unaffected by the sight
　Of great success, nor by its loss o'erthrown."—*Havergal.*

WHILE at the plough "Elijah cast his mantle upon him"
(1 Kings 19. 19). Having been overshadowed with the
prophetic mantle, is the sure evidence of being "Called of
God." Elisha did not preach as a candidate. The "Call"
of God is always accompanied with the needed fitness (see
Lev. 8. vv. 1, 6, 13, 24, 30; Isa. 6). Let us look at Elisha
as a type of the faithful servant of Christ. He—

I. Follows his Master's Footsteps. "As thy soul

liveth, I will not leave thee" (vv. 2-6). He followed his master from Bethel—the House of God—to Jordan, the place of Death and Separation. Personal devotion ought to keep us walking closely with the Master (Ruth 1. 16). Peter followed afar off, and we know the consequence.

II. **Shares his Master's Victory.** "The waters were divided, and they two went over on dry ground" (v. 8). As with Elijah, so with Christ, the dark waters of death (Jordan) rolled between him and his ascension into Heaven, but he went through them. We, His followers, now share His victory (Rom. 6. 4; Gal. 2. 20; 1 Cor. 15. 55-57).

III. **Seeks his Master's Spirit.** "Let a double portion of thy spirit be upon me" (v. 9). He loved to be with his master, now he seeks to be like him. This is always the outcome of knowing Jesus—the desire to be made conformable (Phil. 3. 10). Every Christian has the common portion of the spirit (Rom. 8. 9). How few seem to have the double portion (Acts 19. 2; 1 John 2. 27). Covet earnestly the best gifts.

IV. **Witnesses his Master's Glory.** "Behold there appeared a chariot of fire, and Elijah went up into Heaven. And Elisha saw it" (vv. 11, 12). Having followed Christ unto death and burial by faith, we become eye-witnesses of His Resurrection Glory (Rom. 6. 11; 2 Peter 1. 16, 17). Elisha must follow his master over Jordan to see him taken up. Before Christ lives in us we die with Him (Gal. 2. 20). It was such a sight as made him rend his own clothes in pieces (Gen. 37: 29).

V. **Receives his Master's Gifts.** "He took up the mantle of Elijah that fell from him" (v. 13). The mantle falling from the ascending master seems emblematic of the Holy Spirit's coming after Jesus was glorified. This holy mantle may be accepted or left-unused. To Elisha it was the token of his receiving a double portion of his master's spirit. Without this gift we can never, as we ought, beseech men in Christ's stead (2 Cor. 5. 20).

VI. **Overcomes in his Master's Name.** "He took the mantle and smote the waters, and they parted hither and thither" (v. 14). He overcame by the gift from above. In the name of our Risen Lord, and with the anointing from above, great and mighty things are to be done (Eph. 3. 20). See what Peter accomplished after the mantle of power fell upon him (Acts 2. 14).

VII. **Manifests his Master's Likeness.** "When the sons of the prophets saw him, they said, The spirit of Elijah doth rest on Elisha" (v. 15). He did his master's works, and so reflected his master's image. Does our life and testimony call forth such a confession (Acts 4. 13). Let us rend our own clothes (self-will) in pieces and take up the mantle (Spirit) of our glorified Lord and Master, that we may show forth the power of His resurrection by doing His works (John 14. 12-13).

ELIJAH AND CHRIST.
2 KINGS 2. 1-15.

"Arise, for the day is passing,
And you lie dreaming on;
The others have buckled their armour
And forth to the fight are gone.
A place in the ranks awaits you,
Each man has some part to play;
The past and the future are nothing
In the face of a stern to-day."—*Procter.*

ARISE, the whole course of the Christian life is one grand ascension out of darkness into His marvellous light: out of the self life into the life of God; a forgetting of the things that are behind, and a pressing onward and upward after those things that are above. A resurrected life implies resurrected affections. The manner of Elijah's departure forcibly reminds us of our Lord Jesus Christ, and leads us to think of some other points of resemblance between them. He was like Christ—

I. In the Character of his Ministry. Like our Saviour, Elijah was very much alone in the fulfilment of his mission. Both had a definite message from God, both had power to close or open the heavens. Elijah, like our Lord, was reckoned an enemy by those whom he came specially to help. Both were despised, while yet they were dreaded. Elijah's ministry, like Christ's, began by the showing of himself as one whose character had hitherto been unknown (1 Kings 17. 1), and ended with a translation.

II. In his Glorious Prospect. Elijah evidently knew that he was to be suddenly taken into Heaven by a whirl-wind (vv. 1, 2). He had the blessed hope of passing, in bodily form, into the Kingdom above. So was it also with Jesus Christ after He had passed through the Jordan of death. He said unto Mary, "Touch Me not, for I am not yet ascended unto My Father" (John 20. 17). Is this not the hope that is set before us? "We shall not all sleep (die), but we must all be changed. In a moment, at the last trump, this mortal shall put on immortality." He that "hath this hope in him purifieth himself, even as He is pure" (1 John 3. 3).

III. In his Victory over Jordan. The deep, dark waters of Jordan rolled between him and the place of his glorious ascent to the heavenly mansion. They were divided hither and thither when smitten by his mantle. The mantle was the symbol of the prophetic office turned into a weapon of divine power. Jesus Christ overcame the Jordan of death by smiting it with the mantle of His sacred body. "The waters saw Thee, O God, the waters saw Thee; they were afraid: the depths also were troubled" (Psa. 77.16). By His death on the Cross the waters of sin fled, and the depths of Hell were troubled.

IV. In his Relation to his Followers. "So that
they two went over on dry ground." Elijah and his
successor were undivided in Jordan. Elisha went down
with his master, and, for the time, became buried together with him in this new-made grave. If he had
stopped short of this he would have missed the "double
portion." We must be planted together in the likeness of
Christ's death if we would be also in the likeness of His
resurrection (Rom. 6. 5, 6). Self must go down into
death with Christ if we would rise in newness of life,
clothed with His mantle of divine authority (Gal. 2. 20,21).

V. In his Gracious Offer. "Elijah said unto Elisha,
Ask what I shall do for thee before I be taken from thee"
(v. 9). His loving master is about to vanish out of his
sight, but ere he goes he, as it were, throws the door of
Heaven open, and gives his servant a glimpse of its
treasures and the opportunity of "asking what he will."
This Christ did when He promised the Holy Spirit to His
disciples before He was taken away from them. As Elijah
had to go before he could send down the mantle, so Christ
had to depart before the Spirit could be given (John 16. 7).
In promising the Holy Spirit, Christ was like Elijah, putting
within the reach of His followers the possibility of "asking
what ye will, and it shall be done unto you" (John 15. 7).

VI. In his Glorious Homegoing. "Elijah went up
into Heaven,...and he saw him no more" (vv. 11, 12).
"The time was coming that He (Christ) should be received
up" (Luke 9. 51); "and while they beheld," like Elijah,
"He was taken up, and received out of their sight"(Acts 1.9).
Like Enoch, he walked with God, and he was not, for God
took Him. Blessed are all they who are so firmly assured
of the glorification of their Master: "Eye-witnesses of His
Majesty" (2 Peter 1. 16).

VII. In his Special Gift. "Elisha took up the

mantle that fell from Elijah, and went back, and smote the waters" (vv. 13-15). Like the disciples in the upper room, he tarried till he had received his master's gift from above—that gift, in the power of which wonders were to be wrought in His name. His master was gone, but now "greater works" were to be done through this heavenly gift, which was to be to him a "double portion." Have we so eagerly appropriated that mantle that has fallen for us in His gift of the Holy Ghost, that the works of our ascended Master may be reproduced by us? Elijah wrought seven miracles, but Elisha with the "double portion of his spirit" was able to perform fourteen (John 14. 12). "Have ye received the Holy Ghost?" (Acts 19. 2).

THE HEALING OF THE WATERS.
2 KINGS 2. 19-22.

> "He always wins who sides with God,
>   To him no chance is lost;
> God's will is sweet to him when
>   It triumphs at his cost."—*Faber*.

JERICHO had come under the blight of the divine curse. Like this sin-ruined world, it could only be restored by the sacrifice of a first-born (Josh. 6. 26; Col. 1. 14, 15). All the wealth and wisdom in Jericho could not remove its plague of "bitter waters," neither can the power or wisdom of men stop the outflow, or change the nature, of the bitter waters of sin. The power of the LORD alone is sufficient for all this (v. 21). The need of this city represents the need of every sin-polluted life—divine healing.

I. **Its Condition.** This is viewed in two different aspects—

1. ITS SITUATION WAS PLEASANT (v.9). As far as outward privileges were concerned, everything was favourable. The soil was rich in possibilities, the climate was the finest,

the site of the city was delightful. What a picture of a sinner in the midst of favourable circumstances! What possibilities lie within the reach of the soul of man! "The situation is pleasant" of all who are surrounded with Gospel privileges. But these in themselves are not enough.

2.—ITS GROUND WAS BARREN. Labour as they may, their toil did not bring satisfaction. Those "brackish" waters continually failed to yield them the desire of their hearts. Such is the state of those whose hearts have not been healed by the Word of God. The figs of true satisfaction and the grapes of holy joy cannot grow on the thistle and thorns of man's unrenewed nature. Out of the heart are the issues of life (James 3. 11). An evil heart will always send out bitter waters in the sight of God (Matt. 15. 19, 20). Who can bring a clean thing out of an unclean?

II. The Remedy.

1.—ITS NATURE. "A new cruse with salt therein" (v. 20). This "new cruse" may be a fit emblem of the New Testament, with Christ as the salt of salvation therein. The prophet here signifies that the salt represents the healing virtue of Jehovah (v. 21). This salt has never lost its savour. "There is none other name under Heaven given among men, whereby we must be saved."

2.—ITS APPLICATION. "He cast the salt into the spring" (v. 21). He did not attempt to heal the streams apart from the fountain. He went straight to the source of the evil at once. The salt could work no healing miracle on the spring until it got into contact with it. Those who go about to establish their own righteousness are trying to purify the stream while the spring remains unhealed. It is not Christ in the Bible that saves, but Christ in the heart. Our Lord cast the salt into the spring of life when He said to Nicodemus, "Ye must be born again!" "Have salt in yourselves" (Mark 9. 50). "Christ in you the hope of glory" (Col. 1. 27).

III. The Results.

1.—THERE WAS HEALING. "So the waters were healed" (v. 22). The streams were healed, because the fountain head was regenerated. Make the tree good and the fruit will be good. If the heart springs are pure, the streams of action will be pure and healthful. The waters may not be more copious than they were, but they will be much more welcome and beneficial. So will it be with the outcome of the life when Christ comes into the spring of the heart and renews the waters of actions. The healed waters may abide in the same channel, but oh, how different the results! It is a passing from death unto life.

2.—THERE WAS FRUITFULNESS. "There shall not be from thence any more death or barren land" (v. 21). Death and barrenness are turned into life and fruitfulness when the power of the divine transformer gets into the being. It is easy to bring forth good fruits when the disease of sin and uncleanness have been taken out of the life. Fruit is the outcome of what we are more than of what we do (John 15. 4). A polluted heart makes a barren heart. These poisonous waters were changed suddenly, they did not gradually grow better. It was the expulsive power of a new infection. If any man have not the Spirit of Christ he is none of His.

FLOODS OF BLESSING IN NEW-MADE DITCHES.
2 KINGS 3. 6-25.

"Feeble hands and helpless,
Groping blindly in the darkness,
Touch God's right hand in that darkness."—*Longfellow.*

AFTER the death of Ahab the king of Moab refused to pay his tax of 100,000 lambs and 100,000 rams, with the wool, to Jehoram, the son of Ahab. This led to the union

of the three kings and a declaration of war against Moab.
Several singular things happened which may be full of
significance for us.

I. **A Great Need.** "There was no water for the host" (v.9).
The number of the host was great, and thoroughly equipped
with all the implements of warfare, but they were powerless
because perishing of thirst. A picture of a Church,
thoroughly organised and fully equipped with all the means
of warfare, but utterly helpless because the refreshing stream
of God's saving power is not among them (Acts 1. 8).

II. **An Urgent Inquiry.** "Is there not a prophet of
the Lord, that we inquire of the Lord by him?" (vv. 11-14).
What a scene—three kings begging a favour from a man
who had but lately left the plough. If the water had been
plentiful they would have acted quite independently
either of God or Elisha. It was when the prodigal "began
to be in want" that he thought of his father's house. The
faithful man of God does not fail to remind the king of
Israel of his hypocrisy in serving other gods in the day of
his prosperity, and then seeking the help of Jehovah when
the wells were dry (v. 13). It is the old story of man's
pride and poverty. The Lord and His servants are often
ignored till the day of affliction comes.

III. **A Strange Demand.** "But now bring me a
minstrel" (v. 15). The prophet respects the presence of
Jehoshaphat, and is willing to hear what God the Lord will
speak to them through him. His spirit is perhaps somewhat troubled at this unexpected turn of events in the
attitude of these kings, and he knows that to hear the
"still small voice" of God there must be perfect calmness
of soul in His presence. The minstrel might help him to
be still that he might know the mind of the Lord (see 1 Sam.
16. 23). Music has its place in the service of God, but the
mischief in our days is that the people get more interested in

the minstrels than in the message of God. In fact, the minstrel is now sometimes found taking the place of the prophet. But the great need of the people is the Word of God.

IV. **A Definite Message.** "Make this valley full of ditches;...that valley shall be filled with water" (vv. 16, 17). Ditch-making is a very humble work; but the deeper they dig the larger the blessing. Room must be made for the fulfilment of the promise of God. It is but a "light thing in His sight" to send floods of blessing in an unexpected way. The digging of the ditches was an evidence of their faith in God's Word, and that their expectation was from Him. They believed, and therefore prepared the way for the promised waters. Are we making any ditches in the valleys of our Christian experience, where the river of God might enter and remain as an abiding blessing? Prepare ye the way. Make room for God.

V. **An Abundant Supply.** "In the morning, when the meat-offering was offered, . . . the country was filled with water" (v. 20). This labour of faith was abundantly rewarded, for every man's ditch became a well of water. The blessing of God, it made them rich. Of His fullness did they all receive. There was no excuse for their continuing in a state of paralysing thirst after God had given them this great gift. They would not be such fools as to refuse to accept the gift until they could understand its source, and course, and character. It was the river of life to them; it was nigh even in their own ditches, and there was all-sufficiency for all. God's answer to the prayer of faith will always be to the full. Give to Him, and it shall be given unto you again "full measure, pressed down, and running over" (Luke 6. 38).

VI. **A Twofold Result.** The Moabites deluded, and the Israelites saved (vv. 21-25). That which was the means of bringing deliverance to the one brought destruction to the other.   The same Gospel, which is a savour of life to the believer, is a savour of death to the doubter. These waters, which brought salvation to the host, appeared to the Moabites only as the blood of the slain.   There are those still who can see nothing in God's great provision, as revealed in Calvary's Cross, but the blood of the martyr. Because of their sin God had sent these Moabites a strong delusion, so that they all believed a lie, that they all might be condemned (2 Thess. 2. 11, 12).   For if our Gospel be hid, it is hid to them that are lost (2 Cor. 4. 3, 4).   This stream of salvation, like the pillar of cloud, was not what it seemed to be in the eyes of the ungodly.   So with the preaching of the Cross; to them that perish it is foolishness, but to the saved it is the power of God.   "Now, therefore, Moab to the spoil" was their cry, as soon as they believed that the host had been "smiting one another."   Whenever the Lord's people take to smiting one another the enemy will hasten to the spoil.   But in this case they walked by sight, and were deluded and defeated.   The leaders of the host believed the message of God at the lips of Elisha, prepared the ditches, and in answer to the cry of these empty channels the gift of God came, and was received; then, in the strength of that gift, they overcame.   "Thanks be unto God who giveth us the victory through our Lord Jesus Christ" (1 Cor. 15. 57).

THE WIDOW'S OIL;
Or, Grace Sufficient.
2 Kings 4. 1-7.

'"It may be hard to gain, and still
    To keep a lowly, steadfast heart,
Yet he who loses has to fill
    A harder and a truer part."—*Procter*.

Seasons of affliction are common to all, but only the children of God have wonders wrought for them in such experiences. It is on the cloudy day that the rainbow of His promise is most easily seen. There is always a fruitful "afterwards" to those whose souls are exercised in the day of trouble (Heb. 12. 11). It was while the Israelites were in the desert that they saw the glory of God's goodness in giving them bread from Heaven and water from the flinty rock. This widow of one of the sons of the prophets has been brought into deep water, but see how God in His infinite grace and power was able to supply all her need. Observe the order—

I. **Destitution Confessed.** "She cried, saying, The creditor is come to take my two sons to be bondsmen" (v. 1). Her husband is dead, and being hopelessly in debt, her sons, who are her only hope for the future, are about to be sold. What a sorrowful plight! Yet she honestly confesses the whole truth. Such were some of us when the law as a merciless creditor came suddenly upon us, saying, "Pay me that thou owest" (Matt. 18. 28), and when we discovered that we had "nothing wherewith to pay" (Luke 7. 42), that we were already "sold under sin." Being shut up to faith, what else could we do but cry unto Him who is the true Elisha, "the mighty to save?"

II. **Grace Offered.** "What shall I do for thee?" (v. 2). Elisha, as God's representative, flings back, as it were, the door of heavenly privilege that she might ask what she will. It was the offer of grace sufficient for all her need. So poor was she that she had nothing in the house "save a pot of oil." But poverty is no obstacle in the presence of Almighty grace and fullness (Luke 18. 41). It is those who think that they have need of nothing who shut the Saviour outside of their lives (Rev. 3. 20). What shall I do for thee? "Open thy mouth wide, and I will fill it" (Psa. 81. 10).

III. **Preparation Needed.** "Go, borrow thee vessels,

empty vessels, not a few" (v. 3). As yet, she had no
room for the great blessing God was about to give her. It
is wonderful how even our neighbours, by their kindness or
otherwise, may supply us with that which will enrich us
with heavenly blessing. The borrowing of empty vessels
was an exercise of faith. She believed that she might see.
It was so with the Israelites when they made the "valley
full of ditches" (2 Kings 3. 16-20). The relative value of
each vessel to her was according to its capacity for receiving.
This is also God's manner of dealing with His vessels of
grace (2 Cor. 12. 10).

IV. Faith Rewarded. "She poured out, and the
vessels were filled" (vv. 5, 6). It was a great crisis in
this woman's life when she "shut the door upon her and her
sons," and ventured, as in the presence of God alone, to
claim the promise by faith. When one has made up his or
her mind to "shut the door" and definitely prove God,
there will surely be a marvellous outpouring of the oil of the
Holy Spirit (Matt. 6. 6). She could not make the oil, any
more than we can manufacture the saving grace of God, but
she could hold the vessel and trust God to cause the outflow. Her faith was rewarded to the very uttermost, for
every empty vessel was filled.

V. Blessing Hindered. "There was not a vessel
more; and the oil stayed" (v. 6). As long as there was
an empty vessel, and faith to use the gift of God, there was
no lack. His grace was made sufficient. We are never
straitened in God, but always in ourselves, when the flow
of His blessing is stayed. Whenever our conscious weakness
gives place to self-satisfaction, then the oil of His Spirit's
power is hindered and arrested (Micah 2. 7). The blessings
of His grace, although in Him there is infinite fullness, yet
are they too precious to be poured out and spilt where there
is not the empty vessel of a needy heart. Grace can only

be given to meet a real need (2 Cor. 12. 9). There are
those who talk joyfully of the times past, when the God-
given oil flowed freely. But why is it stayed now?
(Judges 16. 20). No more emptiness!

VI. **Deliverance Accomplished.** "Go, sell the oil,
and pay thy debt" (v. 7). Having received the gift of
God, she is able now to meet all the claims of the creditor.
She and her sons were saved by grace alone. The claims of
a broken law can only be fully met by us through the
infinite grace of God brought to us by Jesus Christ; by that
love of God which is shed abroad in our hearts by the Holy
Ghost, and which is the "fulfilling of the law." If these
sons were asked how they were saved from bondage, they
could truly say, by the "gift of God." It is not otherwise
with us (John 3. 16).

VII. **Provision Made.** "Live thou and thy children
of the rest" (v. 7). The oil, which saved them from debt
and slavery, was also to sustain them day by day. The
children of Israel were not only saved by the blood of the
lamb, but sustained by feasting on it (Exod. 12. 8). Christ
came not only to redeem us from the curse of the law, but also
to satisfy us daily, as the "bread of God" which came down
from Heaven. Live thou and thy children by faith upon
the Son of God, who paid all thy debt upon Calvary's Cross.
What is still left, through His grace for thee and thine, is
sufficient for all your needs, both for time and eternity.

THE GREAT SHUNAMMITE;
OR, FEATURES OF A CHRISTIAN WOMAN.
2 KINGS 4. 8-37.

SHUNEM lay on the road between Samaria and Carmel,
where was a school of the prophets. How refreshing would
the little chamber and the Shunammite's care be after a
weary tramp of thirty miles in the heat and over the warm

dust of an eastern road. The Lord has many a way of digging wells of refreshing for heavenly pilgrims. Those who give even a cup of cold water in the name of a disciple, like this good Shunammite, they shall not lose their reward. This woman was great in the sight of the Lord. Observe wherein her greatness consisted. She was:

I. **Benevolent.** "She constrained him to eat bread" (v. 8). The love of God is not in our heart if our charity acts only like an echo. The love of Christ did not wait to be solicited (Rom. 5. 8).

II. **Discerning.** "I perceive that this is a holy man of God" (v. 9). Being herself pure in heart, she could see God in the prophet (Matt. 5. 8). Pride and self-conceit so blind the minds of some that they cannot distinguish between a prophet and a profligate. Devotion is branded as cant (John 10. 20).

III. **Contented.** "What is to be done for thee?" she answered, "I dwell among mine own people" (v. 13). A grumbling wife makes a cloudy home. Godliness, with contentment, is great gain. The divine recipe for discontent is given in Hebrews 13. 5, 6.

IV. **Sober-minded.** She said, "Thou man of God, do not lie unto thine handmaid" (v. 16). The promise of a son seemed too much for her to expect. So she reminded Elisha that he was a man of God, and as such he should not flatter for favour. In her soul she hated unreality, and loved the truth. She would have been poor company for clamouring gossips.

V. **Submissive.** She said, "It shall be well" (v. 23). Although her beloved child had died, with impressive resignation she said, "It shall be well." The greatest of all Sufferers, when in the flood of affliction, "opened not His mouth," knowing that "It shall be well." Ye have heard of the patience of Job.

VI. Believing. When asked, "Is it well with the child?" she answered, "It is well." It is easy saying, "It is well," while the tide of prosperity continues to flow. It takes faith to say it amidst the gloom of death (Job 13. 15). Doubtless this is one of the women we read of in Hebrews 11. 35. Faith is always rewarded.

VII. Persevering. "I will not leave thee" (v. 30). She had faith in the prophet, and would not go without a blessing. Think of the effect of Jacob's faith (Gen. 32. 26). We have no unjust judge to deal with; then why do we prevail so seldom? (Luke 18).

VIII. Successful. He said, "Take up thy son. She went in and fell at his feet" (v. 37). She was not so taken up with the blessing as to forget the blesser. Mother, beware lest you be more concerned about the prosperity of your family than the honour of your Lord and Master (Matt. 6. 33).

LIFE THROUGH THE LIVING;
Or, How to Win Souls.
2 Kings 4. 18-35.

"I am young, happy, and free.
I can devote myself; I have a life to give."—*Browning*.

THAT was a dark and cloudy day for this woman of Shunem, when her only son died suddenly on her knees "at noon" (v. 20). In her distress she hastens to him through whom she had been blessed, whose promise she had already tested. "Call upon Me in the day of trouble, and I will deliver you, and ye shall glorify Me." This far-seeing woman would neither trust the prophet's servant nor the staff on which he leaned, her faith was in himself (v. 30). It would be good for every troubled one to learn the same lesson. Christ Himself is the source of blessing, not His servant, nor even the staff of His Word. Without the Spirit of Life, even the Word on which He leaned as on a staff will be powerless to waken the dead in sin (2 Cor. 3. 6). It was undoubtedly the will of God that this child of promise should be raised and restored. We have here two efforts made to do this—the one a complete failure, the other a perfect success.

I. **Gehazi, or the Failure of Formalism.** This man seems to be typical of a class of Christian workers that are not uncommon in our own days. He was—

1. OBEDIENT. He was ready to run at any moment at his master's bidding. He has a powerful conviction that he ought to obey (v. 26). No man is more important than he is when about his master's business. He is faithful to the letter of the word, "saluting no man by the way" (v. 29). He will magnify his office if he should never be the means of helping a soul out of the darkness of death into the light of life.

2. UNSYMPATHETIC. He had no word of encouragement for this sorrowful woman, but would have "thrust her away," had not his gracious master said, "Let her alone" (v. 27). He had no eye to see a "vexed soul," but was quick to discern anything irregular or disorderly in her manner. He would stick up for rule and order, even when burdened souls are agonising for the Spirit of Life. He is the brother of those who are destitute of spiritual discernment, and who work for the master because they are paid for it.

3. PRAYERLESS. "Go thy way, and lay my staff upon the face of the child" (v. 29). It would appear that Elisha sent his servant with his staff, either to test the woman's faith, to humble the servant's pride, or perhaps just to get rid of him for the time being. At anyrate, Gehazi went off with the staff, and was evidently so full of self-importance and conceit that he felt no need of crying to God for His mighty power to accompany his effort in trying

to awaken the dead. Self-confidence is inconsistent with the prayer of faith.

4. POWERLESS. "The child is not awaked" (v. 31) It was the prophet's staff right enough, but the prophet was awanting. It is not enough that ye preach the truth, the mere letter of the Word will not raise the dead any more than the staff of the prophet. It is the Spirit that quickeneth. We may lay the very Word of Christ, like a staff, upon the face of a congregation fifty times a year, but none will be "awaked" unless there is the prayer of faith and the laying on of ourselves for the salvation of men. Those who think that they are doing their duty by going through the form of religious service are not likely to see the dead raised by their instrumentality.

II. **Elisha, or the Victory of Faith.** The manner of this man of God is in sharp contrast to the formalism of his heartless servant. There was—

1. REAL SYMPATHY. His heart was deeply stirred on behalf of the sorrowing woman (v. 27). He felt keenly the great importance of the occasion, although the Lord had hid the secret of it from him. Until the heart of the servant of God is moved with compassion by that cry of need, so often raised at our own feet through sin and death, there is little hope of that servant ever accomplishing any great deliverance in the Name of God.

2. BELIEVING PRAYER. "He went in and shut the door, and prayed unto the Lord" (v. 33). Human sympathy is good, but not enough to meet the needs of the case. Brotherly love is sweet, but brotherly love will not raise the dead. It is the man in whose heart the love of God is who is most deeply conscious of his own weakness, and of the need of the forthputting of the power of God. We can say our prayers when we

don't expect anything special to be done; but if we
would see souls delivered from the dominion of death,
there must be a definite dealing with the Living God
for this one thing (Matt. 6. 6).

3. PERSONAL CONSECRATION. "He went in and
stretched himself upon the child" (v. 34). It was not
his staff or anything else that he possessed, but himself that
he gave for the carrying out of this great work. Was not
the Lord Jesus Christ stretching Himself upon the face of
this dead world's need when He submitted to be stretched
upon the Cross? Christ gave Himself for us; Elisha gave
himself for the child. There is no other way of winning
souls but by believing prayer and personal consecration to
the work. The spiritually dead need the embracing of the
living (Acts 20. 10). Embrace them in your heart's
affections and in your prayer of faith before God. Give
thyself to the work, and look to God for the life-giving
power. Son of man, can these bones live? Thou knowest.
Prophesy (Ezek. 37. 3, 4).

4. GOOD SUCCESS. "The child opened his eyes" (v. 35).
He believed and laboured to see the goodness of God in
his revival, and he saw it. He went forth, as it were,
weeping in sympathy, bearing the precious seed of believing
prayer and self-sacrificing effort, and he comes back
rejoicing, bringing the sheaf of victory with him. Believe,
and thou shalt see the glory of God in raising the dead
(John 11. 40). Sometimes preachers are led to say, like
the despairing Corinthians, "How are the dead raised
up?" (1 Cor. 15. 35). Let us learn here that they are not
raised up by the application of forms and ordinances and
dead works, but by the power of the Living God, through
a living, believing, consecrated life. All life has its
source in the living. Spontaneous generation is unknown,
both in nature and in grace.

DEATH IN THE POT.

2 KINGS 4. 38-41.

"Life is too short to waste in critic peep or cynic bark,
Quarrel or reprimand : 'twill soon be dark.
Up! mind thine own aim, and God speed the mark."
—Emerson.

ELISHA came back to Gilgal, from whence he started his
memorable journey with Elijah (chap. 2. 1). The sons of
the prophets are "sitting before him," and although there
was a "dearth in the land," there seemed to be no dearth in
their souls. After Elisha had finished his lecture to the
students he gave orders to his servant to "set on the great
pot." Seeing that "all Scripture is given by inspiration of
God, and is profitable for doctrine," we may surely look for
some profitable doctrine in this miraculous healing of the
poisoned food. We would not dare to say that the pot is a
type of the "faith once delivered unto the saints," but it
might be profitable for us to look at it as an illustration
of it.

I. **The Great Pot.** Like the faith once delivered unto
the saints—

1. IT WAS COMMON PROPERTY. It belonged to no one in
particular, but was the property of the whole school of
prophets, and every one was bound to care for it. The
Gospel ministry has not been committed to any individual
or sect, but is the property of the whole Church of God.

2. IT WAS THE CENTRE OF A COMMON INTEREST. Especially at dinner time, they all received out of the one pot.
In this time of famine there was no other source whereby
their hunger could be appeased. What the great pot meant
to their empty stomachs the Gospel of God should mean
to our hungry souls. The Gospel is always a centre of
interest to those who are experiencing a dearth in their
land.

II. The Startling Discovery. "O thou man of God, there is death in the pot." The poison of death had got into the pot, although—

1. IT WAS PUT IN UNINTENTIONALLY. The man who went out and gathered his lap full of wild gourds and shred them into the pot knew them not. They looked harmless, and so their pernicious character was not discovered. Seeing that these were new things and their nature unknown to them, surely they ought to have been tested before they were passed as wholesome food. Because a man claims to be a son of the Church, that is no reason why he should be allowed to empty the wild gourds of his "destructive criticism" into the Gospel pot. He may be doing it, like this son of the prophet, with an honourable purpose, but it is poisonous all the same. The man who put them in was not more blameworthy than those who consented to him doing it. They were all alike guilty, for we read that "they knew them not."

2. IT SPOILED ALL THAT WAS IN THE POT. There were, no doubt, many good and wholesome things in the pot, but when this new death-working element was introduced it vitiated the whole. The good things lost all their virtue in the presence of this powerful deadly thing. Do we wonder that the truths of the Gospel are being neutralised in our days, when so many new, unproven, and poisonous theories are being shred into the Gospel ministry. The general effect is just the same as the wild gourds in the pot—the whole is spoiled, and nobody is the better of it. The Gospel will never be helped by our putting into it things that we know not.

3. IT PUT AN END TO THEIR EATING. As soon as they discovered that the contents were polluted at once they gave up taking it. They could not satisfy themselves with poisoned food. Who would blame them for refusing all

that was in the pot when once they had found out that there was "harm" in it? Who shall ever be able to satisfy their conscience with a poisoned Gospel? As soon as men believe that the Word of God is untrustworthy they will cease to take it. The inevitable consequence of allowing the self-gathering and pernicious thoughts of men to mingle with the pure, soul-satisfying thoughts of God is to taint the whole with poison and make it an unpalatable mixture good for nothing.

4. IT WAS INSTANTLY REPORTED. They did not whisper to one another to say nothing about it, and that it would come all right in the end. Immediately they tasted it they cried out, "O man of God, there is death in the pot." They never thought of attempting to minimise the mischief wrought by praising the good qualities of the man who had gathered the "wild gourds." Actuated by common sense, they said the sooner this deadly thing is exposed and removed the better.

III. **The Effectual Remedy.** The prophet's answer was, "Then bring meal." The meal was cast into the pot, "and there was no harm in the pot." The—

1. MEANS APPOINTED. "Meal." That which was perfectly sound and wholesome. The emblem of a pure Gospel. But the meal had to be cast "into the pot." It could not save the pottage by remaining in the barrel. It must be brought into contact with those evils which it is meant to heal. Moreover, the meal must be accompanied with the power of God, for, of itself, it could never counteract the destructive influence of the deadly gourds. So it is with the pure, nutritious Gospel of Christ. It is not enough to cast it into the deadly pots of men's minds; unless it is accompanied with the transforming power of the Holy Spirit, the death-working power of error and sin will not be overcome. The sons of the prophets were not asked to make the meal, they had but to bring it.

2. RESULTS PRODUCED. "There was no harm in the pot." The evil had been overcome with the good. The meal, like the incorruptible seed of the Word in the heart, puts all right, and gives these hungry souls a satisfying feast. The Gospel of Christ is the power of God to every one that believeth; for "the foolishness of God is wiser than men" (1 Cor. 1. 25).

NAAMAN, THE LEPER.
2 KINGS 5. 1-15.

"Man should be humble: you are very proud,
And God dethroned has doleful plagues for such. "—*Browning*.

NAAMAN, the leper, occupies pretty much the same place in the Old Testament as the "Prodigal Son" does in the New. The story is both well-known and well-worn, and has been the means of bringing the light of salvation into many a soul. These are wonderful words of life, let us tell them over again. See here a—

I. **Blighted Life.** Naaman had almost all that a man of the world could wish in the way of honour, and fame, and success, but there was a sore in his life that all the praise and wealth of the world could not heal—"he was a leper" (v. 9). Like the rich young ruler, there were many things which he did not lack, but he did lack "one thing"—purity. He was unclean. Wherever sin has dominion, it casts its withering blight over the whole character; but not until it becomes a conscious presence does it mar the false peace of the heart.

II. **Faithful Testimony.** This "little maid" had evidently profited by her godly upbringing. The God of "the prophet that was in Samaria" was to her an Almighty Saviour. She had convictions that were both real and deep, and she was not afraid to speak them out. "Would God that my lord were with the prophet that is in Samaria, for he would recover him of his leprosy" (v. 3). This was a simple, child-like testimony, but it is the kind of testimony that is everywhere needed, and that is sure to be blessed. It was the testimony of faith given at the right time and in the right spirit. "We speak that we do know." This "little maid" was the first "girl preacher."

III. **False Interpretation.** "The king of Syria said, Go, and I will send a letter unto the king of Israel." So Naaman departed. Sent by a king to a king, and taking with him the princely gift of something like the value of £12,000, seemed to them the proper way to go about the matter of salvation from the curse of leprosy (vv. 5, 6). Yes, this is that "worldly wisdom" which completely sets aside that Gospel of Grace preached by the little maid, and which is still preached through Jesus Christ. "It is not by works of righteousness which we have done, but according to His mercy He saves us" (Luke 18. 13, 14). Those guided by mere natural wisdom make no allowance for the grace of God. They will not buy "without money" (Isa. 55. 1).

IV. **Merciful Message.** "Go and wash in Jordan seven times, . . . and thou shalt be clean" (vv. 8-10). Nothing but trouble and disappointment could come by going to the king instead of the prophet. There was none other Name given among men whereby he could be saved (Acts 4. 12). The means was within easy reach. "Wash in Jordan." The promise was sure. "Thou shalt be clean." The prophet kept himself out of sight that Naaman's faith might be in God and not in man. The true herald of the Gospel does not seek the honour of men, but he will have a definite message of certain salvation for every anxious inquirer. "Believe in the Lord Jesus Christ, and thou shalt be saved."

V. **Rebellious Spirit.** "Naaman was wroth, . . . and

went away in a rage" (vv. 11, 12). Why did this God-sent message of salvation from the lips of the prophet come to his heart like a spear thrust instead of a healing balm? Because of his pride and false notions of the God of salvation. He said, "I thought he will surely come out to ME," etc. No, that proud "I" and that haughty leprous "me" must be broken down before God's saving power can be enjoyed. The simple message of the Gospel of Christ cuts at the roots of all preconceived opinions and self-efforts of men. Naaman, or any other man, may wash as often as he likes in the "rivers of Damascus," but there is no regenerating virtue in them, because there God hath not put his promise. All our own works are godless, therefore utterly powerless to save us.

VI. **Surrendered Will.** "Then went he down and dipped himself seven times in Jordan" (v. 14). Then! When? After he had been reasoned with by his sensible servants. These simple-minded men were quick to see that their master, the "mighty man in valour," was stumbling at the simplicity of the remedy. He was quite prepared to do "some great thing," but not this self-abasing foolish thing. But he changed his mind, and "then went down" with the definite purpose of putting the Word of God given to him through the prophet to the test. As soon as his mind was made up to accept this new way of cleansing, the rest was easily and quickly done. His going down was the evidence that he had now believed the message of grace sent him. The faith that does not lead to a personal acceptance of Christ is a dead faith. "Ye will not come to Me that ye might have life" (John 5. 40).

VII. **Changed Man.** "His flesh came again like unto the flesh of a little child, and he was clean" (v. 14). He became a new creature through the obedience of faith (Matt. 18. 3). His faith was also evidenced by a cleansed life. "The flesh of a little child" signifies not only perfect cleansing from his foul disease, but the renewing of his youth. What a perfect illustration this is of the wonder-working power of the Gospel of Christ! "If any man be in Christ he is a new creation: old things have passed away; behold, all things have become new." This great change was followed, as it ever should be, by an open confession. "Behold, now I know that there is no God in all the earth but in Israel" (v. 15). Truly may those, who have been loosed from their sins by the Blood of Christ, say, like the king of old, "There is no other God that can deliver after this sort" (Dan. 3. 29). "Ye shall be witnesses unto Me."

GEHAZI;

OR, SIN FOUND OUT.

2 KINGS 5. 20-27.

"My very thoughts are selfish, always building
  Mean castles in the air;
I use my love of others for a gilding
  To make myself look fair.
Alas! no speed in life can snatch us wholly
  Out of self's hateful sight."—*Faber*.

EVERY attempt to build a God-pleasing character on the foundation of self-interest is to build a "castle in the air." These castles only look substantial in the eyes of the foolish builders, they have actually no existence in the sight of God. Take heed where you build as well as what you build (Matt. 7. 26, 27). Gehazi tried this kind of castle-building, but was doomed to a fearful disappointment. Mark his—

I. **Special Privilege.** He was "the servant of Elisha, the man of God" (v. 20). The name Gehazi means a "valley of vision," and very fitly represents his honourable position. Many a vision of the power and goodness of God did he get through the acts and words of his divinely-

anointed master. Although he lived and moved in a
spiritual atmosphere, yet it seemed to be with all the pride
and self-importance of an unconverted beadle. Spiritual
influences and opportunities have about as little effect on
some souls as the sunshine has on a toad. They can sit for
years under a Gospel ministry and yet be nothing the
better of it in the end.

II. **Selfish Purpose.** "As the Lord liveth, I will run
after him and take somewhat off him" (v. 20). No
doubt the temptation was exceptionally great to a covetous
man. Here was an unprecedented opportunity of making
himself rich without robbing his master just by inventing
a simple plausible pretence. But this "I will" of his was
an act of rebellion against the spirit and honour of his
master and of his God. In a few moments, and within the
domain of his own soul, was the battle between good and
evil fought, which resulted in the surrender of his will to do
the evil thing. In making such a decision he revealed a
sinful distrust in God; a desire to usurp His providence.
"The love of money is the root of all evil."

III. **Deceitful Work.** As soon as his mind was made
up to do this dastardly deed he goes into it with all earnestness, so he runs after Naaman, and begins his lying tale
with "My master hath sent me," etc. (vv. 21, 22). After
the poison had entered his heart, his first utterance is
a lie against his master. No servant of Christ can act
falsely without bringing grief to his Master's heart, even if
it should not at the time cast any dishonour upon His
Name in the eyes of men. As soon as the love of money
strikes its roots into the heart, covetousness and falsehood
must appear in the life as seen by God. Satan is an unchangeable adept in the black art of lying (Acts 5. 3).
Resist him.

IV. **Seeming Success.** His plan to get for himself

the silver and the garments succeeded beyond his expectation. Instead of getting one talent of silver he got two, and, moreover, two of Naaman's servants to carry the spoil back to his own house. How very fortunate (v. 23). What are his thoughts as he walks behind those servants carrying the bags and garments all for his own use? Does it pay to be a hypocrite? Are bags of silver and garments of beauty sufficient compensation for a violated conscience? To be clothed in purple robes and to fare sumptuously every day is not the Kingdom of God (Luke 16. 19). "The Kingdom of God is righteousness, and peace, and joy in the Holy Ghost." Asaph said, "I was envious when I saw the prosperity of the wicked....Until I went into the sanctuary of God, then understood I their end" (Psa. 73. 3-17). Will the eternal end justify the means? Will success atone for sin?

V. Unexpected Discovery. "He went in and stood before his master" as he had often done before, and as if nothing had happened to mar their fellowship or hinder his service. Have we never been guilty of the same thing in seeking to maintain our standing before our Master while there is unconfessed sin in the heart? Be not deceived, God is not mocked. Be sure your sin will find you out in rendering you unfit for service. Elisha said unto him, "Whence comest thou?" and Gehazi said, "Thy servant went no whither" (v. 25). Here is an attempt at self-justification, the fatal refuge of a backslider. He that covereth his sins shall not prosper, but he that confesseth and forsaketh his sins shall find mercy. Elisha's words must have come with a pride-withering effect when he said, "Went not mine heart with thee?...Is it a time to receive money?" etc. (v. 26). His secret sin is naked and bare before the eyes of his master. Does not the heart of our Lord and Master always go with us? Must we not stand before Him too to give an account of the deeds done

in the body? Shall our final appearing bring shame or
reward? Is this a time to be seeking after selfish gain and
honour when we ought to be seeking only the glory of
God? "Ye are not your own" (1 Cor. 6. 19).

VI. **Terrible Punishment.** "He went out from his
presence a leper as white as snow." His covetousness
led him to err from the faith, and to pierce himself through
with many sorrows (1 Tim. 6. 10). (1) There was the
sorrow of a personal humiliation and shame. "He was a
leper." (2) The sorrow of being alienated from his master.
"He went out from his presence." (3) The sorrow of
bringing his offspring into the same condemnation. "The
leprosy of Naaman shall cleave unto thee and unto thy
seed" (v. 27). No man liveth unto himself. Gehazi, having
loved this present world, and having denied God for greed of
gain, seems to have become a castaway from the service of
God. "What shall it profit a man if he shall gain the whole
world and lose his soul?" What is a man profited in the
end if he lays up treasures on earth and is not rich towards
God? And what shall it profit his children though, if they
inherit his earthly riches, they also inherit his earthly spirit?

THE BORROWED AXE;
Or, Lost Power.
2 Kings 6. 1-7.

"So should we live that every hour
May die as dies the natural flower—
A self-reviving thing of power;
That every thought and every deed
May hold within itself the seed
Of future good and future need."—*Houghton*.

THE hypocritical Gehazi had gone out smitten with the
leprosy of Naaman; branded with a life-long shame and
dishonour (vv. 5-27). Surely it is significant that in the
very next verse we should read, "Behold, now the place

wherein we dwell with thee is too strait for us" (v. 1).
The little meeting-house suddenly became too small when
the false professor is excommunicated. The Church of God
ought to be a growing concern, for it is the most important
and best-established business on earth. The incoming of
new members into the society of "the sons of the prophets"
sets them all astir to seek the enlargement of their place.
Fresh converts are sure to bring fresh blood and interest
into a congregation. But how is the thing to be done?
They propose not to have a bazaar or a sale of work, but to
have a deal of work. "Let us go into Jordan, and take
thence every man a beam." Every member of this Church
was a worker, but some were wiser than others, for one said
to Elisha, "Be content to go with us." The others seemingly would have been content to go without the master.
Alas! that this class of worker should be so numerous.
Interested in the "building fund," and in the general good
of the 'Church, but indifferent about the presence and
fellowship of Christ. This one who took to praying for the
master's presence with them was the one who did most
for the work. If the master had not been there when the
head of one of their few axes fell in Jordan, their special
effort would have been seriously hindered. Moses prayed,
"If Thy presence go not, carry us not up hence" (Exod.
23. 15). They that wait on the Lord shall exchange
strength. Except the Lord build the city they labour in
vain that build it. Let us now see what lessons we may
learn from the man who lost his axe. The vital point of
interest in this incident finds its centre here.

I. **He Lost his Power for Service.** As soon as the
"axe-head fell into the water" he became helpless for
effective work. Once he had power, now it is gone, and
gone suddenly and quite unexpectedly. It is possible for
a Christian worker to lose his or her power in service for
God. There is a something that every servant of Christ

ought to have which corresponds to the "axe-head," and
without which our labour will only be a piece of useless
formality—that something is the presence of the Spirit of
God.   Where the Spirit is grieved, there power for service
is lost (Judges 16. 20).

II. **He Lost his Power while Working.** It was
while he was "felling a beam" that the axe-head fell off.
His power was not lost through laziness or idleness.   He
had a mind to work, but had no mind to watch that the axe
was not slowly slipping off the haft.   It is good to be
willing to work; it is safe to be willing to pray.   It is
possible to be so carried away with the desire for doing as to
be forgetful of the spirit in which the thing should be done.
Any uprising of pride and self-interest in the heart while
doing service for God is a slackening of the axe-head of
spiritual power, which may end in total separation if not
attended to at once.

III. **He Lost that which was not his Own.**   "Alas,
master! for it was borrowed."   This point is beautifully
applicable to the Christian worker, because all his power for
service is borrowed power, and he is accountable to his
Lord for how it is used.   The Lord Jesus Christ has given
to His servants that with which they are to trade in His
Name till He comes (Luke 19. 13-22).   The gift of the
Holy Spirit is, as it were, a loan made over to every servant
of Christ, by which they may accomplish great things for
the honour of His Name.   Have you borrowed and lost this
wonder-working gift.   In ourselves we have no power to
lose.   In me, that is, in my flesh, dwelleth no good thing.
"All power is given unto Me" (Matt. 28. 18), says the Risen
One, therefore go ye borrowing from Me.

IV. **He was Painfully Conscious of his Loss.**   "Alas!"
As soon as the axe-head disappeared he felt that further
effort was useless, and, like a sensible man, he gave it

up at once until things were put right again. Any amount of eloquence, earnestness, and good intentions will never make up for the loss of the keen-cutting edge of spiritual power. If the man had gone on swinging the headless handle as if nothing had happened he would have been looked upon by his brethren as one beside himself. Yet in reality he would not have been more silly than the preacher who continues the round of religious services destitute of the power of the Holy Ghost. Of course, those who go to this work, without borrowing this heavenly implement, will go on slaving away, beating the air, quite unconscious of the fact that they are attempting to fell trees with a headless haft. When will the servants of God learn to stop and examine themselves and their methods when they see their work fruitless? Tarry till ye be endued with power from on high.

V. **He Immediately Appealed to his Master.** "Alas, master!" To whom else could he go? If the man of God cannot help him, who can? If you find that you have lost power to make headway in the work of the Lord, do not sit down and try to content yourself with the thought that it cannot be helped. It can be helped. Take it to the Lord in prayer. Tell Him plainly that you have lost your power to win souls, and that you can do nothing until this power is restored. What a dishonour it would be to God if Elisha was not able to restore! Shall your Master fail to make good that which you ought to have for the glory of His own Name if you so commit your case into His hands?

VI. **He had it Miraculously Restored.** "The man of God said, Where fell it? and he showed him the place. He cut a stick and cast it in,...and the iron did swim,... and he put out his hand and took it" (vv. 6, 7).

1. HE GOT IT WHERE HE LOST IT. There was no other

place where he could find it. There is no use of seeking for lost power in longer prayers and better sermons when it has been lost through worldliness and self-seeking. If power for God has been lost through the worry and excitement of much serving, it can never be regained by an increase of that worry and excitement. You will find your lost power for service back at that place where you failed to reckon on the Holy Ghost, and went on in your own wisdom and strength.

2. HE GOT IT THROUGH A MIRACLE. Elisha made the "iron to swim." Every enduement of power is a miracle of grace wrought through the casting in of that stick called the Cross. It is the gift of God, and always comes in a supernatural way. If God has made this gift of power to swim before your eyes as a great possibility brought within your reach, then, like this man, "put out your hand and take it."

A BLIND SERVANT.
2 KINGS 6. 8-17.

"Thou who hast given me eyes to see,
And love this sight so fair;
Give me a heart to find out Thee,
And read Thee everywhere."—*Gell.*

THE weapons of a "man of God" are not carnal, but spiritual. Elisha was able through his wonderful spiritual insight to save the king of Israel, "not once nor twice" from the trap set for him by the king of Syria (vv. 9, 10). They go to spy the prophet out, and come back, saying, "Behold he is in Dothan." Therefore a great host is sent by night to compass the city and capture the man of vision. This praying man is a mightier obstacle to the king of Syria than the army of Israel. Oh, what power lies within the reach of that one who is in favourable contact with God! Elisha was a man whose eyes God had opened to

see invisible things, but he had a servant who was spiritually blind. A "young man" (v. 17) who had just lately
come into office after the deceitful Gehazi had gone out
a leper. There are some lessons of vital importance here.
We may learn that—

I. There are Unseen Realities. Elisha said, "They
that be with us are more than they that be with them"
(v. 16). This man of God lived by faith and endured,
like Moses, as seeing the forces that are invisible. We
look not at the things which are seen, but at the things
which are unseen and eternal. To have this vision that
discerns spiritual things is to be saved from the fear of
man, and to be always confident of victory in the Name
of God. "Greater is He that is in you, than he that is in
the world." "If God be for us, who can be against us?"
(Rom. 8. 31). These spiritual things are not created by
faith, but revealed to faith, as light does any earthly object.
Did not our Lord believe that there were more than twelve
legions of angels ready at His bidding to defend Him?
(Matt. 26. 53).

II. Some Men are Blind to these Realities. When
Elisha's servant saw that host of Syrians compassing the
city he said, "Alas, master! how shall we do?" (v. 15).
Like the unbelieving spies, this young man could only see
with those carnal unanointed eyes which can never see
God's way of deliverance. The heavenly host was also there,
but the servant had no eyes to see it. To him their condition was hopeless. "The natural man receiveth not the
things of the Spirit of God" (1 Cor. 2. 14). Spiritual
blindness, if it does not lead to fear and despair, will
certainly lead to pride and self-confidence. "How shall
we do?" Shall we surrender to these forces of evil that
are round about us, or shall we make a desperate effort to
escape? Shall we allow ourselves to become captive to the

power of this world, or shall we fight them in our own strength?   Uttered or unuttered, this is all the salvation that the unenlightened know.

III. **The Lord Alone can Give this New Vision.** "Lord, I pray Thee, open his eyes that he may see" (v. 17). Elisha did not argue with his servant; he knew that spiritual things could only be seen through spiritual eyes. "Things which eye saw not...God hath revealed unto us through the Spirit" (1 Cor. 2. 10, R.V.).   Secret things belong to God   Those hidden treasures of spiritual strength—mountain full of horses and chariots of fire— can only be seen and trusted by those who have received the holy eye-salve of Him who has all power in Heaven and on earth (Rev. 3. 18).   No amount of learning or scholarship will ever be able to do the work of this eye-salve, which is the Holy Spirit.   It is the Spirit that quickeneth.

IV. **Spiritual Sight Might be Given in Answer to Prayer.**   "Elisha prayed, and said: Lord, I pray Thee, open his eyes."   How confidently that man can pray who lives and moves with opened eyes, as in the presence of God, and among the realities of eternity.   It is easy for the man of God to pray the prayer of faith (James 5. 17).   Blessed is that servant who has such a Master.   Is it not your heavenly Master's will that your eyes should be so opened that you might see clearly those unfailing forces that are for you, that you might be more than conquerors? To pray a servant's eyes open, that he may see that cloud of witnesses, with which he also is compassed about, is to bring him into newness of life.   If this is "the second blessing" it is a great one.

V. **Opened Eyes Brings Rest and Satisfaction.** "The Lord opened the eyes of the young man, and he saw the mountain full of horses and chariots of fire round about

Elisha." Before he could only see the enemy round about the city. The host of God was there, not to preserve the city, but the man of faith. Ye are the salt of the earth. What a revelation this was to that young man trembling with fear, and what a cure it would be for all his doubts and alarms! He could now truly say, "God is my salvation, I will trust and not be afraid" (Isa. 12. 2). This great saving vision now centres round the Cross of Christ. It is there on Mount Calvary, the opened eyes can see the hell-conquering chariots of God's mercy, grace, and power. This is the vision that delivers from the fear of death and the fear of man, that brings peace and rest to the soul, that inspires to praise and service, and with the hope of eternal victory. "Believe, and thou shalt see!"

THE LEPERS' DISCOVERY.

2 KINGS 7. 1-16.

"In contemplation of created things
By steps we may ascend to God. "—*Milton.*

THE famine was so great in Samaria that the almost fleshless head of an ass was sold for fourscore pieces of silver, and some women went the length of boiling and eating their own offspring (vv. 6, 25-29). The whole city was overshadowed with a dismal death-cloud, when suddenly a message of hope and salvation is heard from the lips of the man of God. "To-morrow a measure of fine flour shall be sold for a shekel" (v. 1). This was God's Gospel to a perishing people. How the tidings would fly among the famishing inhabitants! But who would believe the report? How could this thing be? This message was not revealed to reason, but to faith. So it is with the Gospel of salvation. Believe, and thou shalt see! We shall view this incident in connection with these four lepers. Note their—

I **Miserable Condition.** "There were four leprous

men at the entering in of the gate" (v. 3). According
to Jewish tradition these men were Gehazi and his three
sons. If so, it is a terrible sequel to the sin of deceit
and greed of gain (vv. 5-20). Their state, like every
one outside the Kingdom of God's saving grace, is pitiful
in the extreme. They were unclean; they were outcasts;
they were helpless and hopeless; they were ready to perish
as they sat by the gate of a famine-stricken city. This
is not an overdrawn picture of the man who is, by personal
uncleanness, guilty before God, and who sits waiting for
help at the gate of a world that is famishing for lack of
that knowledge of God, which is the "Bread of Life."

II. **Intense Anxiety.** "Why sit we here until we die?"
They are now fully awakened to a sense of their terrible
plight. They used to be quite content to sit still and
take things as they came, but now they realise that to
continue in this indifference means for them certain death.
They are now ready to do anything, if so be that they
might be saved. Although they were unclean, they were not
now unreasonable, for they were quite prepared to accept the
only hope of salvation set before them (v. 4). Their only
possible way of escape was to "fall unto the host of Syrians,"
and they decide to do it. Salvation from sin, and from that
death which is the wages of sin, is never afar off from those
who, in like manner, seek for it. "What must I do to be
saved?" (Acts 16. 30) is the language of one who was prepared
to do anything, or go anywhere, to get salvation.

III. **Joyful Discovery.** "They went to the uttermost
part of the camp of Syria, and behold, there was no man
there" (vv. 5-7). It must have been with great fear and
trembling that they made their way to the first tent.
But the Lord had wrought a wonderful deliverance. Everything was there that they needed, and nothing and nobody
to stand in their way. They found a full and free salvation.
"The Lord had made the Syrians to hear the noise of a

great host"—perhaps that host which Elisha saw at
Dothan (vv. 6-17). It is easy for God to smite His
enemies with the fear of death, and make them to flee when
no man pursueth. This is the terrible fear with which God
may smite the finally unrepentant sinner. When we, like
these lepers, enter in at the only door of hope set before us,
we shall find, like them, that we are saved by the judgment
and mercy of God. Our salvation has come through a
divinely-wrought victory. The silent Cross of Christ, like
the silent camp of Syria, speaks to us, does it not, of
judgment, of victory, and of mercy? Have you made this
soul-satisfying discovery? Whosoever will, let him take.

IV. Selfish Behaviour. The conduct of these lepers,
immediately after they had discovered God's great provision for famishing souls, was most blameworthy. They
ate and drank, and took to hiding treasure for themselves
(v. 8). For the time being they were utterly indifferent
about the salvation of others. This great and merciful
salvation of God had not yet got beyond their own personal
needs and selfish aggrandisement, as if this Heaven-sent
deliverance was exclusively for themselves. This conduct
was indeed Gehazi-like. Alas! that there should be so
many Christians who never seem to get beyond this first
experience of eating, drinking, and hiding. All for self,
nothing for others. So busy looking after their own ease
and comfort that they forgot the perishing multitude, and
neglected to publish abroad the tidings of salvation. Eat
the "Bread of Life," drink the "Water of Life," and hide
the treasures of God's Word in your heart; "but mischief
will come upon you" if that is the end of your faith
(1 Peter 1. 9, leaving out the word *your*).

V. Merciful Consideration. "They said one to
another, We do not well; this day is a day of good tidings,
and we hold our peace....Come, that we may go and tell"
(v. 9). These lepers had two different awakenings within

the space of a few hours. The first was to a sense of their own need, the second was to a sense of the need of others. It takes some of the Lord's people a very long time to get from this one experience to the other, although, with some others, these experiences are almost simultaneous. The counterpart of eating and drinking is going and telling. To "hold our peace" in this "day of good tidings" is to be guilty of the blood of souls. As in Samaria, so round about us, there are many perishing for lack of that knowledge which we possess. Here is bread enough and to spare, yet they perish with hunger. Go and tell (Mark 16.15).

VI. **Successful Testimony.** "So they came and told them (v. 10),...and the people went out" (v. 16). They simply told what great things had been done for them, and, although the king at first doubted the statement, thinking it too good news to be true, yet afterwards the multitude rushed out and claimed every one a portion. The gospel that these leprous men preached, like the Gospel of Christ, is exactly suited to the needs and conditions of the people. It was the news of ample provision, without money and without price. Oh, that men were half as anxious to go out by faith and take those blessings, brought within their reach through that great deliverance which God hath wrought for us on Calvary's Cross, where the enemy of our souls has been routed, and where the spoils of salvation are lying for the lifting!

LESSONS FROM THE DEATH OF ELISHA.
2 KINGS 13. 14-24.

"Teach me to live! 'Tis easier far to die—
　Gently and silently to pass away—
On earth's long night to close the heavy eye,
　And waken in the glorious realms of Day."

ELISHA was now about ninety years of age. Forty-five years have gone since he performed his last public act in connection with the anointing of Jehu. There are some practical lessons we may learn from this portion. That—

I. The Most Useful Life Must Come to a Close. "Now Elisha had fallen sick of his sickness whereof he died" (v. 14). It is appointed unto men once to die; there is a second death, but this is within the realm of man's own appointment. Elisha's master passed away without tasting death, but he must go the way of all the earth. No matter how great our gifts and privileges are, the solemn end is never far out of sight. Lives of great men do remind us of the tremendous possibilities of a single lifetime. Redeem the time.

II. The Past Achievements of the Aged should Encourage the Young. "Joash the (young) king... came and wept, and said, O my father, my father, the chariot of Israel, and the horsemen thereof" (v. 14). This was a timely reminder of a great event in the life of Elisha, fifty-seven years ago (2 Kings 2. 12). The young king's heart was melted at the thought of it, as he gazed on the pale face of him who once had such power with God that he became a terror to royal evil-doers. There is hope for a young man who respects the wisdom and experiences of an aged saint, and who is conscious of the fact that the mightiest weapon on earth is faith in God (Mark. 9. 23).

III. Confession of Need is the Way into a Life of Success. The dying prophet fully understood the deeper meaning of the king's confession. He desired victory over his enemies. "Take bow and arrows," said Elisha, "and Elisha put his hands upon the king's hands, and said, Open the window—shoot; and he shot" (vv. 15-17). That arrow was the symbol of the "Lord's deliverance." The hand of Elisha may have been weak and trembling, but it was a hand not to be despised by the young and the strong who sought victory in the Name of God. The hand of youthful vigour is powerless in the work of God without the hand of faith. The hand of the man of God is truly an "helping hand."

IV. It is Dishonouring to God to be Satisfied with Partial Success. "The man of God was wroth with him, and said, Thou shouldest have smitten five or six times" (vv. 18, 19). What an opportunity the king got, when he was assured that for every time he smote the ground with an arrow he would have a deliverance. Yet he only "smote thrice and stayed." He got according to his faith (v. 25). But why did he stop short of all that God was prepared to do for him? Was it pity for the enemy, or a self-satisfying confidence that three victories would be quite enough to serve his purpose? Why do we stop short of the fullness of the blessing when we might be more than conquerors? Are there not many like Joash, that are perfectly content with just as much of the grace and power of Christ in their lives as enable them to get along with some honour and credit to themselves. Every arrow of believing prayer means a deliverance by the power of God. "Men ought always to pray and not to faint" (Luke 18. 1).

V. God can Make His Servants a Blessing to Others even when Dead. "And when the man...touched the bones of Elisha he revived, and stood up on his feet" (v. 21). This nameless man, buried in a hurry, was born anew in the grave of the prophet. He being dead, yet speaketh life into the dead. The posthumous influence of a holy man is in the hands of God. He who blessed the handkerchiefs and aprons that were brought into contact with the body of Paul (Acts 19. 12) will see that the memory of His justified ones is blessed. The glory of some lives is scarcely realised until they are gone. The prodigal son, who, on returning home, found his mother dead and buried, and who went and flung himself on her new-made grave, confessing his sin, knew by experience the power of this influence. What we know not now we shall know hereafter. All who come into contact with the death of the Lord Jesus Christ are made alive again by the miraculous power of God. "You hath He quickened who were dead." Every true servant of Christ, as well as their Master, shall see of the travail of their soul, and shall be satisfied.

HEZEKIAH; or, DARE TO DO RIGHT.

2 KINGS 18. 1-8.

MAZZINI uttered a great truth when he said, "God created us not to contemplate but to act. He created us in His own image, and He is thought and action, or rather in Him there is no thought without simultaneous action." The wise man is he that doeth the will of God. Such was Hezekiah. Theorists are plentiful, but men of action are rare. His mother's name is given (Abi, or Abijah, possessor of Jehovah, 2 Chron. 29. 1) because, perhaps, through her influence he was what he was. The reformation in Judah may be traceable to the God-fearing mother of the king. The cause of God has always owed much to mothers. As for Hezekiah, he—

I. **Chose the Right Motive.** "That which was right in the sight of God" (v. 3). He was not so foolish as to trust in his own heart, or to be guided by the light of his own eyes. It takes some daring to square one's life with that which is right in the sight of God. Any dead or sickly fish can go with the stream. Joshua made the same choice when he said, "As for me and my house, we will serve the Lord" (Joshua 24. 15).

II. **Put Things in their Right Place.** "He removed the high places, and brake the images, and cut down

the groves" (v. 4). He also caused "all uncleanness
to be cast out of the temple, " and all the vessels to be
restored (2 Chron. 29. 16-18). The things which dishonoured God were broken down and cast out; while those
things which were honouring to Him were set up. The
hindrances to the service of God must be removed, as well
as the helps received. Are there no "places" or "images"
in our own hearts or homes that occupy a higher position in
our esteem than the things of God. Put things in their
right place by putting first things first, as Moses did
(Heb. 11. 25, 26). "Seek first the Kingdom of God and
His righteousness, and all other things shall be added"
(Matt. 6. 33).

III. **Called Things by their Right Name.** "He
brake in pieces the brazen serpent,...and called it Nehu-
stan"—a piece of brass (v. 4). Some had been calling
it a piece of God, and burning incense to it. Idolatry
is a blind and stupid minister that would exalt every
useless relic to the place of God. A silver cross is not
a whit better than a brazen serpent as an object of worship.
Call brass, brass; and sin, sin. The worshippers of
money, pleasure, or worldly honour are as much idolaters
as those who adored the brazen serpent, the golden calf,
or the symbol of the cross. These be thy gods which
control the affections of the heart.

IV. **Put his Confidence in the Right Person.** "He
trusted in the Lord God of Israel" (v. 5). All great
reformers have found the spring of their strength in the
same source—Savonarola, Luther, Knox. Hezekiah's
reformation was social as well as religious, for the turning
of the hearts of the people to God implied their deliverance
from social oppression and degradation (see vv. 11, 12).
He that trusteth in his own heart is a fool.

V. **Walked in the Right Path.** "He clave to the

Lord, and departed not from following Him" (v. 6). There can be no cleaving unto Him without following Him, for His presence means progress. If we would abide in Him and with Him, then we must be prepared to obey Him. "If any man," says our Lord, "would come after Me, he must deny himself, and take up his cross, and follow Me" (Matt. 16. 24). It is always safe to follow where He leads. He leads beside the still waters.

VI. **Enjoyed the Right Kind of Success**. "The Lord was with him, and he prospered whithersoever he went forth" (v. 7). There can be no failure when He is with us. Defeat means self-confidence (Num. 14. 44, 45). All godless prosperity is after the "wood, hay, and stubble" sort; it will end in eye-blinding smoke and eternal disappointment. The success that succeeds is that gained through faith in Him who is able to do exceeding abundantly above all that we ask or think. If we are with Him, He will be with us, "working with, and confirming the Word, with signs following" (Mark 16. 20). True success is always in the line of the will of God. To delight in His will is to see of the travail of the soul, and be satisfied.

VII. **Showed the Right Kind of Independence**. "He rebelled against the king of Assyria, and served him not" (v. 7). The man who is most dependent on God is the man that is most independent of man. Let the time past suffice for the service of the flesh and that enemy the Devil. We can easily afford to rebel against all the principalities and powers that are opposed to the progress of the Kingdom of the Lord Jesus Christ, for greater is He that is with us than all that can be against us. "His servants ye are to whom ye obey," therefore "yield yourselves unto God," and say to every other master, as the three Hebrew youths said to the king of Babylon, "Be it known unto thee, we will not serve thy gods" (Dan. 3. 18).

HEZEKIAH; or, PREVAILING PRAYER.

2 Kings 19.

Hezekiah began his reign in a noble fashion. He expected much from God, and attempted much for God. Through faith he "rebelled against the king of Assyria," and "prospered whithersoever he went" (chap. 18. 7). But thirteen years after, through fear of the Assyrian monarch, he cowardly recanted, and now we see him stripping the "House of the Lord" of its silver and gold to atone for the offence of his independence (chap. 18. 14, 15). A back-slider in faith becomes a weakling in testimony. Now, three years after this attempt to satisfy his enemy with silver and gold, he returns with a "great host," demanding the surrender of all (chap. 18. 17-25). Give the world and the flesh an inch, and they will seek a yard. To compromise with evil on one point is to endanger the citadel of our strength for God. However, Rab-shakeh's blasphemous letter seems to have brought Hezekiah back to a sense of his need of divine wisdom and power (vv. 9-14). Only one of two courses is open for him: either submit himself to Sennacherib or submit himself to God. He cannot serve two masters; no more can ye. He chose the better part, and spread out his case before the Lord. We shall now look at his prayer. It was—

I. **Urgent**. The issues at stake were vital and tremendous—national liberty or bondage. Hezekiah was now fully awake to the question of the crisis that had come upon him. "This day is a day of trouble, and of rebuke, and of blasphemy" (v. 3). Have we, as the servants of Christ, as clearly grasped the situation of to-day? Is this not the day of the trouble of indifference, the rebuke of worldly enthusiasm, and the blasphemy of infidelity?

II. **Unreserved**. When Hezekiah received the letter "he went up into the House of the Lord, and spread it before the Lord" (v. 14). This was better than attempting to write a reply. Some letters are like torpedoes, they are sent for the purpose of destruction—the destruction of your peace, happiness, usefulness, or confidence in God. Like the king of Judah, "spread them before the Lord;" allow Him to see and read all that has been said against both you and Him. Commit thy way unto God, and He shall direct your steps. But there are some who have not the courage to write, but would whisper a slanderous story against you. Deal with all evil reports as Hezekiah dealt with the sneering letter.

III. God-honouring. He looks on the language of Rab-shakeh as a "reproach to the living God" (v. 16), and pleads for deliverance, "that the kingdoms of earth may know that Thou art the Lord God" (v. 19). When our personal interests are so vitally linked together with those things which belong to the honour and glory of the Lord Jesus Christ, then may we confidently expect God to do great things for us. "If ye ask anything in My Name," for My glory, "I will do it" (John 14. 14). This is the strong, unfailing basis of all prevailing prayer. All purely selfish purposes must be crucified if His glory is to be the motive of the life and the argument in prayer.

IV. Heard. While Hezekiah was praying, the Lord spake to Isaiah, who sent this message of comfort to the pleading king: "Thus saith the Lord God of Israel, That which thou hast prayed to Me...I have heard" (v. 20). Not only Hezekiah's prayer, but the "rage" of his enemy had come up before God (v. 27). His "I have heard" is sure to be followed with His "I will do" (v. 28). "If we know that he heareth us, we know that we have the petitions that we desired of Him" (John 5. 15).

V. Answered. "That night the angel of the Lord went out and smote in the camp of the Assyrians, and

in the morning, behold, they were all dead corpses"
(v. 35). At the rebuke of God "the stout-hearted are
spoiled, they slept their sleep" (Psa. 76. 5). When they
said peace and safety, then sudden destruction came upon
them. When the Israelites arose in the morning, behold,
their formidable enemy had become an army of pale-faced
corpses. Who shall be able to stand when He appeareth
with the flaming sword of judgment in His hand? Thus
the prayer of the man of God proved more powerful than
Sennacherib's host. It was such an answer to prayer as
would vindicate the Name and power of God, in all coming
ages, as the Great Deliverer in the day of His people's
trouble and trust. Whatever be the means used, God is
always ready to work, so that it may be clearly seen that the
work is of God, and that we may glorify Him. Prayer is
the mightiest weapon ever put within the reach of man.

A SUDDEN CALL.
2 KINGS 20. 1-11.

"There are things
Known but to God, and to the parting soul
Which feels His thrilling summons."—*Hemans.*

I. **A Solemn Announcement.** "Set thine house in
order, for thou shalt die" (v. 1). This solemn declaration
must have come with startling suddenness to the young
king, after such a marvellous victory as that recorded in
the previous chapter. Great prosperity is no guarantee of
a long life. Some of the most useful and brilliant lives
have been short ones. One of the most urgent duties of
life is to set the house of the heart, or the home, in order
for that great change which may come as unexpectedly to
us as to Hezekiah. His house was the house of the kingdom. Having no son to succeed him, there was need for
this timely warning to set it in order. It is not enough for
us that we live and die, there are responsibilities resting

on us in connection with those who shall succeed us. Our
deeds are not buried with our bones.

II. An Earnest Prayer. "Then he turned his face
to the wall, and prayed,...and wept sore" (vv. 2, 3). The
tidings he had received were most unwelcome. He had
only reigned fifteen years, and was still a young man of
but thirty-nine years old. He felt that as yet he was
quite unprepared to submit willingly to this command
of God. In turning his face to the wall he was turning
his back to all human help and hope, and casting himself
as a bewildered and peevish servant at the feet of his
Lord. There is a selfish, petulant tone in his petition
so very different from his last recorded prayer (chap.
19. 15). There he pleads in the Name of God; here he
pleads in his own name. "I have walked before Thee in
truth with a perfect heart" (2 Kings 20. 3), he groans, as
if, because of this, his life should be prolonged. Although
Hezekiah struggled against this revelation of the will of
God concerning him (which we think was his sin), yet, at
the same time, his prayer shows a familiarity with the
Lord, which is in itself refreshing.

III. An Abundant Answer. Before Isaiah had got
outside the royal court the answer came, an answer that
was exceedingly abundant beyond all that the dying king
had asked. He was to be healed, and fifteen years added
to his life; and the city defended "for His own Name's
sake, and His servant David's sake;" but, notice, not for
Hezekiah's sake (vv. 5, 6). Even this is not all. A
miraculous work is wrought in the "dial of Ahaz" to
reassure his doubting heart (vv. 8-11). We may be
wrong, but we cannot resist the feeling that there is a
measure of irony in all this, a holy and divine sarcasm that
might teach us to be content with the will of God, even
when it does seem unkind and unfair, cutting at the roots

of all our future plans and prospects. A peevish, fretful child may cry for sugar until the mother is compelled just to give it the bowl and let it sip till it sickens at it. Hezekiah's life has evidently become self-centred (2 Chron. 32. 25). He is quite ready to say, "Good is the Word of the Lord," as long as there is to be "peace and truth in his day" (v. 19). But look at the results!

IV. A Sorrowful Consequence. If those fifteen years added to his life were given as a blessing, surely there would have been much blessing in them; but instead they were fruitful of the most terrible evils It would have been good for both Hezekiah and the nation if he had died of that sickness, meant as God's good messenger to take him away from the evil to come. In the very first year of his new lease of life he showed those wily spies from Babylon all that was in his house, which tempted them in later years to come and "carry all into Babylon" (v. 17). About three years after he was recovered there was born unto him a son, of a woman, who, judging by her name (Hephzi-bah, my delight is in her), was to him more than his God. This son (Manasseh) set himself to undo all the good that his father (Hezekiah) had done. "He built up again the high places which his father had destroyed,...and worshipped the host of Heaven, and served them;...and built altars in the House of the Lord....He used enchantments, and dealt with familiar spirits and wizards....He wrought to provoke the Lord to anger;...and seduced them to do more evil than the nations whom the Lord destroyed.... Moreover, he shed innocent blood very much, till he filled Jerusalem from one end to the other" (chap. 21. 1-16). If Hezekiah had been content to die of his sickness, Manasseh would never have been born, and these moral horrors might never have been committed. The story is told of a mother who cried to God to save her son (who was dying) at any cost. The son lived, but the mother had the unspeakable anguish of seeing him hanged as a criminal If Hezekiah could have seen all that was to happen as the result of his prolonged life as God saw it, surely he would have said, "Not my will, but Thine be done" (Luke 22. 42).

JOSIAH AND THE BOOK.

2 KINGS 22.

"Woe to the man who wastes his wealth of mind,
And leaves no legacy to human-kind."—*Coleridge.*

MANASSEH had a godly father, yet for about fifty years he lived a wicked life. Josiah had a wicked father, yet he proved to be one of the choicest of Old Testament saints. The true value of a human life depends on its relationship to God. All lasting virtue comes through our being in touch with the Lord Jesus Christ. Even the hem of His garment is full of power. Let us look at some of those features in this young man's character which have made his name great in Israel (vv. 23-25).

I. **Chose a Good Example.** "He walked in the way of David his father" (v. 2). "While he was yet young he began to seek after the God of David" (2 Chron. 34. 3). He did not seek after the gods of his father Amon, for what did they do for him? Nor did he seek after the God of Hezekiah, for even the good life of his grandfather was not a perfect model; but, in the truthfulness of his soul, he went back to him who was a "man after God's own heart." He desired a God like unto the God of David, and David's God was found by him; and the works that David did, he did also, in establishing the Kingdom in righteousness. In this Josiah is an example to us. Let us go back, not to our godly forefathers, but to Christ, the (perfect) Man after God's own heart, and if His God is our God, the works of Christ will be also manifest in our lives. He hath left us an example that we should follow in His steps.

II. **Revered the Word of God.** "When the king heard the words of the book of the law, he rent his clothes" (v. 11). It was a great discovery Hilkiah, the priest, made while looking after the repairs in the temple. He found the book of the law written by Moses. The Word of God may be burned or buried, but, in some way or other, it will have a resurrection, and, in due time, manifest its authority and power. While the scribe read it to the king, it was to him as a message direct from the Court of Heaven (Deut. 29. 25-27). In token of his belief in it, "he rent his clothes." The Word of God has usually a self-humbling, self-stripping effect before it becomes the inspiring motive of the life. It is most significant that when Josiah began to seek after God, the written Word should be brought and read in his hearing. This is in perfect harmony with the teaching of Jesus Christ (Luke 16. 31). Wherever there is faith in the Word of God, there will be a rending of the heart when it is read or preached in the energy of the Holy Spirit.

III. **Sought to Know the Mind of God for Himself.** "Go ye, inquire of the Lord for me, and for the people" (v. 13). As king of Judah he was anxious to know what God would have him and his people to do. He had learned from the book a lesson which this present generation sadly needs—that the "wrath of the Lord is kindled against those who will not hearken unto the words of this book" (v. 13). The words of Scripture and the God of the Scriptures are one (vv. 16-17). When Josiah met the book, he felt as really in the presence of God as Saul of Tarsus did when he cried out, "What wilt Thou have me to do?" (Acts 22. 10). But it was not enough for him merely to believe the book, the tidings of the book constrained him to seek the God of the book, and to have his own life brought into conformity with His will. It was the complaint of Christ that the scribes and Pharisees of

His day searched the Scriptures, but they would not come
to Him for life. "They are they which testify of ME"
(John 5. 39), he said. Nor was the king disappointed; the
answer came in a definite promise from the Lord (v. 20).

IV. Published Abroad the Tidings from God.
"The king gathered unto him . . . all the men of Judah,
. . . and he read in their ears all the words of the book
of the covenant" (chapter 23. 1, 2). He was not ashamed
of his faith in the book. Believing it to be God's message
to all, he read it out in the ears of the nation. The
book had moved him as no other book could, and it
was able also to move others, and to so move them that
their lives would be surrendered to its influence, and the
whole nation saved thereby. The best way to defend the
Bible is to read it and preach it as God's present-day
message to the people. The best way to defend a caged lion
from a pack of yelping dogs is to let it loose, and it will
splendidly defend itself. Let the Bible loose in all its
native and original majesty, and wonders will certainly be
done. If you cannot preach the Word, you can read it.
Hearers seldom sleep while the Word is being read. Ezra
read out of the book "from morning until mid-day, and
the ears of all the people were attentive" (Neh. 8. 1-3).
Our Lord will be ashamed of us if we are ashamed of Him
and of His Word (Mark 8. 38).

V. Consecrated Himself to do the Will of God.
"The king stood by a pillar, and made a covenant with
the Lord to walk after the Lord, . . . and with all his heart
and soul to perform the words that were written in this
book "(v. 3). He took a bold stand, and launched out into
the deep of God's revealed will. It is one thing to believe
the words; it is quite another to perform them. The
faith that does not lead to action is a dead faith. The
consecration of ourselves to the will and work of God is

surely the logical and legitimate outcome of faith in His
Word.   It was manifestly so in the Apostolic times, why
not now?   The measure of the power of God's Word upon
our hearts is seen in the measure of our personal surrender
to the doing of that Word.   It is not he that sayeth, "Lord,
Lord!" but he that doeth His will that enter into that
Kingdom where the Christian life becomes a power, a
glory, and a blessing.   He was not disobedient to the
heavenly vision, but fearlessly carried on the work of God.
He cleansed the temple of the Lord, put down idolatrous
priests (vv. 4, 5), and reinstituted the Passover of the Lord
(v. 21).   Ye are the temple of God!   Are ye cleansed
from all your idols, and has the Passover Lamb got His
true place in all your work for Him?

JEHOIACHIN; or, SAVED BY GRACE.

2 KINGS 25. 27-30.

"She sat and wept; with her untressed hair
She wiped the feet she was so blessed to touch;
And He wiped off the soiling of despair. "—*Coleridge.*

THE divine threatenings in Leviticus 26 find their terrible
fulfilment in the reign of Jehoiachin.   "Be not deceived,
God is not mocked."   Sin brings to ruin every nation and
individual that yields to its dark and foulsome dominion.
The king of Babylon was Jehovah's sword of vengeance in
the punishment of Judah for their rebellion against Him.
Jehoiachin was taken captive and thrown into a Babylonian
prison, where he remained for the long period of thirty-
seven years.   But Babylon's new king, Evil-merodach, had
mercy on him, and in grace wrought a marvellous change
for him, giving us an illustration of the wonder-working
grace of God.

I. **Delivered**.   "He did lift up Jehoiachin out of
prison" (v. 27).   This was his first necessity.   He could

in no wise lift himself up. The grace of God which bringeth salvation has a mighty uplifting power. "He brought me up out of an horrible pit, out of the miry clay" (Psa. 40. 2); and from the darkness and thraldom of Satan into the Kingdom of God's dear Son. As with the king of Judah so with us; there is no uplifting into liberty without the exercise of Royal Authority.

II. **Comforted.** "He spake kindly to him." The law has no kind word of comfort to speak, but grace has. By grace are ye saved. All those ransomed by the power of Christ are comforted by the ministry of the Holy Spirit. The religion of man attempts to speak comfortably to men in the prison of sin; the religion of God first saves, then comforts. The blood of His victory goes before the water of His consolation. He knows how to speak a word to the weary. In all the coming ages God's people will show forth His kindness towards them through Christ Jesus (Eph. 2. 7).

III. **Exalted.** "He set his throne above the throne of the kings that were with him in Babylon." Jehoiachin had the pre-eminence among the othei kings who were as captives in Babylon. The whole incident may be prophetic of Judah's future exaltation and glory, as it is suggestive of the spiritual uplifting enjoyed by those who are risen and exalted into heavenly places in Christ Jesus. Abounding sin and failure is conquered and overcome by the much more abounding grace of God. If man's fall through sin has been great, his uplifting through grace has been greater. He can make the homeless beggar of the dunghill meet to sit among the princes of Heaven. "Oh, to grace how great a debtor!"

IV. **Clothed.** "He changed his prison garments." The prison garments speak of guilt, defeat, shame, and bondage; but now they are gone, and garments of beauty take their place. So it is with those whom grace hath saved. The old things which spoke of failure, degradation, and imprisonment, are put off, and those things have been put on which tell of glory, honour, immortality, and eternal life. A change will soon be evident when once a soul has been emancipated from the law of sin and death—the filthy rags of self-righteousness gives place to the righteousness of God, which is unto all and upon all them that believe (Zech. 3. 3).

V. Honoured. "He did eat bread continually before him." He had the daily privilege of having fellowship with him who had delivered him from the house of bondage. The prisoner was now the constant companion of his saviour. The grace of God not only saves and transforms, but brings into abiding fellowship with Himself. The kindness of David wrought the same gracious work for Mephibosheth (2 Sam. 9. 7). The door of our King's banqueting-house is always open for His own specially-invited guests. Eat, O friends!

VI. Supplied. "His allowance was a continual allowance given him of the king, a daily rate for every day, all the days of his life."

1. It was an *allowance*. It was not a reward, or something given as wages. It was something placed at the disposal of him whom the king delighted to honour. It was the provision of grace. How much has God placed at the disposal of those who have been saved by His grace? All the unsearchable riches of Christ.

2. It was a *daily* allowance. "A daily rate for every day." Take no thought for your life. "My grace is sufficient for thee." To-morrow's allowance will come with to-morrow's need.

3. It was given him *of the king*; out of the king's fullness,

and from his own gracious hand were all his wants
supplied. "My God shall supply all your need"
(Phil. 4. 19).

4. It was an allowance *for life.* "All the days of his
life." The royal promise covered his every need. All
is yours, for ye are Christ's.

THINE ARE WE.

1 Chronicles 12. 16-18.

"Oh, Lord, that I could waste my life on others,
  With no ends of my own;
That I could pour *myself* into my brothers,
  And live for them alone. "—*Faber.*

The "love of Christ" is the mightiest motive power that
ever touched a human soul, in constraining to self-sacrifice
for the good of others. The true Christian is not a self-
centred mystic, but a Christ-centred evangelist. He is not
only a consumer of the things of God, he is a producer of the
fruit of the Spirit. In the light of such like teaching, let
us look at this portion. It involved a—

I. **Decided Step.** "There came of the children of
Benjamin and Judah to the hold unto David." This may
have been the cave of Adullam, or some such secret place
of refuge, but to those who came to David it meant on their
part a willingness to take their stand for him, and to share,
if need be, the shame of rejection with him. The pros and
cons about this step would likely be closely discussed before
any definite action was taken. Those who would identify
themselves with the rejected Son of God will do well to
count the cost, but they will do ill if they go on counting
and never come.

II. **Conditional Offer.** "David went out to meet
them, and said, If ye be come...to help me, my heart

shall be knit unto you. " David is more anxious for
quality than quantity. He well knew that it would not be
for the good of his cause to have a heartless crowd following
him. All who are prepared to help in the cause of the
Lord Jesus Christ may depend on having His heart's
affections knit unto them. The Lord's work, like David's,
must be heart work. David could see but two motives they
could possibly have in coming to him—either to help or to
betray; they must be either for him or against him. His
heart was open to embrace all who were ready to help him
in the cause of God. Did not Christ also declare that "He
that is not for Me is against Me?" (Matt. 12. 30). Is not
His heart also ready to receive all who come unto Him in
sincerity and in truth?

III. **Personal Surrender.** "Amasai said, Thine
are we, David, and on thy side. " He said this after the
"Spirit came upon him. " It was a Spirit-indited confession; it was a Spirit-led act. There was no uncertainty
about it. It implied the yielding of their lives to David for
the furtherance of his cause and the fulfilment of his will.
In giving themselves to him, they were no longer their own
they became his instruments for the carrying on of his work.
To be on David's side was to become a sharer of his sorrows, as well as of his resources ; a partner in his
tribulations, as well as his victories. To become a partner in
the resources and triumphs of David's Lord and ours
we must also yield ourselves wholly to Him, as those ready
to suffer for His sake, if so be that His will might be done
in us and by us. His servants ye are to whom ye yield
yourselves (Rom. 6. 16). Consecration of service will
surely follow when, like Amasai, we are clothed with the
Spirit (v. 18, *margin*).

IV. **Confession of Faith.** "Peace be unto thee,
and peace be to thine helpers; for thy God helpeth thee. "

They were convinced that the God in whom David trusted was with him, and that He is greater than all that were against him. Perhaps it was the evidence of this fact that led them first of all to think of joining his band. Somehow or other men will be drawn to those whom God undoubtedly helps. The man or the cause that is espoused by the Almighty is absolutely certain to succeed. They are wise who join themselves to that movement which has God in it, and that cannot be defeated. Such a movement we have in the work of the Greater David—the Lord Jesus Christ. Did not His God mightily help Him, and are not all His helpers helped of God? What an abundant proof there is that God was in Christ, and that the help that is mighty was laid upon Him. This is seen in His words and works, and especially in His being raised again from the dead. As we can truly say of Him, "Thy God helpeth Thee," (1 Chron. 12. 18), so let us also add, "Thine are we, Jesus, Thou Son of God; peace be to Thine helpers." Those who would serve the Lord must not only believe in Him, but also possess such a spirit as will make for peace with all His helpers.

V. Successful Issue. "Then David received them, and made them captains of the band." They came in the right spirit, and they found an open door into the heart and service of their Lord. This was no formal reception. They were received as Christ also receives those who so come to Him—into the affection of His heart, and into the sacred business of His life. All who come to the Lord Jesus Christ are welcome to His love and service. But, as it was in David's case, so is it now; these two, favour and service, go together. If these children of Benjamin would enjoy the love of David they must join his service. He made them captains, for they that honour Him shall be honoured (Acts 1. 8).

A SONG OF THANKSGIVING,

AND WHAT IT TEACHES.

1 CHRONICLES 16. 7-36.

"Thou, O Christ, our way hast known;
When alone we're not alone;
I've felt it all, and songs I'll raise,
The garment I'll put on of praise."—*Grosart.*

THIS chapter throbs with vital teaching. The song of praise and thanksgiving comes after the Ark of God has found its rightful place "in the midst of the tent that David had pitched for it," and after sacrifices had been offered unto God, and the people blessed in the Name of the Lord (vv. 1-3). Thankfulness is sure to come when God has got His rightful place in the life. This song teaches us—

I. What we Should Seek. "Seek the Lord and His strength; seek His face continually" (v. 11). There is here a threefold object set before the seeker.

1. Seek the *Lord*; seek Himself for salvation. He that findeth Me, He says, findeth life. This is eternal life to know Him.

2. Seek His *strength* for service. They that wait on the Lord shall exchange strength. To them that have no might He increaseth strength.

3. Seek His *face* continually for fellowship. To have the light of His face is to have the light of His presence. "Seek and ye shall find."

II. What we should Sing. "Sing unto Him, sing psalms unto Him" (v. 9). If "all the earth" should sing unto the Lord (v. 23), how much more so those who have been redeemed by His Son, and strengthened by His grace and Spirit. Those whose hearts are brimful of thankfulness to God are never at a loss to know what they shall sing. They have songs which can only be sung by lips touched with live coals from the holy altar. They have many psalms to sing unto the Lord: the psalm of deliverance, the psalm of forgiveness, the psalm of peace, another of hope, another of joy, and that other, which is the sweetest of all, the psalm of His presence. We would not be asked to sing unto the Lord if the Lord did not hear and take pleasure in our singing. He hears our singing as well as our praying.

III. **What we should Give.** "Give thanks unto the Lord" (v. 8). "Give unto the Lord glory and strength" (v. 28). "Give the glory due unto His Name" (v. 29). The best thanks we can give to the Lord is to live a life of grateful trust in Him day by day. We give Him "glory and strength" when we act as those who believe in His glory and depend on His strength. We cannot give Him "the glory due unto His Name" by merely talking about it, but by allowing that glory so to fill us that His Name will be glorified in us. "Freely ye have received, freely give." Give out that light and love so freely given in Christ Jesus.

IV. **What we should Remember.**

1. "Remember His marvellous *works*; His wonders" (v. 12). The Israelites were never to forget the pit out of which they had been digged, nor the manner in which they had been brought out. They were saved by such marvellous works and wonders as can find their only antitype in the life, death, and resurrection of the Lord Jesus Christ.

2. "Remember the judgments of His mouth." Remember His *words*. The works and words of God our Saviour are inseparably bound together. The words of Christ are "spirit and life," so are His works. The Jews wept when, in their affliction, they remembered Zion; we may rejoice at every remembrance of Christ.

3. Remember His *faithfulness*. "Remember His covenant for ever: the Word which he commanded to a thousand generations" (v. 15, R.V.). He is the same yesterday. to-day, and for ever. Remember His covenant of grace

in Jesus Christ, and reckon on His faithfulness to all His promises. The sin of forgetfulness is a very common one.

V. What we should Speak. It is well to remember God's works for us, and His words to us, but with the mouth confession is to be made.

1. We are to speak to *one another* of "all His wondrous works" (v. 9). "They that feared the Lord spake often one to another, and the Lord hearkened and heard." The conversations of God's own people with each other are often such as must grieve the heart of the Divine Listener. If the works of our Lord are not really wondrous in our eyes, we shall not be inclined to talk much about them. Let your conversation be as becometh the Gospel—that Gospel which is the greatest wonder in heaven, earth, or hell.

2. We are to speak of "His glory *among the heathen*; His marvellous works *among all nations*" (v. 24). We who are witnesses unto Him, as our redeeming Lord and Saviour, must seek to spread abroad the savour of His saving Name. Fellowship one with another ought to lead up to missionary enthusiasm for the cause of Christ. Blessed are all they whose consecrated lives sing this song of thanksgiving.

THE KING'S REQUEST;

OR, CONSECRATED TO SAVE.

1 CHRONICLES 21. 22-28.

"Whate'er I render Thee, from Thee it came;
And if I give my body to the flame,
My patience, love, and energy divine
Of heart, and soul, and spirit—all are Thine.
Oh, vain attempt to expunge the mighty score!
The more I pay, I owe Thee still the more!
            —*Madame Guyon.*

SATAN sought to oppose Israel, and he did it by "provoking David to number the people" (v. 1). It is still a wile of

the Devil to get us to trust in numbers instead of in God.
Glowing reports of numerical strength are very gratifying
to the flesh, and may lead to the lessening of faith in God.
David's act of unbelief led to awful consequences—70,000
men perished. But David's confession was followed with
this message of hope: "Set up an altar unto the Lord in
the threshing-floor of Ornan" (vv. 17, 18). This way of
escape from the judgment of God was a revelation from
God Himself. Who else could do it? "Look unto Me, and
be ye saved, for I am God" (Isa. 45. 22)

I. **The Request**. "David said to Ornan, Grant me the
place of this threshing-floor" (v. 22). It was a big demand
to make at that moment when "Ornan was threshing
wheat." It was no mere idle floor, for the treasures of
the owner were on it and in it. Does not our Lord and
King sometimes make sudden and strange demands of
us when He asks for the full control of our business, or
of that scheme in which we are presently engaged. Like
David, He will not take it by force; He will give us the
privilege of granting it to Him.

II. **The Reason**. "That I may build an altar unto the
Lord...that the plague may be stayed from the people"
(v. 22). The royal request was accompanied with reasons
abundantly worthy of it. Because of sin a plague was
mowing down the people as a sword in the hand of the
messenger of divine vengeance. A place and an altar were
needed that a sacrifice might be offered unto the Lord, that
judgment might be averted and the people saved. Ornan
possessed that place, and was now asked to surrender it as
a means in the hands of the king of delivering the people
from death. This great salvation could only be secured by
Ornan's place of business being converted into a place of
sacrifice unto the Lord. The threshing-floor must give
place to the altar. There are some men's minds that are

mere threshing-floors, nothing more. Their chief business
is to thresh out problems and theories. The King of
Heaven demands that such threshing-floors should have an
altar, that the plague of sin may be arrested, and sinners
saved. The intellect can become something more useful
than a mere threshing machine.

III. **The Response.** "Ornan said unto David, Take it
to thee,...and do that which is good in thine eyes; lo, I
give thee the oxen also...and the threshing instruments...
I give it all" (v. 23). He might have made many excuses,
such as "The time is not convenient," or "I will need to
think over it," etc. ; but no, he grasped the situation at
once; his whole soul was captured for the cause. He not
only offered the threshing-floor, but all that was on it—
the oxen, the instruments, and the wheat. "I give it all."
This is the language of one who evidently has the best
interests of the people at heart. It is the expression of a
truly missionary spirit. He yields his own personal
claims to the greater claims of God and of his perishing
fellow-creatures. The mercenary bargaining spirit is
allowed no place in Ornan's mind in his answer to the
kingly call. Are we ready at the call of our King to yield
to Him the threshing-floor of our hearts as an altar; the
faculties of our mind and intellect as threshing instruments
to spread the fire of His holy sacrifice; and the wheat of our
riches as a meat offering unto the Lord? May not the love of
Christ and love to perishing souls constrain us? (Rom. 12. 1).

IV. **The Result.** The result was a threefold success.

1. ORNAN WAS REWARDED. "David gave to Ornan for the
place six hundred shekels of gold." The price mentioned
in 2 Samuel 24. 24—fifty shekels of silver—was for the
threshing-floor alone. This six hundred shekels of gold
(£2400) was for the whole place, and was in all likelihood a
second transaction. This is in beautiful correspondence

with the parable of the treasures in the field. The whole field
is bought for the treasure it contained (Matt. 13. 44). Ornan
was willing to give it all to David, but he is like the greater
David who bountifully rewards those who yield their all to
Him. "Give, and it shall be given unto you; good measure,
pressed down, and running over." Surely this is "full price."

2. GOD WAS SATISFIED. "The Lord answered him from
Heaven by fire upon the altar" (v. 26). The sacrifice for
sin was accepted, and the fire from Heaven that fell upon
the altar, consuming the offering, was God's token of peace.
What a comfort to Ornan to know that his gift of the
threshing-floor and its contents was a means in bringing
from Heaven the assuring fire! We never know all that our
gifts to the cause of God may accomplish. "Prove Me, and
try Me, if I will not pour out a blessing upon you."

3. JUDGMENT WAS AVERTED. The plague was stayed.
"The Lord commanded the angel, and he put up his sword
again into the sheath thereof" (v. 27). David's sin of
numbering the people was a sin against God, and, explain
it as we may, God demands sacrifice for sin. There is no
way of securing deliverance from His wrath, and gaining
the assuring token of His favour, but by the altar of atoning
blood. The Cross of the Lord Jesus Christ is God's final
effort to put away sin by the sacrifice of Himself. Only
when the Sacrifice is accepted and trusted by the individual
soul will the sword of judgment be sheathed. "When I
see the blood I will pass over you."

A CALL FOR CONSECRATED SERVICE.
1 CHRONICLES 29. 1-9.

"With bowed heads and open hearts we may offer ourselves. We
can do no more, and we dare do no less."—*Westcott.*

IT is a great privilege to be able to do anything for God.
There is not an angel in Heaven but what glories in every

opportunity of service. Why should not His angels on
earth do the same? David had an earnest desire to build
a house unto the Lord, but this was not permitted him
because he had been a "man of war" (chap. 28. 2, 3). War
and worship never go easily together. Although not
allowed to build the temple he made great preparations for
it. He gathered gold to the value of £547,500,000, and
silver to the amount of £342,000,000 (Newberry, chap. 22.
14.) Why should our interest in God's work be lessened
because we are not permitted to do that piece of work which
we so much desire to do? Some slacken their efforts for
Christ's cause at home because their way has not been
opened for going abroad. There are others who, if not
asked to do some great thing, they will do nothing. Note—

I. **The Work.** "The work is great, for the palace is
not for man, but for the Lord God" (v. 1). It is a great
work to prepare a palace for the King of Heaven. David
was anxious that God should have a house worthy of His
Name, and the Lord Himself greatly desired this. But let
us not forget that God was as great when in the bush as
when in the temple. The glory does not consist in the
character of the house so much as in the character of the
occupant. "Know ye not that your body is the temple,
the palace of God, and that God dwelleth in you?" (1 Cor.
6. 19). Does not He desire that you should be a house
worthy of His great and glorious Name? This is a "great
work." It is the work of the Spirit of God, in union with
our spirits. Ye are not your own. Like this palace, ye are
"not for man, but for the Lord God."

II. **The Example.** David does not ask others to con-
secrate their service unto the Lord without having first set
a worthy example before them. He says, "I have prepared
with all my might for the house of my God" (v. 2). And
again, "I have set my affection to the house of my God.

Moreover, I have of mine own...gold and silver given to the house of my God" (v. 3). David's private gift amounted in gold to £16,420,000, and in silver to £2,394,000 (v. 4). His example was one of love and liberality. He sought first the Kingdom of God. How does this example compare with that of David's greater Lord? Did He not prepare with all His might for the new spiritual House of God? Did He not set His affection upon this great work? Did He not give of His own untold wealth of grace and suffering? Has He not left us an example that we should follow His steps?

III. **The Call.** "Who then offereth willingly to fill his hand this day unto the Lord?" (v. 5, R.V., *margin*). This was a call for full hands and willing hearts. There are multitudes who are ever ready to fill their hands with service for their own personal profit, but how few are willing to have full hands for God. Full hands imply whole-heartedness. Half empty hands mean half empty lives. Who, then, is willing? It is a call for voluntary self-sacrificing service. It is also an urgent call—"This day." The King's business requireth haste. What thou doest, do quickly, for the day of service and holy privilege will soon be past.

IV. **The Response.** "Then the chief of the fathers,... the captains,...with the rulers, offered willingly" (v. 6). "With a perfect heart they offered willingly to the Lord" (v. 9). When the heart is perfectly yielded to the claims of God's work, the hands will soon be filled with voluntary offerings. The "perfect heart" is needed to make the service acceptable unto the Lord. "The Lord loveth a cheerful giver." The gifts were different in value, but all were needed and acceptable. "Gold, silver, iron, precious stones" (1 Cor. 3. 12). Iron may have been the best that some had, but they gave it. There would never be any lack in the house of God if those connected with it had this "perfect heart" toward the Lord. The outstanding characteristic of the great majority of professing Christians is that they "mind earthly things. "

V. The Result. "Then the people rejoiced,...and David the king also rejoiced with great joy" (v. 9). They rejoiced because the offerings were given "willingly, with perfect heart. " Joy is the fruit of the Spirit, and is the outcome of the heart made perfect toward the Lord and His cause on the earth. The happiest Christians are those who willingly fill their hands for God. Joy in the Lord is power, "for the joy of the Lord is your strength"(Neh. 8.10). "The Kingdom of God is righteousness, and peace, and joy in the Holy Ghost" (Rom. 14. 17).

SOLOMON'S PRAYER.
2 Chronicles 6. 22-42.

"A man's reach should exceed his grasp,
Or what's Heaven for?"—*Browning.*

This is the longest prayer in the Old Testament, and may be fitly compared with the longest in the New, as recorded in John 17. Both are intercessory and provisional. This temple, prepared for God and filled with His glory (v. 14), is a wonderful type of the person and character of the Lord Jesus Christ. What the temple was to Israel, Christ is to the world. What Solomon did on the brazen scaffold (v. 3), Christ did on the accursed tree—open the way for others into the place of blessing. This prayer of Solomon, like the work of Christ, revealed a large and cosmopolitan heart. In it, there was provision made for the—

I. Maligned. "If a man sin against his neighbour,... and an oath be laid,...then hear Thou and judge" (v. 22). To sin against our neighbour is to sin against God, so those sinned against may confidently appeal to Him, and expect

that He will "requite the wicked, and justify the righteous
(v. 14). As in Solomon's prayer there was provision made
for the maintenance of the character of the righteous, so is
there also in the intercession of Christ. Those wronged by
their neighbours should believingly commit their case unto
the Lord. He will avenge His own.

II. **Defeated.** Those "put to the worse before the
enemy" (v. 24). This is a numerous class. Many there
be who have fallen before the power of the enemy, "because
they have sinned against God." Sin always leads to defeat
(Joshua 7. 10, 11). For God's people to be put to the worse
before the enemy is to bring dishonour upon the Holy
Name. He would have us to be "more than conquerors."
But at the temple altar there was a way back for the van-
quished to forgiveness and victory. By their returning and
confessing God would hear and forgive, and restore them
again to the land which He gave them (vv. 24, 25). It
mattered not how far they had been driven away by the
enemy if they turned their faces towards the House of
God, confessing their sins, then deliverance was to be
granted them. So may those be saved who have been
overcome by temptation and sin, by turning the eye of
faith to the provision made by Jesus Christ at the altar of
the Cross.

III. **Thirsty.** "When the Heaven is shut up, and there
is no rain, because they have sinned against Thee" (v. 26).
God had different ways of manifesting His displeasure at
sin. In a spiritual sense Heaven is still shut up, so that
no refreshing rain comes upon the soul of the disobedient
and the backsliding. A silent and irresponsive Heaven is
a fearful calamity to a thirsty soul, but this thirst is meant
to bring us back in heart to the place of confession and
blessing. "Then hear Thou, and forgive,...and send rain"
(v. 27). The way to escape the horrors of a closed-up Heaven

is to keep in "the good way" of the Lord.   Abide in Him.
If spiritual dearth has come, there is still in Christ provision for restoration and refreshing.   "Look unto Me, and
be ye saved. "

IV. **Oppressed.**   "When the enemies besiege them in
the cities of their land;... when every one shall spread forth
his hands towards this house, then hear Thou" (vv. 28-30).
The people of God were not exempt from trial and suffering,
even in their own cities—in the very midst of all their joys
and privileges.   Solomon believes that, if the enemy is
permitted to besiege them and oppress them, it would be
on account of their sin, for in his prayers he says, "When
Thou hearest, *forgive.* "   No enemy is able to besiege and
imprison any soul that is walking in fellowship with God.
It is ever a wile of the Devil to get between us and Him
who is the home of our hearts.   But if you are really
besieged so that you have no *liberty* to go out and in, in
your service for God—out of communication with head-
quarters—then here is the remedy: Spread forth the hands
of your faith toward the dwelling-place of God, and
forgiveness and deliverance will be yours.

V. **Stranger.**   Even "the stranger which is *not* of
Thy people" finds a place in the large heart of this King
of Peace.   What good news it would be to the stranger
who had "come from a far country, " drawn by the influence
of God's "great name" and "mighty hand, " to find that
the gate of divine blessing was open for him, and that
God was willing to do "according to all that the stranger
called to Thee for" (v. 33).   Did not the Ethiopian take
advantage of this provision when he came to Jerusalem
for to worship? (Acts 8. 27).   It is still true that those
born in the far country of sin, and who are strangers to
God and to His people, may have their needs supplied by
calling upon the Lord.   "Him that cometh unto Me, I will

in no wise cast out. " "Ho! every one that thirsteth, come ye to the waters. " "Ye who sometimes were far off are made nigh by the Blood of Christ" (Eph. 2. 13).

VI. Warrior. "Then if Thy people go to war...by the way that Thou shalt send them, and pray unto Thee toward this city,...then hear, and maintain their cause" (vv. 34, 35). It is of the utmost importance that in going out in holy warfare we should go *by the way* that God has sent us. The Christian life is a warfare, but not with carnal weapons. Put on the whole armour of God, that ye may be able to stand. Praying always with all prayer, that "He may hear from the Heavens your prayer and supplication, and maintain your cause" (v. 35). In Solomon's prayer, as in the work of Christ, there is provision made for certain victory in battling for the Lord. Warriors for God; keep your face towards the holy place of sacrifice and fellowship, and He will maintain your cause.

VII. Captives. "If they sin against Thee,...and their enemies carry them away captives, yet if they bethink themselves...and turn and pray unto Thee,...then hear Thou, and maintain their cause, and forgive" (vv. 36-39). The Lord's people could never be taken away as captives so long as they were obedient to His will. Sin leads to separation from God, and when separated from Him we become an easy prey to the enemy. The only hope for those led captive by the Devil, or the pleasures of the world, is to bethink themselves, and turn to the Lord, saying, "We have sinned, we have done amiss. " If we confess our sins, He is faithful and just to forgive. The fire that "came down from Heaven" (chap. 7. 1) when Solomon had made an end of praying was the token that his prayer was heard, and that God was ready to do all that had been asked. The coming of the Holy Ghost from

Heaven, after Christ had finished His work, is the proof
to us that God is ready to fulfil to us all the desires of His
heart. "If ye ask anything in My Name, I will do it."

ASA'S FAITH AND FAILURE.

2 CHRONICLES 14-16.

"Belief's fire, once in us,
Makes all else mere stuff to show itself;
We penetrate our life with such a glow
As fire lends wood and iron."—*Browning.*

IN these chapters we have a faithful biography of Asa.
The features of his character, both good and bad, are
equally prominent. In the Bible there is no touching up
of the negative to give the photograph a more pleasing
appearance. As an historian the Spirit of God knows
nothing of the art of flattery. As a man is in his heart so
is he before God. The life of Asa is full of encouragement
and warning to us. We observe his—

I. Good Character. "Asa did that which was good
and right in the eyes of the Lord his God" (chap. 14. 2).
This was a noble start. He refused to be guided by the
light of his own eyes, or by the opinions and prejudices of
others. It is a good thing to remember that the eyes of
the Lord are ever in search of those whose hearts are right
with Him, that He might show Himself strong in their
behalf (chap. 16. 9). Right thinking will lead to right
acting, and God's strength is on the side of the righteous.
Asa not only "broke down the images," he also "commanded Judah to seek the Lord God of their fathers." It is
not enough to put away the wrong. We must seek the right.
To give up our idols will avail us nothing unless we turn to
God (1 Thess. 1. 9).

II. Great Faith. Asa's faith was put to the test when
his army of 580,000 was met by 1,000,000 Ethiopians

and 300 chariots, but it stood the test. "Asa cried unto the Lord his God, and said, Lord, it is nothing with Thee to help, whether with many or with them that have no power. We rest on Thee, and in Thy Name we go against this multitude" (vv. 11, 12). He looks upon the many as nothing, but the "help of God" as everything. To have God's help is to get an almighty lift. The way to secure His help is to "rest on Him," and go in His Name. This is the work of faith, and faith gains the day, for the "Lord smote the Ethiopians before Asa." He did it, for Asa rested on Him, and trusted in His Name to do it. "This is the victory that overcometh the world, even our faith."

III. **Timely Warning.** "The Spirit of God came upon Azariah, and he went out to meet Asa, and said, Hear ye me, Asa, the Lord is with you while ye be with Him...Be ye strong therefore,...for your work shall be rewarded" (chap. 15. 1-7). This is emphatically a Spirit-inspired message. Why did it come to Asa immediately after his great victory of faith? Because the Spirit of God knew that at that moment there was a danger of him being lifted up with pride, and of falling back into a state of self-confidence. Oh, how anxious the Holy Spirit still is to maintain our faith in God, that His Name might be honoured by doing great things for us! "If thou wouldst believe, thou shouldest see the glory of God" (John 11. 40). Take heed how you hear.

IV. **Mighty Influence.** "They fell to him out of Israel in abundance, when they saw that the Lord his God was with him" (v. 9). Many strangers from the kingdom of Israel joined the ranks of the king of Judah when they saw that God was on his side. Those who gain victories by faith are the most influential of all leaders. All are not born leaders. Many are ready to follow a tune who could never raise it. But the supernatural element must be self-evident in the divinely appointed leader.

"My sheep," says Christ, "hear My voice, and they follow Me." Are there not many who would fall out of the kingdom of darkness to-day if they could but see that the Lord our God is with us? Not with us in theory, but in mighty conquering deeds. Asa's influence was not only attractive, but it was most effectual in turning the whole heart of Judah unto the Lord (vv. 12-14). He constrained them to seek the Lord until "He was found of them." He used his great influence for the best of all purposes—to bring men to God.

V. Sudden Failure. When "Baasha, king of Israel, came up against Judah . . . Asa brought out silver and gold out of the treasures of the house of the Lord, and sent them to Ben-hadad king of Syria" (chap. 16. 1-4). This was a bribe sent to the king of Syria to help him against the king of Judah. Has he forgotten already that Spirit-inspired message of Azariah? (chap. 15. 1, 2). Where is his faith now? He began in the spirit. Is he going to end in the flesh? His present unbelief leads him to desecrate the things of God (chap. 15. 18). When in his greater trouble with the Ethiopian host he cried unto the Lord and rested on Him, but this is not such a formidable affair, so he thinks to manage it by his own skill and stratagem. God is ignored, and Asa has fallen from grace. Our greatest dangers do not always lie in our greatest temptations, for when we are made conscious of our own helplessness in the face of a great trial, we fortify ourselves by leaning upon God. It is thinking ourselves wise enough and strong enough for the petty occasion that our greatest danger lies. "In all thy ways acknowledge Him, and He will direct thy paths" (Prov. 3. 6).

VI. Rebellious Attitude. When Hanani the seer rebuked Asa "because he had relied on the king of Syria, and not relied on the Lord his God," Asa, we read, "was wroth with the seer, and put him in a prison house, for he was in a rage with him because of this thing" (chap. 16. 7-10). It is an infallible sign of backsliding when a man gets

into a rage at the seer of God because he tells him the truth.
Casting the man of vision into the prison does not make
the vision any the less true.   The man of faith will always
be a seer, while the man of unbelief will always be blind.
Asa makes no attempt to bribe the seer, but he attempts
to bridle his lips.   Instead of repenting his folly in putting
his trust in an arm of flesh, he seeks to justify himself, even
to the condemnation of the warning voice of God.   To get
beyond repentance is to get beyond the hope of recovery.
"If we sin we have an Advocate with the Father—Jesus
Christ the Righteous" (1 John 2. 1).

VII. Miserable End.   "Asa . . . was diseased in his
feet, until his disease was exceedingly great, yet in his
disease he sought not the Lord, but to the physicians"
(v. 12).   His sin lay not in seeking the help of the physicians, but in not seeking the help of the Lord.   Had not his
heart been diseased as well as his feet this sin would never
have been laid to his charge.   A physician may be a gift
from God as much as a seer, but when we trust the gift
instead of the Giver, we dishonour God, and expose ourselves to failure and death.   It is a melancholy fact that
this otherwise great and good man's life is closed with these
sorrowful words, "He sought not the Lord."   "Let him
that thinketh he standeth take heed lest he fall" (1 Cor.
10. 12).   Remember the words of the son of Oded, "The
Lord is with you while ye be with Him" (2 Chron. 15. 2).

JEHOSHAPHAT, THE BACKSLIDER.
2 Chronicles 17, 18.

"The whole Cross is more easily carried than the half.   It is the
man who tries to make the best of both worlds who makes nothing
of either."—*Drummond.*

Of how many of God's people it may be said, as was said of
the Galatians, "Ye did run well: who did hinder you that

ye should not obey the truth?" Although there are
always about us hindrances in abundance, that is no reason
why those gifted with the wings of faith should be hindered
in their spiritual life. Jehoshaphat, like Asa, began well,
but his bright morning soon became clouded with the
sorrows of failure. His character affords us both encouragement and warning. We see him—

I. Highly Honoured. "The Lord was with him"
(chap. 17. 3). The presence of God with us is an absolute
guarantee of success and sufficiency. The reason why God
companied with him was "because he walked in the first
ways of his father David." The first ways of David, and of
his father Asa, were their best days, when their hearts were
simple and perfect toward the Lord. He did not make
their sins an excuse for not following after the righteousness of God. The blemishes of others are often made a
stumbling-block to their virtues. Christ is the only perfect
example.

II. Greatly Encouraged. "His heart was encouraged
in the ways of the Lord" (v. 6, *margin*). When Uzziah
was made strong, his heart was lifted up to his destruction
(chap. 26. 16). When pride lifts the heart, it is lifted out
of the ways of the Lord into the way that leads to defeat
and death. It is while we are in the ways of the Lord that
we may confidently expect His uplifting. The Lord is not
going to encourage that man whose manner of life is
opposed to His will. "Delight thyself in the Lord, and
He shall give thee the desires of thine heart" (Psa. 37. 4).

III. Unequally Yoked. "Now Jehoshaphat joined
affinity with Ahab" (chap. 18. 1). Now, when he "had
riches and honour in abundance." Ahab was well known
as an enemy to Jehovah. "He did more to provoke the
Lord God of Israel to anger than all the kings that were
before him" (1 Kings 16. 33). After the friendship was

formed there came, of course, the fellowship. "He went down to Ahab to Samaria." The ungodly Ahabs are ever ready enough to have the servants of God to come down to their level. Nehemiah joined no affinity with Tobiah and Sanballat. His answer to them was, "I am doing a great work, so that I cannot come down." Be not unequally yoked with unbelievers. What fellowship hath light with darkness? The darkness may need the light badly, but the light can have no fellowship with the darkness. While Christ lived on earth He was constantly walking amidst the dense darkness of human sin and guilt, but He had no fellowship with it. No more can ye.

IV. **Wholly Surrendered.** Not to God, but to the scheming, unprincipled Ahab. How are the mighty fallen? "Wilt thou go with me," said Ahab, and Jehoshaphat answered him, "I am as thou art" (chap. 18. 3). Compromising has resulted in a voluntary captivity. Yet, at bottom, this answer is false, for the man who has known the power and fellowship of God can never be as that man who has ever been a stranger to God. We sell our liberty in Christ whenever we become the bondslaves of any man, or the tool of prejudice or fashion. The fear of man bringeth a snare. As long as Jehoshaphat was pledged to help Ahab, he was useless to help the cause of God. One is your Master, even Christ. Say to Him, "I am as Thou art" (2 Chron. 18. 3).

V. **Secretly Dissatisfied.** When Jehoshaphat proposed that inquiry should be made at the Word of the Lord, Ahab at once "gathered together of prophets four hundred men" (v. 5). These unsent prophets were quite unanimous that it was the mind of Jehovah (whom they knew nothing about) that they should "go up." To the king of Judah the testimony of those four hundred prophets sounded so formal and hollow that he knew there was no message from God in it. Neither numbers nor unanimity can constitute the àuthority of God. Ahab's prophets were ordained to preach "smooth things," and they did it. Jehoshaphat said, "Is there not a prophet of the Lord besides that we may inquire of him?" (v. 6). Four hundred worldly, men-pleasing preachers may be enough to keep an ecclesiastical machine going, but they are not enough to meet the needs of one single anxious soul who desires to know the mind and will of God. Words are not enough to bring settled conviction into the soul. The Christian who is satisfied with a formal powerless ministry has gone farther away from God than Jehoshaphat.

VI. Shamefully Exposed. "The captain of the chariots compassed him about, but Jehoshaphat cried out, and the Lord helped him" (vv. 30, 31). The king of Israel disguised himself, but an arrow shot at a venture found him out. Jehoshaphat confessed and was saved. Be sure your sin will find you out. But what a sorry part the king of Judah plays in this affair! What a picture of abject helplessness in the face of the enemy—he is utterly demoralised. Who is so powerless in the presence of temptation or opposition as the backslider? Yet, when their sin and folly is acknowledged before God, how ready He is to stretch forth His hand and help. Unbelief makes cowards of us all (v. 32).

JEHOSHAPHAT, THE OVERCOMER.

2 CHRONICLES 19, 20.

"Faith needs no staff of flesh, but stoutly can
To Heaven alone both go and lead."—*Herbert.*

ALTHOUGH Jehoshaphat, through his affinity with Ahab, fell into the mire, we do not find him wallowing in it. He must have been deeply ashamed on his return to Jerusalem, when Jehu, the son of the seer, met him with that sharp rebuke, "Shouldest thou help the ungodly?" (v. 2). But this good thing was found in him; he had already "prepared his heart to seek God" (v. 3), and God had already marked his repentance. As we have noted in our last study his steps down to failure and shame, we shall note now his upward steps of faith to victory and joy. His work of faith is seen in—

I. **Seeking the Restoration of Others.** "Jehoshaphat went out again through the people,...and brought them back unto the Lord God" (chap. 19. 4). If they had been led away from the Lord through his evil example, now that he was restored in heart, he loses no time in using his influence for their good. The best work we can do for our fellowmen is to bring them back to God. In bringing them to Him, we bring them to the source of peace, power, and plenty. We may bring them back to sobriety, and to the Church, without bringing them back to God. Those who seek to bring men to God show their faith in Him.

II. **Justifying the Ways of God.** "Now let the fear of the Lord be with you,...for there is no iniquity with the Lord our God, nor respect of persons, nor taking of gifts" (v. 7). These words were spoken to the judges in the land. The basis of their actions was to be the righteousness of God. There is no false dealings with Him, no respect of persons, no taking of bribes. Jehoshaphat found this out to his sorrow and loss when he joined affinity with Ahab, and went to war with him, although Micaiah had warned him in the Name of God about it. But he has learned a lesson, so he now testifies that there is no unrighteousness with God. He will not be bribed to "help the ungodly." "He is the Rock, His work is perfect, a God of truth and without iniquity, just and right is He" (Deut. 32. 4).

III. **Warning them of the Evils of Backsliding.** "Warn them that they trespass not against the Lord,

and so wrath come upon you, and upon your brethren"
(v. 10). "Burnt bairns dread the fire." The king has
learned by bitter experience that there is a vital
connection between the trespass of men and the wrath
of God. Man cannot sin with impunity. He that goeth
over the fence of God's will, the serpent of sin will
surely bite him. Outside the will of God is always
forbidden ground; it leads to Doubting Castle and the
tortures of Giant Despair.

IV. Seeking the Help of God in the Day of Trouble.
"After this the children of Moab and the children of
Ammon...came against Jehoshaphat to battle" (chap.
20. 1). After this—after he had decided to follow the
Lord fully—the testing time came. The trial of your faith
is more precious than gold. The time was when he might
have appealed to Ahab for help, having made a treaty
with him, but he looks away from man, and "sets
himself to seek the Lord" (v. 3). His example is
followed by the whole nation, for they "gathered
themselves together to ask help of the Lord" (v. 4).
Nations, as well as individuals, must believe in the
Lord to be saved. The man of faith knows no other
refuge than God Himself (Psa. 46. 1). He appeals to
God (1) as the *Almighty* One (v. 6); (2) as the *Faithful*
One (v. 7); (3) as the *Trusted* One. "Our eyes are
upon Thee" (v. 12). Whatever thy trouble is, seek help
from God, and expect it.

V. Answered Prayer. Jehoshaphat's faith in God
is further evidenced by this sudden answer to his prayer.
The Spirit of the Lord came upon Jahaziel, as he stood in
the midst of the congregation, with this message, "Be not
afraid nor dismayed by reason of this great multitude, for
the battle is not yours, but God's" (vv. 14, 15). As soon
as Jehoshaphat had put his trust in the Lord the battle

became His. God takes over the responsibilities of those who cast all their care upon Him. All the man of faith had to do was to "stand still and see the salvation of the Lord" (v. 17). How this was to be done they knew not; it was enough for him that God had promised to do it (Exod. 14. 13, 14). Christ fought for us the battle of sin and death. "Ye shall not need to fight in this battle."

VI. **Humble Acceptance.** In acknowledgment of God's wondrous grace, he "Bowed his head with his face to the ground,... worshipping the Lord" (v. 18). The revelation of God's saving power has always a head-bowing and heart-hallowing effect upon those to whom it comes in answer to faith and prayer. The true attitude of spiritual victors is that of worshippers. The more deeply we drink of the river of His grace, the more readily shall we bow and worship. He who humbled Himself to the Cross for us has given the death-blow to our pride and self-sufficiency.

VII. **Faithful Testimony.** "Hear me, O Judah, Believe in the Lord your God, so shall ye be established; believe His prophets, so shall ye prosper" (v. 20). Jehoshaphat has proved for himself the truth of this, he speaks from experience. Faith in God must lead to faith in His prophets. The fruit of faith is not weakness and instability, but strength and prosperity. The Bible affords us many examples of those who have been strengthened and made successful through their faith in God (see Heb. 11). "Therefore be not slothful, but followers of them who, through faith and patience, inherit the promises" (Heb. 6. 12).

VIII. **Joyful Expectation.** "Faith laughs at impossibilities, and says, It shall be done." He believed God, and rejoiced in the hope of a glorious victory. This is seen in his "appointing singers unto the Lord, to go out

before the army, and to say, Praise the Lord" (v. 21).
Happy is that man who can sing praise to God for His bare
word of promise, and go on expecting miracles to be
wrought.   He shall not be disappointed.   "Believe, and
thou shalt see. "   "When they began to sing and to praise,
the Lord set ambushments against the enemy,... and they
were smitten" (v. 22).   "Then they returned with joy"
(v. 27).   If the singers had been defeated, then might
the enemies of the Bible rejoice; but the God of the Old
Testament never fails to fulfil the expectations of all those
who trust Him.   This is the victory that overcometh the
world, even our faith.

UZZIAH; or, FAILURE THROUGH PRIDE.

2 CHRONICLES 26.

"The fall thou darest to despise—
May be the angel's slackened hand
Has suffered it, that he may rise
And take a firmer, surer stand;
Or, trusting less to earthly things,
May henceforth learn to use his wings. "—*Procter*.

UZZIAH was but a lad of sixteen when he was crowned king
of Judah.   His reign was a long one, extending over fifty-
two years.   It was good for him that he came under the
godly influence of the clear-visioned Zechariah, the
burden of whose message was, "If ye forsake the Lord
ye cannot prosper" (chap. 24. 20).   Who can reckon up
the full value of that life, which has been illumined
with a definite message from God.   Zechariah's word
had burned its way into the heart of young Uzziah,
for in his days he sought God (v. 5).   The story of
his life reveals to us—

I. **An Encouraging Testimony.**   The writer of the
Chronicles tells us that, "As long as he sought the Lord,
God made him to prosper" (v. 5).   As long as God got

His true place in the life and work of Uzziah, there were
no interruptions to the steady march of his rising prosperity. All true and abiding prosperity is "God-made,"
and the condition of it is seeking to know and how to do
His will. Mark that it was "as long as he sought the
Lord," and no longer that the divine benediction rested
on him and his work. It is ours to go on trusting; it is His
to go on blessing.

II. **An Assuring Confirmation.** "He was marvellously helped till he was strong" (v. 15). God helped
him against the Philistines, and against the Arabians
(v. 7), to build towers, and to dig many wells (v. 10).
He also gave him a great host "that made war with mighty
power to help him against the enemy" (v. 13). The
help of God is intensely practical. They are always
marvellously helped that are helped of God. It is surely
God's purpose to make those strong who seek Him, that
His will may be done in them. God will still bear them
witness, both with signs and wonders, and with divers
miracles and gifts (distributions) of the Holy Ghost (Heb.
2. 4). "Be ye strong in the Lord, and in the power of
His might."

III. **A Terrible Fall.** "But when he was strong, his
heart was lifted up to his destruction" (v. 16). It is a
great privilege to be helped of God and made strong, but
every privilege has its corresponding temptation and
danger. Peter was made strong to walk on the sea, but
even then he began to sink. Elijah was made strong to
overcome the wicked works of Ahab, yet afterwards he fled
before the wrath of Jezebel. Yes, Uzziah fell.

1. THE CAUSE. "His heart was lifted up." Lifted up
through pride and self-confidence. As long as he sought
the honour of the Lord, God lifted him up, but now that he
seeks to honour himself by assuming the priestly office he

falls from the grace of God (v. 18). His position as king
gave him no right as priest. A man's worldly position
gives him no authority or fitness for the holy ministry.
Uzziah, in his presumption, was setting aside the revealed
will of God. He must have known that the Levites had
been chosen of God from among the children of Israel to do
the service of the tabernacle. A solemn warning had also
been given: "The stranger that cometh nigh shall be put
to death" (Num. 18. 6, 7). But, in his own name, and in
his own strength, he would go, so his pride led to his fall.
It is of the nature of self-righteousness to despise the work
and office of the Priestly Saviour.

2. THE EFFECT. "He was a leper unto the day of his
death" (v. 21). He was wroth, and would not go back
when Azariah the priest remonstrated with him, but when
the Lord smote him with leprosy "he hasted to go out"
(v. 20). Instead of his work being accepted of God, he
was smitten with a curse, and driven out from His presence
with a lifelong brand of sin upon him. Like many other
lepers, the plague was in his head. Having been smitten
with a sense of his presumption and sin, God did not need
to cast him out of His holy place, for he himself hasted to go
out. The holy presence of God is no place of comfort and
rest for the unforgiven sinner. Heaven is no home for those
who ignore the work of Christ, who is our Great High
Priest. He is the One Mediator between God and man;
the Way, the Truth, and the Life; no man can come unto
the Father but by Him. It was Uzziah's own sin that "cut
him off from the house of the Lord" (v. 21). It is the sin
of putting proud self in the place of the Lord's Anointed
that kindles the wrath of God, and cuts that soul off from
fellowship with Him. The man who sets aside God's
appointed way of life does it to his own destruction.
"There is none other name under Heaven given among
men whereby we must be saved."

HEZEKIAH; or, FEATURES OF A REVIVAL.

2 CHRONICLES 28, 29.

"Teach me, my God and King,
  In all things Thee to see;
And what I do in anything,
  To do it as for Thee!
All may of Thee partake,
  Nothing can be so mean,
Which with this tincture (for Thy sake)
  Will not grow bright and clean."—*Herbert.*

LAMENNAIS says, "Faith demands action, not tears; it demands of us the power of sacrifice—sole origin of our salvation; it seeks Christians capable of saying, 'We will die for this;' above all, Christians capable of saying, 'We will live for this.'" The man who can truthfully say, "To me to live is Christ," is revealing Christianity in its sublimest form. Ritual and dogma may have their place, but if the individual life does not manifest itself in bringing glory to God and eternal blessing into the lives of sinful men, they are clouds without water. Hezekiah's revival work was the outcome of his own faith in the Living God— the faith which worketh by love. We shall try and find some helpful lessons here. We observe some—

I. Evidences that a Revival was Needed.

1. HOLY THINGS ARE CUT IN PIECES. "Ahaz...cut in pieces the vessels of the House of God" (chap. 28. 24). These sacred things which had been so useful in the House and service of God became the objects of the wrath and hatred of those who despised Him, whose instruments they were. All those who are seeking to cast discredit upon the books of the Bible are, in their own way, attempting to "cut in pieces the vessels of the House of God." These sixty-six books, which compose the Bible, are so many vessels needed in the House of God for the work of the ministry. Every servant of God is also a vessel in His

House, and the ungodly still try, with the sharp tongue of
scorn and calumny, to cut their testimony in pieces.

2. THE WAY OF ACCESS IS CLOSED. "He shut up the
doors of the House of the Lord" (v. 24). It is surely a
sign that a revival is needed when men seek to block the
way of others from worshipping God. Ahaz denied
Jehovah, then sought to shut others out from the acknow-
ledging of Him as God. There are doors in the temple of
every man's heart that may be closed to his own loss and
destruction. The door of communion with God may be
shut by our love of, and delight in, the things which He
hates. Our own unfitness is as a self-closed door. The door
of Divine love and light may be closed by our own pride
and prejudice. The door of faith and prayer is shut up
by the unbelief of our own hearts.

3. THE LIGHT OF TESTIMONY IS QUENCHED. "They put
out the lamps" (chap. 29. 7). The lamps of God, aflame
with the holy oil, became unbearable to those who loved the
darkness of falsehood rather than the light of truth. The
Christian's testimony for God is as a flame kindled and
sustained by the oil of the Holy Spirit. When this is "put
out," it is an insult to God and a grieving of that Spirit,
whose character and mission is to make us as a flame of
fire. It was a sad experience the foolish virgins had when
their lamps went out. It is even the work of the world, the
flesh, and the devil to put out the lamp of truth, and to
quench the light of testimony, that the darkness of death
and desertion may settle down in the House (Church)
of God.

4. THE OFFERING OF INCENSE IS GIVEN UP. "They have
not burned incense" (v. 7). When the lamp of testimony
has been put out, the offering up of the incense of prayer
and adoration will speedily cease. These two are vitally
connected—they live or die together. Testimony for God

will be but as sounding brass and tinkling cymbals where the sweet incense of believing prayer is awanting.

5. THERE IS A GENERAL DEPARTING FROM THE WORSHIP OF GOD. "Our fathers have forsaken Him, and have turned away their faces from the habitation of the Lord, and turned their backs" (v. 6). There is great need for a revival when the multitude turn their backs upon the House of God. Of course we do not wonder at many turning away their faces from God's House when the doors are shut up and the lamps out. Polished stones, carved wood, and all sorts of material finery have no attractions for a soul hungering for the Bread of Life. But there are many who turn their backs upon God's provision because they prefer the broken cisterns of their own hewing. To turn the back on God is to turn the face to destruction.

II. **Evidences that a Revival had Come**. There was—

1. A PERSONAL CONSECRATION. "Hezekiah did that which was right in the sight of the Lord" (chap. 29. 2). He began by getting himself put right in the eyes of the Lord. It is one thing to pray for a revival, it is quite another to yield ourselves definitely to God, that His will and work may be done in us and by us. A coming shower of blessing is sure to be heralded by drops falling on some individual soul. Seek to be that soul by personal consecration.

2. THE OPENING OF CLOSED DOORS. "He opened the doors of the House of the Lord" (v. 3). Every avenue of the soul that has been closed through indifference and unbelief will be immediately thrown open, and the light of God's truth will have free access to the heart, which should be the House of the Lord. "Clear the darkened windows, and let the blessed sunshine in." All revival comes from the PRESENCE of the Lord, who waits outside the closed door, saying, "Behold, I stand at the door and knock, if any man hear, and open, I will come in."

3. A CASTING OUT OF THE UNCLEAN. "Sanctify
yourselves, and sanctify the house...and carry forth
the filthiness out of the holy place" (v. 5).   "And the
priests went into the inner part, and brought out all the
uncleanness" (v. 16).   It is an unmistakable evidence that
the power of God's Spirit is moving mightily when His
servants take to the work of cleansing the inner part.   Out
of the heart are the issues of life.   If God the Spirit is to
dwell in us, the inner sanctuary of the life must be purged
of all that is unbecoming in His presence.   The common
Levites had no power to deal with those abominations that
were in the inner parts of the temple, the priests had to go
in and bring them out to the court, before the Levites could
remove them (v. 16).   There are evils and hindrances to
the work and worship of God that can be seen and dealt
with only by those who have had the anointing of the Holy
Spirit.   Others, like the Levites, may see the sinfulness
of certain things, when they have been pointed out,
and put them away.   "Cleanse Thou me from secret faults"
(Psa. 19. 12).

4. REALISATION OF THEIR TRUE POSITION BEFORE GOD.
"The Lord hath chosen you to stand before Him, to
minister unto Him, and that ye should be His ministers,
and burn incense" (v. 11, R.V.).   A revolution is certain
when God's people realise their true relationship to Him as
chosen ones.

(1) They are chosen *by the Lord*—called by His grace.

(2) They are chosen to *stand before Him*—to wait before
Him, and to receive His Word.

(3) Chosen to *minister unto Him*—to do all in His Name
and for His glory.   "Ye are not your own."

(4) Chosen to *be His ministers*—to carry His Word and
will to others.

(5) Chosen to *burn incense*—to offer unto God the sweet incense of intercessory prayer. Ye know your calling, brethren; are ye walking worthy of it?

THE ROYAL MESSAGE.

2 CHRONICLES 30. 1-12.

"Matter exists only spiritually, and to represent some idea and body it forth."—Carlyle.

ALL Scripture is given by inspiration of God, and is profitable for doctrine. Let us see if we cannot find some profitable doctrine from the historical facts here chronicled for our spiritual advantage. Observe the—

I. Great Provision. "The priests made an atonement for all Israel: for the king commanded that the burnt-offering and the sin-offering should be made for all Israel" (chap. 29. 24). This was the great day of atonement, when reconciliation was made for the people by the blood of sacrifice. The sin-offering speaks of guilt put away, while the burnt-offering declares acceptance with God. There was no message of hope and blessing to the people until the question of sin had been settled. The Gospel of Salvation could only be preached by the apostles after Christ had suffered for us, as the sin-offering; and had risen again, as the burnt-offering. It is through Him we have received the reconciliation (Rom. 5. 11, R.V.).

II. Urgent Message. These letters, sent from the king, and carried by the posts throughout all Israel, contained—

1. A CALL TO REPENTANCE. "Ye children of Israel, turn again unto the Lord God of Abraham" (v. 6). No turning is effectual that is not unto God. The Thessalonians "turned to God from idols.." A man may rend his garments and turn to idols, but those whose hearts have been rent will turn to God (Joel 2. 13). Repentance is

needed, for all have gone astray. God hath commanded all men everywhere to repent and believe the Gospel.

2. A CALL TO SURRENDER. "Yield yourselves unto the Lord" (v. 8). This royal letter demanded, not only repentance toward God, but a personal consecration of the life to Him. The yielding of ourselves unto God is the evidence that we have in heart turned to Him. "Know ye not that your bodies are the members of Christ" (1 Cor. 6. 15). We turn to God·for life, then we are to yield ourselves unto Him, as those that are alive from the dead, and our members as instruments of righteousness unto God (Rom. 6. 13).

3. A CALL TO SERVICE. "And serve the Lord your God" (v. 8). Acceptable service is the outcome of a consecrated life. Turn, yield, serve—is the royal order. If ye are redeemed by the precious Blood of Christ, therefore glorify God in your body and your spirit, which are God's. If ye can say, "Whose I am," ye ought also to add, "Whom I serve" (Acts 27. 23).

4. A WORD OF ENCOURAGEMENT. "For if ye turn unto the Lord, your children shall find compassion...for the Lord your God is gracious and merciful, and will not turn away His face from you" (v. 9). This letter, like the Gospel of Christ, contained the only way into a life of true happiness and usefulness.

III. **General Invitation.** The king's message was to be "proclaimed throughout all Israel, from Beer-sheba even to Dan" (v. 5). From the southern to the northern extremities of the land. Like the Gospel, it was to be preached to every creature (Mark 16. 15). All were invited to "keep the Passover unto the Lord." It was for the glory of God that they should keep in memory that terrible night in Egypt, when they were saved through the blood of the lamb. How much more is it to His glory that we should remember the "Blood of His Cross?" To share in this great deliverance, the Gospel of God invites us.

IV. Twofold Result.

1. SOME MOCKED. "They laughed them to scorn, and mocked them" (v. 10). The poor postmen had to bear their sneers, but it was the God of Israel, who inspired the message, that was mocked and laughed at. The posts, who passed from city to city as itinerant preachers, were not responsible for the message they carried; they were doing the king's business, and with him they had to do. The messengers of the Cross and the King of Glory are so closely linked together that to despise the one is to despise the other. "Inasmuch as ye have done it unto one of the least of these, ye have done it unto Me" (Matt. 25. 40). Saul was persecuting the saints when the Lord said to him, "Why persecutest thou Me?" (Acts 9. 4).

2. SOME BELIEVED. "Nevertheless divers...humbled themselves and came to Jerusalem" (v. 11). No doubt this call was a humbling one. It implied a confession of their sins and a turning away from their own wilful, wicked works. It was much easier for some to laugh at the messenger than to do this. Any fool may sneer, but it takes a wise man to repent. Although the Gospel is to be preached to every creature, that does not prove that every creature who hears the message will be saved (Acts 16. 34). Only those who repent and believe—who "humble themselves and come" —can partake of the benefits of this Great Passover. Christ, our Passover, sacrificed for us. Whosoever will may come.

MANASSEH'S CONVERSION.
2 CHRONICLES 33. 10-13.

"He that finds his Heaven must lose his sins."—*Cowper*.

SOME lives are virtually blighted and ruined before they are born, because of hereditary tendencies. Manasseh had everything in his favour, being the son of a godly father, yet, in point of principle, he was a moral wreck. How much his mother or his counsellors were to blame for this it is difficult to say, but he proved himself to be an enemy to his father and to his God. We note his—

I. Rebellion. To all who feared the Lord, his reign was the "reign of terror." There was an utter disregard to his father's godly example. "He built again the high places which his father had broken down" (v. 3). But not only so, he was possessed with such an evil spirit that he would have his own will and way, to the dishonour and defiance of God, by setting up his own idol in the House of God (v. 7). The essence of rebellion against the Lord is: Not Thy will, but mine be done. The Dagon of self is often set up in the temple of God. It is said that Sir John Sloane had the heartless sayings of his unnatural son pasted together, framed and glazed, and hung up on the wall, with these words printed underneath: "Death-blows given to his mother, by George Sloane." Is not every sin a death-blow given by the sinner to the grace and mercy of God?

II. Warning. "The Lord spake unto Manasseh, and to his people, but they would not hearken" (v. 10). In some way or other God made the young king to know that he was living a life at enmity with Him. If he had no special message sent by the prophet Isaiah, whom he probably caused to be sawn asunder, he had the commandments and ordinances given by the hand of Moses (v. 8). In mercy, God warns before He strikes in judgment. The warning may come through some providential earthquake, or by the still small voice of conscience, or, perhaps, through the lips of some heaven-sent messenger. Not to "hearken" is to continue an unholy warfare against the Almighty.

III. Defeat. "They took Manasseh among the thorns (hooks), and bound him with fetters" (v. 11). Because he denied the Lord, the Lord brought the host of Assyria against him. National backsliding brought national defeat. This is an established principle in the government of God, as the book of Judges, and all past history, clearly teach. As it is nationally, so is it individually. The soul that sinneth, it shall die. Defeat and bondage like ravenous wolves, will, sooner or later, overtake the God-defying sinner. The Lord has many an unexpected way of "hooking" His enemies. He hooked Saul of Tarsus on his way to Damascus, with the light of truth. Manasseh was hooked with the irons of affliction and reproach (Psa. 107. 10, 11). What is man that he should boast himself against God? At any moment He may thrust in His hook of authority, and hurl back the rebel into everlasting doom.

IV. Surrender. "When he was in affliction he besought the Lord his God, and humbled himself greatly before God" (v. 12). While in his affliction and solitary confinement, his guilty past, in all its ghastliness, stares him in the face. He sees that the forces against him are overwhelming, and yields himself a prisoner unto God. Never did an enemy sue for peace more earnestly than did the subdued Manasseh. His repentance was real—he humbled himself and sought the Lord. Before, he sought to slay the truth of God by resisting it; but the truth has conquered. A drunken sailor was once brought to his knees by a Christian worker tenderly saying to him, "Jack, you had a mother." Sometimes memory, as well as patience, has its perfect work. There can be no real repentance that does not lead to God. A man might tremble, as Felix did, or be as deeply convicted as Agrippa, and yet never repent. Feeling sorry for sin, and resolving to do better in the future, is not the repentance that brings life. If our bitterness of soul does not constrain us to seek the forgiveness of God, and to yield ourselves to Him, it is a repentance that needs to be repented of. The evidence of the prodigal's repentance was that "he came to his father" (Luke 15).

V. Victory. "The Lord heard his supplications, and brought him again to Jerusalem, into his kingdom" (v. 13). He comes back a new man to live a new life. Old things have passed away; all things have become new. His was a great deliverance, as all God's deliverances are. He was emancipated from a wicked self and a terrible past by being made a new creation through the grace of God. He only now begins to live; his past life has brought forth nothing but failure and shame. Manasseh is the Saul of the Old Testament. God can save the worst of sinners, but only by the way of repentance and faith. Although this is an example of the grace of God, there is no encouragement to continue in sin, that grace may abound. If one dying thief was saved, that is no proof that other dying thieves will. Although one Blondin crossed the Niagara on a rope, that is no guarantee that anybody could do it. God hath commanded all men to repent and believe the Gospel. "Then Manasseh knew that the Lord, He was God" (2 Chron. 33. 13). He knew Him now because he had experienced His saving and restoring power.

THE STIRRED-UP SPIRIT.
Ezra 1. 1-11.

"Not to the rich He came, and to the ruling
  (Men full of meat, whom wholly He abhors);
Not to the fools grown insolent in fooling—
  Most, when the lost are dying at their doors.
Nay! but to her who, with a sweet thanksgiving,
  Took in tranquility what God might bring;
Blessed Him and waited, and, within her living,
  Felt the *arousal of a holy thing.*"—*Myers.*

THE clock of God's providence may seem at times to go slow, but it always strikes at the proper minute. During the seventy years of the Jews' captivity, the cup of Babylon's iniquity was being filled, so that the time of their deliverance synchronised with the time of Babylon's downfall. The quiver of the Almighty is full of arrows. In the first year of his reign, Nebuchadnezzar carried many into captivity. He reigned forty-five years; his son (Evil-merodach), twenty-three; and his grandson (Belshazzar,) three years—which make up the seventy predicted years of their bondage. In the third year of Belshazzar, Darius, the Mede, captured the city of Babylon, and Cyrus, the king of Persia, became ruler (Dan. 5). The accession of Cyrus to the throne was another marvellous fulfilment of prophecy (Isa. 44. 28). The very name of the Jews' liberator was mentioned one hundred and fifty years beforehand. This is no mere coincident or random occurrence, it is an indisputable proof of inspiration. At this crisis three distinct prophecies found their fulfilment:

1. The punishment of the king of Babylon (Jer. 25. 12).

2. The end of the seventy years' captivity (Jer. 29. 10; Dan. 9. 2).

3. The coming of the deliverer named. We may use these words, "The Lord stirred up the spirit of Cyrus," as a key to unlock some of the treasures of this chapter.

I. **The Spirit Needs Stirring Up.** "The Lord stirred up the spirit of Cyrus" (v. 1). The will of God will never be done by us until the spirit within us is stirred up to do it. Man is not a machine. Cold, mechanical service is an insult to the living God. Selfishness is death in His sight. It is possible to have the form of godliness while the spirit is sleeping the sleep of death. You hath He quickened who were dead in trespasses and sin.

II. **God Alone can Effectually Stir up the Spirit.**

"The Lord stirred up the spirit of Cyrus." The source of all spiritual life and power is with Him. Every God-quickened spirit is a spirit raised from the dead, that He might work in that spirit both to will and to do of His good pleasure (Phil. 2. 13). There is a divine purpose in every divinely-awakened soul. It is the Spirit that quickeneth.

III. **The Means by which the Spirit was Stirred up.** There was (1) the Word of God. Daniel understood by books the number of the years...that the Lord would accomplish seventy years in the desolations of Jerusalem (Dan. 9. 2). Daniel may have showed Cyrus the prophet's reference to himself, as the divinely-appointed shepherd by whom the temple was to be built, and the captives freed without a price (Isa. 44. 28; 45. 1-13). (2) The providence of God. The fact that Cyrus was now made Governor of Babylon, he was in a position to carry out the prophetic declaration. He discovered that the means of accomplishing these purposes of God were committed to him. Woe must come upon him if he obeys not the heavenly call. Thus, God still stirs up the spirits of men, by making them to know and feel that His word has special reference to themselves in the doing of His will. No man will heartily obey the Gospel of God unless he has, like Cyrus, been powerfully convinced that it is for himself, as if there were no other to whom it could be so applied, and whose only alternative is to obey or sin against the clearest Light. A woman was once led to claim the bare promise of God through receiving a letter addressed to another woman of the same name. She concluded that, if her name had been written in the Bible, she could never have believed that it was her that was meant. When the Holy Spirit applies the word of God, it is always unmistakably luminous and personal.

IV. **The Evidences of a Stirred-up Spirit.**

(1) There is faith in the word of God. Cyrus said, "The Lord God of heaven . . . hath charged me to build Him an house at Jerusalem" (v. 2). The king of Persia was no more clearly and urgently charged to build the temple than we are to believe on the Lord Jesus Christ, and serve Him without fear, in holiness, all the days of our life (Luke 1. 74-75). This call to us is quite as personal and imperative as the call that came to Cyrus. Have we as heartily believed it?

(2) There is confession of the purpose of God. "He made a proclamation through all the land" (v. 1). When we discover what the will of God is concerning us, we should not be ashamed to make it known publicly what our attitude is toward this revealed will. Has he not warned us that "Whosoever is ashamed of Me and of My word, of them will I be ashamed."

(3) There are liberal things devised for the honour of God. The large-heartedness of Cyrus is seen in his offer to let all the captives go who desired the restoration of Jerusalem (v. 3). in his providing for the sojourners by the way (v. 4), and in his delivering up of "all the vessels of the house of the Lord" into the hand of "the prince of Judah" (vv.7-8). The liberal deviseth liberal things (Isa. 32. 8). The spirit that has been stirred up by God will surely be constrained to do God-like things. The spirit of Carey was powerfully stirred up when he said, "Expect much from God, and attempt much for God." Moody said, "God never uses a discouraged worker." The stirred-up spirit is always on the alert for opportunities of helping on the work and people of God, and deviseth means whereby His banished ones may be restored. Such spirits seek first the Kingdom of God and His righteousness, and God worketh in them both to will and to do of His good pleasure.

THE SECRET OF SUCCESS IN THE LORD'S WORK.

Ezra 6. 14.

"First, seek thy Saviour out, and dwell
Beneath the shadow of His roof,
Till thou have scanned His features well,
And known Him for the Christ by proof. "—*Keble*.

"THEY prospered through the prophesying of Haggai and Zechariah." Those words may be taken as the key to the whole situation, as described in chapters 3 to 6. Including servants and maids, who had gone with their masters and mistresses, over forty-nine thousand accepted the offer of Cyrus, to leave their captivity and go up from Babylon to Jerusalem. They counted themselves blessed, on hearing such a "joyful sound" (Pas. 89. 15). (See Luke 4. 18). Now, look at—

1. The Work to be Done. "To build the house of the Lord God of Israel" (chap. 1. 3). This house was for the honour of God: it was to be a testimony to His holy Name. We may learn from this that it is the prime duty of those who have been delivered from bondage to seek that the name of God might be magnified among the heathen. Every redeemed one should build for Him an house of testimony.

II. The Start Made. The first thing they did was to set the altar upon his bases (chap. 3. 3). They began with the altar. This is the sure basis of all acceptable work for God. The atoning sacrifice must have its true place if the great house of God's Church is to be built up and established. The altar of the Cross is not upon its proper basis when it stands on the wisdom of men instead of the wisdom of God. The true basis of the Cross of Christ is to put it where God has put it, between sin and salvation. Then they laid the foundation (chap. 3. 10). After the burnt-offerings came the laying of the foundation. Those who lay the foundation, and go on with the building before the altar of the Cross is placed upon its right basis, are vainly working outside the gracious purposes of God. The foundation of God's house is laid on the rock of Christ's atoning sacrifice. God's order is, first, reconciliation, then stability and progress. After this they praised the Lord (chap. 3. 11). This was not formal Psalm-singing, it was the spontaneous outburst of hearts filled to overflowing with joy and thanksgiving. "They shouted with a great shout" (Josh. 6. 5). Such a result surely proves that this is the right method and spirit in which to do the work of God.

III. **The Adversaries.** When the people of God begin to shout and praise, then the enemy will be stirred up to envy and opposition. "The adversaries of Judah came... and said, Let us build with you" (chap. 4. 1, 2). They professed to be seeking also the honour of the God of Israel. These may have been the "fathers" referred to by the woman of Samaria in John 4. 20. The work so far has been a success, and now they wish to become partners in the business. But the answer of those divinely commissioned ones was fearless and unequivocal. "Ye have nothing to do with us to build an house unto our God; but we ourselves will build" (chap. 4. 3). Those sent ones were not going to be unequally yoked with unbelievers. What part hath he that believeth with an infidel? (2 Cor. 6. 14-16). When they saw that they were to have neither part nor lot in the matter, then they sought to "weaken their hands...and trouble them;" they also "hired counsellors to frustrate their purpose" (chap. 4. 4, 5). But one thing they forgot, or refused to believe, and that was, that "their purpose" was God's purpose. The cause of God cannot be properly advanced but by those who know that they have been called of God.

IV. The Temporary Interruption. "Then ceased
the work of the house of God which is at Jerusalem" (chap.
4. 24). The wicked may have their day of triumph, but
their time is short. How was the work stopped? Those
"hired counsellors" wrote a letter to the new king of Persia,
representing Jerusalem as a "rebellious and bad city," and
that these Jews who had lately come from Babylon were
rebuilding it for the purpose of fortifying themselves
against the power and authority of Babylon. The king on
receiving the letter made search, and found "that the city
of old time hath made insurrection against kings" (chap.
4. 19), and because of the city's past glory and power he
"gave commandment to cause these men to cease." This
must have been a staggering blow to those enthusiastic
men. What could it mean? Does the providence of God
contradict His Word? In the time of perplexity, wait.

V. The Renewed Effort. "Then the prophets Haggai
and Zechariah prophesied unto the Jews that were in
Jerusalem,...then they began to build the house of God"
(chap. 5. 1, 2). This revival came through the word
spoken "in the Name of the God of Israel." There is need
for a prophet to ring out the message of God when His
work has come to a standstill. These discouraged workers
needed to be reminded that they were saved out of Babylon
to serve the Lord in Jerusalem, and that "the eye of their
God was upon them" (chap. 5. 5). The prophets doubtless
made it clear to them that this was God's work, and that
they had been called of Him to do it, so in His Name the
work is resumed with more determination than before, for
"with them were the prophets of God helping them" (chap.
5. 2). Nor was it in vain, for Darius the king discovered
in "the house of the rolls" the decree of Cyrus concerning
the Jews and the house of God, and straightway sent a letter
to the "adversaries" saying, "Let the work of the house of
God alone" (chap. 6. 7). So "they prospered through the

prophesying of Haggai and Zechariah" (chap. 6. 14). And the house was finished (v. 15). The remedy for our helpless hands and feeble knees is a clearer apprehension of God's purposes of grace in our individual lives, and a fearless, whole-hearted devotion to the fulfilment of the same. He giveth power to the weak, and to them that have no might he increaseth strength.

EZRA: HIS LIFE AND CHARACTER.
Ezra 7. 10.

"Thou canst not choose, but serve; man's lot is servitude,
But thou hast thus much choice—a bad lord or a good."
—*Trench.*

Ezra, who led the second party from Babylon to Jerusalem, was both a priest and a scribe—a minister of the sanctuary and an exponent of the law of Moses. Between the first and second detachments there is a period of fifty-seven years. The last four chapters of the book are descriptive of the work done under the personal guidance of the author. In looking at this man and his work we shall find much that stimulates to faith and service. Observe his—

I. **Preparation.** "Ezra prepared his heart to seek the law of the Lord, and to do it, and to teach" (chap. 7. 10). The preparations of the heart belong to man (Prov. 16. 1, R.V.). When a man is prepared in his heart to seek the Word of God, to do it and to teach it, a great work of revival has already begun. The heart must first be put right with God before the life can become useful for Him. These preparations belong to man, but the revelations belong to God. Christ's first message was Repent, for the Kingdom of Heaven is at hand. Change your mind; prepare your heart for that new order of things which has, in grace, come within your reach.

II. **Qualification.** "The hand of the Lord his God

was upon him" (v. 6). Because of this invisible and powerful hand upon him, the king granted him "all his requests. " The mighty hand of God's guiding and upholding power came upon him after he had prepared his heart to seek those things by which His Name might be glorified. The All-conquering Hand is the accompaniment of the prepared heart. We think of the disciples of Christ preparing their hearts during those ten days in which they waited for the promised power of the Holy Ghost. All who are filled with the Spirit have the hand of the Lord their God upon them.

III. **Provision.** "I, Artaxerxes the king, do make a decree...that whatsoever Ezra shall require of you, it be done speedily, unto an hundred talents of silver" (chap. 7. 21, 22). Here he had the assurance that all his wants would be supplied. Ezra prepared his heart, and God in this singular manner prepared against all his needs. He never sends His servants a warfare on their own charges. The measure of supply was to be unto even "an hundred talents of silver" (£22,000), but the measure of our supply is "according to His riches in glory by Christ Jesus. " Unsearchable riches. "Look unto Me, and be ye saved" from your poverty and powerlessness.

IV. **Commission.** "And thou, Ezra, after the wisdom of thy God, that is in thy hand...teach ye them that know not the laws of thy God" (chap. 7. 25). Those who have the wisdom of God in their hearts must become the "messengers of the Lord of Hosts" (Mal. 2. 7). The counsel of this heathen king would put many professing Christians and religious teachers to shame. If God is to have a chance of gaining moral victories among those who know not His will, surely His Word must be plainly taught to them by those who have experienced the power of it in their own hearts and lives. Faith cometh by hearing, and hearing by the Word of God. The hearing that stirs up faith in God is not the hearing of the words of man's wisdom, but the hearing of that word which is the wisdom of God. Preach the Word.

V. Consistency. "I was ashamed to require of the king soldiers and horsemen to help us against the enemy in the way, because we had spoken unto the king, saying, The hand of our God is upon all them for good that seek Him" (chap. 8. 21, 22) To say the least, this is the simple honesty of faith If our faith is in God, and we know that the cause is His, why should we beg for the patronage of men? Our life should be consistent with our testimony. To preach "faith in God," and be found catering for the favours of the ungodly, is to make the religion of Jesus Christ to stink in the nostrils of reasonable men. If the Lord be God, follow Him. But what did Ezra do? He made it a matter of special prayer, and the Lord of Hosts answered him (v. 23). Cast all your care upon Him.

VI. Devotedness. "The holy seed have mingled themselves with the people of those lands.... When I heard this thing I rent my garment and my mantle, and plucked off the hair of my head, and sat down astonied" (chap. 9. 2, 3). This was a violation of the Divine command (Deut. 7. 3), and the tidings of it came to Ezra as a heart-breaking sorrow. He felt it the more keenly because of the warmth of his own heart towards the Word and ways of God. The depth of our sorrow over the sins of others will be according to the depth and reality of our sympathy with the cause of God. For a people, separated unto God (Deut. 7. 6), to be unequally yoked together with unbelievers, is enough to make every true servant of Christ sit down astonied. It is a paralysing and soul-sickening sight If we had more of Ezra's devotedness we would know more about the sufferings of Christ (Jer. 8. 21).

What else could he do than fall upon his knees and spread
out the case before God (vv. 5-15), for he felt that as long
as they lived in sin they could not stand accepted before
Him (v. 15).

VII. Success. "Then all the congregation answered,
As thou hast said, so must we do" (chap. 10. 12). And
the guilty priests "gave their hands that they would put
away their wives" (v. 19). The earnest prayer and
faithful testimony of this consecrated scribe prevailed, and
a great victory was won for God in the spiritual uplifting
of the people. Some of those "strange wives" may have
been as dear to some of those men as an eye or a right hand,
but they must be cut off. The more closely the affections
become entwined with any forbidden object, the more fatal
is the snare. The secret of Ezra's success is an open one,
and is within the reach of every servant of Christ—true-
hearted, whole-hearted loyalty to God's Word and work.
Have faith in God; the prayer of faith shall save.

SOUL-STIRRING SYMPATHY.
NEHEMIAH 1. 1-4.

> "How was He
> The blessed One made perfect? Why, by grief—
> The fellowship of voluntary grief—
> He read the tear-stained book of poor men's souls,
> As I must learn to read it."—*Kingsley.*

NEHEMIAH, like Moses, was singularly fitted beforehand
for the work God had appointed him to do. Belonging, as
he did, to the "children of captivity," he was in perfect
sympathy with them, and being the "king's cupbearer," he
accepted a position of wealth and influence that gave him
pre-eminence among his brethren. He was fitted, not only
socially, but morally, as a true leader of men—being a man
of great courage, with profound convictions and intense
devotion to the cause of God. In our study of his life and

character we trust there will be, in his example, much to inspire us in our service for Christ, and to follow those who "have obtained a good report through faith."

I. His Position. "I was in Shushan the palace" (v. 1). He had the privilege of being in this great palace because he was "the king's cupbearer" (v. 11). Although he occupied this high position in the Persian court, we have no reason to believe that it was at the sacrifice of any religious principle, but rather because of his attractive and trustworthy character. The "man of God" should be the most dependable of men, although, like Joseph, their virtue may become their only fault.

II. His Sympathetic Inquiry. "I asked them (men who had come from Judah) concerning the Jews...and concerning Jerusalem" (v. 2). Nehemiah was not so far carried away by his own promotion and success as to be indifferent to the interests of his brethren and the city of his God. They are in a sad state who, through prosperity, have had their sympathies withered up for the poor of God's people and the honour of God's Name. Those who desire to help in the cause of God will not fail to inquire into the real nature of the case. If the heart is alive unto God, we will gladly avail ourselves of every opportunity to fit ourselves, even for self-sacrificing service unto Him. Where the love of the world is, the love of the Father cannot be "The love of Christ constraineth us" (2 Cor. 5. 14).

III. The Revelation Made. "The remnant are in great affliction and reproach: the wall of Jerusalem is broken down, and the gates burned with fire" (v. 3). This was sorrowful news, but it is better to know the facts than live under a delusion. The people were suffering from poverty and reproach, and the wall of their defence was broken down. They were still reaping the fruits of their rebellion and idolatry (2 Kings 25). Weakness and

reproach must always characterise the people of God when
the walls of separation are broken down, and the gates
of praise burned up by the enemies' fire. A powerless,
praiseless Christian is a reproach to the name he bears.

IV. **The Effect Produced.** He says, "When I heard
these things, I sat down and wept" (v. 4). All those
generous forces of his soul were arrested on hearing about
this God-dishonouring state of matters. In the warmth of
his sympathy he abandoned himself for the good of his
fellows and the glory of his God. Oh! with what indifference we can see and hear those things that are making the
Church of God to-day a reproach and a bye-word among
His enemies. Paul knew about this holy soul agony when
he said, "I tell you, even weeping, that they are the
enemies of the cross of Christ" (Phil. 3. 18). Is it possible
for us to be baptised into His death, and yet to have hearts
so callous toward His cause amongst men, that we are
never constrained through personal interest to sit down and
weep? It is very easy and natural for us to sit down and
sorrow over our own personal losses and bereavements;
we cannot help feeling it, because our own souls are so
closely and vitally associated with them. Then is it
because we, in our hearts, are not in such close and vital
fellowship with Christ and His cause and people that we
are so difficult to move to tears over the ravages of sin and
the desolation of the sinner? Christ wept over Jerusalem.
If we had His eyes and heart of compassion we would
weep over it too. If Nehemiah's heart had not been moved
and melted first, he never could have done the work which
he afterwards did. Can we possibly be in a fit condition
for serving Christ if we are not able to weep over those
things that dishonour His Name and grieve His Spirit?
A further evidence that his heart was right with God is
seen in the fact that his sympathy constrained him to self-
denial and prayer. "He fasted and prayed before the God

of Heaven." Those who have the interests of God and His kingdom so close to their hearts as Nehemiah had will be ready to deny themselves of everything that would hinder His will from being done in them and by them (Heb. 11. 24-26). He laid aside the luxuries of the palace that he might give himself to prayer. Where else can a trustful, affectionate child go but to his father in the day of perplexity and anguish? Their "great affliction" was not too great for the "God of Heaven." With a heart melted in the love of God, and eyes bedimmed with the tears of brotherly kindness, surely the prayer that comes from such a source, and in such a manner, will be abundantly answered. If we have not compassion enough to lead us to pray for others it is high time to sit down and weep, and fast, and pray for ourselves.

INTERCESSORY PRAYER.

NEHEMIAH 1. 4-11.

"Why have they never known the way before?
Why hundreds stand outside Thy mercy's door?
I know not: but I ask, dear Lord, that Thou
Wouldst lead them now."—*C. F. Tytler.*

"MY prayers," says Trench, "are the one grace which my foe cannot refuse." "I can get at him through the God of Heaven," said a fond mother, in speaking of her wayward, wandering boy. Yes, prayer is one of the greatest privileges and one of the mightiest forces with which the soul of man can have to do. Through prayer Elias shut up the rain of Heaven for three and a half years (Jas. 5. 17); and Peter was delivered from the prison in answer to prayer (Acts 12. 5). Having been made unto our God a kingdom of priests (Rev. 5. 10, R.V.), it is part of our heavenly calling to make intercession for others. In these words of Nehemiah we think we see all the characteristics of prevailing prayer. There was—

I. Earnestness. "He wept, mourned, fasted" (v. 4). This was no formal prayer. It was the outcome of a soul stirred to its utmost depths. Those who draw nigh with the lip while the heart is afar off may themselves be satisfied with a prayer which is nothing but a solemn mockery in the sight of God. As God loveth the cheerful giver, so doth He regard the whole-hearted petitioner. The fervent prayer of a righteous man availeth much.

II. Knowledge. It was because Nehemiah knew God that he could pray thus: "I beseech Thee, O Lord God of Heaven, the great and terrible God, that keepeth covenant and mercy for them that love Him" (v. 5). He believed in God's greatness, His terribleness, His faithfulness, and His mercifulness. He that cometh to God must believe that He is, and that He is a Rewarder of them that diligently seek Him (Heb. 11. 6). To know such a God and in such a fashion is to ask much and expect much. They that do know their God shall be strong and do exploits through the prayer of faith (Dan. 11. 32; see 1 Sam. 12. 18).

III. Importunity. "Hear the prayer of Thy servant, which I pray before Thee now, day and night" (v. 6). Importunity is a vital element in prevailing prayer. It was because of the widow's "continual coming" that she gained her request. This is the lesson our Lord Himself teaches us from that parable of the man begging loaves from his friend at midnight: "I say unto you...because of his importunity, he will give him as many as he needeth" (Luke 11. 8). It was while Moses held up his hand that Israel prevailed. Pray without ceasing. Be not weary in such well-doing, for in due season ye shall reap if ye faint not.

IV. Confession. "Both I and my father's house have sinned, we have dealt very corruptly against Thee" (vv. 6, 7). The sin of dealing falsely with God is a very common one, and very grievous. We pretend to believe His Word, and yet live in fear and doubt; we ask Him for things that we don't expect, and make a profession of loyalty to His cause, while, in heart, we are more concerned about our own personal interests than His. How can we expect to prevail with God in prayer if there is no confession made of that deceitfulness which has made our lives so barren in the past. Spiritual bondage and failure in the Christian life imply that there is sin in the camp, and need for self-scrutiny and confession.

V. **Faith.** "Remember, I beseech Thee, the word that Thou commandest, saying,... If ye turn unto Me, and keep My commandments... I will bring them into the place that I have chosen to set My Name there" (vv. 8, 9). Faith lays hold upon the spoken Word of God. The prayer that is built up by faith on the promise of God cannot be overthrown. In turning to the Lord himself, Nehemiah fulfilled the condition of blessing, then he takes the place of the Lord's remembrancer, saying, "Remember... the Word." This is that beautiful child-like confidence which honours God, and is infinitely well pleasing in His sight. God cannot deny Himself when He finds so much of Himself involved in such pleading. But he goes a step farther, and reminds God of His great work in redeeming His people by His "great power and strong hand" (v. 10). The audacity of faith is astounding. It looks up into the face of God, saying: There is Thy word of promise, and there, in redemption, is the evidence of Thy mighty love and the strong hand of Thy saving grace. Now, therefore, do this thing for me. He that cometh to God must believe, and, in so believing, he must be rewarded.

VI. **Consecration.** "O Lord, be attentive to the prayer of Thy servant, who desires to fear Thy Name"

(v. 11).   In our prayers we shall often ask amiss, it we
are not prepared to yield ourselves unto God, and to live for
the glory of His Name (Jas. 4. 3).   There are three classes
of servants: the slave, who serves through fear; the hireling, who serves for wages; and the son, who serves for
love.   It is the obedient and devoted son who expects
and gets the favour and the fullness of the father.   It is
those who present themselves a living sacrifice unto God
that are able to prove what is that good, and acceptable,
and perfect will of God (Rom. 12. 1, 2).   Those who would
prevail with God to give them the servant's portion must,
first of all, take the servant's place.

ANSWERED PRAYER.

NEHEMIAH 2. 1-8.

"Speak to Him, thou, for He hears, and Spirit
With spirit can meet.
Closer is He than breathing, and nearer
Than hands and feet."—*Tennyson.*

A PERIOD of three months comes in between the month
Chisleu—when Nehemiah heard of the "great affliction" of
his brethren in Jerusalem—and the month Nisan, when his
prayers began to be answered.   All this time he had been
earnestly pleading with God in secret, yet, in his public
service he had hitherto been able to conceal the sorrow of
his heart by wearing a cheerful countenance.   Well he knew
that it was a crime against the king to appear before him
with a sad face.   But in thus seeking to please men we
may be putting away from us the very blessing we so much
desire.   God does not require us to play the hypocrite in
order that His will might be done.   It is always best to be
perfectly honest.   This is clearly proven by what follows.

I. A Startling Question.   "Why is thy countenance
sad,...this is nothing else but sorrow of heart?" (v. 2).
His agony of soul had become too great to be covered

any longer with a smile. The king's question smote him with terror. "Then I was very sore afraid." At that time Nehemiah had become so intensely interested in the well-being of others as to forget himself in the presence of the king. Such deep self-forgetfulness cannot fail to become a channel of rich blessing to many. He had prayed that he might find mercy in the sight of the king (chap. 1. 11), but he could never have anticipated that, through his sadness in the king's presence was to come the dawn of deliverance. "My ways are not as your ways, saith the Lord" (Isa. 55. 8).

II. **A Critical Moment.** After Nehemiah had confessed that his countenance was sad because "the city of his father's sepulchres lieth waste," the king said unto him, "For what dost thou make request?" (v. 4). If the first question filled him with fear, this one was fitted to bewilder him with astonishment. Was this the daybreak of hope falling at last upon that long night of sadness which had overcast his soul? Was this God's door of salvation now suddenly opened before his eyes? Had the time come when all the desires of his heart were to be granted him? "For what dost thou make request?" What an opportunity this is when given by one who is able to satisfy the soul with good. A greater than Artaxerxes has said, "What wilt thou that I should do unto thee?" But observe how this man of prayer faced this new situation. "So I prayed to the God of Heaven." Had he not been living in the spirit of prayer he would not have thought of it at that particular moment. In this little spontaneous act there is a revelation of his true character. Even when taken unawares the holy habit of his soul is to look up to God for guidance. When God becomes the greatest reality in our lives there is nothing more natural than prayer. Those who say they have no time to pray know not the nature of prayer. Nehemiah found time to pray while a king waited

on his answer. It is with prayer as it is with salvation—
"Look and live." "Look unto Me, and be ye saved"
(Isa. 45. 22).

III. **A Great Request.** He had now gained the
favour of a great king, and so he brought large petitions.
He asked definitely for two things—

1. That he may be SENT. "If it please the king...send
me...that I may build" (v. 5). This devoted servant of
God had not only prayed for his brethren and his father's
city, but he had consecrated himself unto God, and was
ready to be used of Him as soon as the door of opportunity
opened. Like Isaiah, he could say, "Here am I, send me."
How can we expect God to do great things for us and by us
if we are not prepared to make a sacrifice of ourselves for
Him. The religion that costs nothing is just worth what
it costs. Our prayers would have a new meaning if we
offered them as from the altar of burnt-offering. Then he
asked—

2. That he may be SUPPLIED. "If it please the king, let
letters be given me," etc. (vv. 7, 8). These letters to the
governors beyond the river, and to the keeper of the king's
forest (royal preserves) were to Nehemiah words of authority
and promise. He had what every God-sent servant ought
to have, a clearly-defined commission, an assurance of
safety (convoy), and the promise of supply. Our Lord and
Master never sends any a warfare on their own charges. He
makes all grace abound that we may have all-sufficiency.
"Ask and ye shall receive" (Matt. 7. 7).

IV. **An Abundant Answer.** "The king granted me
according to the good hand of my God upon me" (v. 8).
The secret of success in the work of the Lord lies here.
When a man's life is in the grip of the "good hand of God"
then signs and wonders will be done. The measure of
blessing will be according to the power of that hand that is

upon us. This mighty, conquering hand laid hold of
Nehemiah that day when he was constrained to "sit down,
and weep and pray" (chap. 1. 4). He did not, like Jacob,
wrestle against that heavenly and divine hand which was
bowing him in sorrow and humiliation at the feet of God.
He yielded himself entirely to the pressure of His heavy,
yet "good hand." Like Ezra (chaps. 7. 6; 9. 28), he was
quite conscious that the hand of God was upon him, as an
instrument by which to accomplish the good pleasure of His
will. All things work together for good to them that love
God, to them who are the called according to His purpose.

PREPARING FOR THE WORK.
NEHEMIAH 2. 11-20.

"Lives of great men all remind us
　　We can make our lives sublime,
And, departing, leave behind us
　　Footprints on the sands of time.
Footprints, that perhaps another—
　　Sailing o'er life's solemn main
A forlorn and ship-wrecked brother—
　　Seeing, shall take heart again."—*Longfellow*.

NEHEMIAH is one of those "great men" whose footprints
have been left deep and distinct on the sands of the past,
footprints that have inspired with fresh courage many a
drooping heart in the service of the Lord. His journey
from Babylon to Jerusalem occupied three months. His
prayers have been so far answered; he is now on the long
coveted field of labour. It will be interesting and profitable
for us to study his method of operation. For he—

I. **Takes Time to Reflect.** "So I came to Jerusalem,
and was there three days" (v. 11). Ezra also waited
three days (chap. 8. 32) before the work began. He
that believeth shall not make haste. It is a great lesson
to learn to wait on God. We imagine these three days

were spent largely in meditation and prayer. Three days
are significant of death and resurrection. The servants of
Christ have often seen their plans and purposes pass from
death into life, while they calmly waited before God.
When a great crisis came in David's life he went and "sat
before the Lord" (1 Chron. 17. 16). In the secret chamber,
Luther, Knox, and many others learned how to conquer.

II. **Surveys the Difficulties.** "I arose in the night...
neither told I any man what my God had put in my heart
to do...and viewed the walls which were broken down"
(vv. 12, 13). Like a wise physician, he begins by making a
thorough diagnosis of the case. No devoted city "slummer"
ever went out of a night to view the desolations of sin
with more eager eyes than did Nehemiah to investigate
those ruined walls and heaps of rubbish. There are many
Christian workers living in a fool's paradise because they
refuse to believe that things are as bad as they really are.
Those who only view the city on a Sunday can know little
about those terrible heaps of broken-down humanity that
are seen on a Saturday night. In many cases faith in the
Word of God, and the habit of going to hear it, have been
broken down, and the gates of praise have been burned
with the fire of unholy criticism. Viewing the difficulties
will be a wretched business and a heart-breaking task,
unless, like Nehemiah, we know that God has put the
remedy within our own hearts (v. 12). The unbelieving
spies will be sure to bring back a God-slandering report.
The ruin must be measured by God's remedy. Man's need
can only be met by the infinite grace and power of the
almighty Saviour.

III. **Makes an Appeal for Helpers.** "Ye see the
evil case that we are in,...come and let us build up the
wall of Jerusalem, that we be no more a reproach" (v. 17,
R.V.). One of the best ways of beginning a work for

God is to set others to work. But observe, he did not say, "Go and build," but "Come, let us build." The great work of restoring Jerusalem (Church) to its pristine glory and power will never be accomplished so long as the leaders (preachers) attempt to do all the building themselves, and seem satisfied if the others will but come, and sit, and listen, and look on. "All at it, and always at it," ought to be the normal condition of the Christian Church. It would take a very expert workman to do as much work in a week as twenty ordinary hands. Besides, as the life of God's people is one, so is their work. Unity of faith should lead to unity of effort. As a ruined Jerusalem was a dishonour to every Jew, so a weak and powerless Church is a dishonour to each individual member. The way to roll away the reproach is to arise and build. Put those displaced stones into their proper place.

IV. **Gives an Encouraging Testimony.** "Then I told them of the hand of my God upon me, as also the king's words, and they said, Let us rise up and build" (v. 18). Personal testimony is a most powerful factor in the service of the living God, but this implies, of course, a real, deep, personal experience of the goodness and faithfulness of God. This, in some measure, every leader in the work of God must have. The Holy Spirit works through us that which He has wrought in us. The fact that God had answered Nehemiah's prayers, and called him to do this work, was an inspiration to the others to "rise up and build." Such is the influence of a consecrated life. Those take too much upon them who try to put all God's servants on the same level, so do those who would monopolise the holy service because they are paid for it. While it is true that some are called of God, as evangelists, pastors, and teachers, it is also true that "to every man his work" (Mark 13. 34).

V. **Meets with Opposition.** "When Sanballat,

Tobiah, and Geshem heard, they laughed us to scorn, and despised us" (v. 19). It was a great grief to them that "a man had come to seek the welfare of Israel" (v. 10). The more Christ-like the life becomes, the more bitter will the enemies of God and His people be. They hated Him without a cause, and the disciple is not greater than his Lord. Sanballat means "strength and courage," and fitly stands for the wisdom of this world. Tobiah—"the Lord is good"—is a true representative of the formal professor, one who has a good name but a bad heart. They laughed to scorn the weak hands that were attempting to rebuild the walls, but they saw not the "good hand of God" that was with them. They mocked and despised, because, as the work proceeded, they found that they themselves were being built outside the city. Everything that makes the ungodly feel their weakness and their isolation from the city and people of God, if it does not lead to repentance, will doubtless provoke to opposition (Luke 23. 2).

VI. Declares the Whole Truth. He meets the scoffers' objections with a simple, brief, fearless statement of the whole case. He declares the truth about God: "The God of Heaven, He will prosper us" (v. 20). This work is associated with the living, faithful, almighty God of Heaven; He is for it, He is with it, He is in it. He declares the truth about himself and his co-workers: "Therefore we, His servants, will arise and build." We are His servants, we are doing His business, and we will go on, say what ye will, do what ye may. He declares the truth about his enemies: "Ye have no portion, nor right, nor memorial in Jerusalem." As for you, ye are strangers to God; ye are not His people. There is nothing belonging to you in the Holy City; ye have no right to any of its privileges, for the things of Jerusalem awaken no sacred memories in you. Ye have neither part nor lot in this matter (Acts 8. 21). When the walls of the New Jerusalem (the Church of God)

are finished, will you be built out or built in? The word
of the Cross is, to them that are perishing, foolishness;
but to us, who are being saved, it is the power of God
(1 Cor. 1. 18, R.V.).

AT THE WORK.
NEHEMIAH 3.

"Knowing ourselves, our world, our task so great,
Our time so brief—'tis clear, if we refuse
The means so limited, the tools so rude,
To execute our purpose, life will fleet,
And we shall fade, and leave our task undone—
We will be wise in time!"—*Browning.*

THERE is a deep truth in the saying of Emerson, that
"every man's task is his life preserver." This truth is
specially applicable to the Christian worker. If any man
will lose his life (in service) he shall save it, is the teaching
of a greater than Emerson. This chapter is crowded with
the names of those who took part in the work of repairing
the wall. Their names are held in everlasting remembrance
because, like Mary, they had wrought a good work for the
honour of His Name. Holy deeds stand like footprints on
the sands of time. Some brief, but important lessons
might be learned here.

I. **There is Need for Work.** "The wall is broken
down" (chap. 1. 3). By faith, the walls of Jericho fell
down, after they were compassed about; but the walls of
Jerusalem are not going to be built up by faith alone.
According to the practical theology of James, there is a
sphere in which "faith without works is dead." Son, go
work to-day in my vineyard. Are there not many stones
(souls) lying about our own doors that are out of their
proper setting, and so failing to fulfil the real purpose for
which they exist?

II. **There is Work for All.** "To every man his work"

(Mark 13. 34). "He that will not work should not eat" (2 Thess. 3. 10). Surely this holds good with regard to spiritual things as well as temporal things. What right has anyone to feast continually on spiritual things if there is no outcome in active service for the Lord, the Giver of all? All may not be able to do the same work, but all can work. The daughters of Shallum (v. 12) could not perhaps do as heavy work as the son of a goldsmith, or the son of an apothecary (v. 8). The priests (v. 1) and the merchants (v. 32) may not be equally expert in the art of building, but in the Name of God they helped in the work. Let every one do something. If you can't handle the trowel, surely you can say, "God bless the builders." Labour in prayer.

III. **This Work was Voluntary.** "They said, Let us rise up and build" (chap. 2. 18). The need was set before them; they took it to heart, and made up their minds to make a start at once. Those professed servants of Christ who loiter about the ecclesiastical market-place in idleness because "no man hath hired them," are to be sincerely pitied. Those who go and work for love to Him will receive from Him "that which is right." "The wise man's heart is at his right hand," ready to manifest itself in action (Eccles. 10. 21). Where the heart has been given to God and His cause, the hand of service will certainly follow. The Lord Jesus Christ does not press His yoke upon us, but He does say, "Take My yoke upon you" (Matt. 11. 29).

IV. **This Work was United.** You will notice that almost every verse in this chapter begins with words such as these: "And next unto him," "Next unto them," "After him," "After them." Every worker joined his work with his neighbour's. Because they were united in heart they willingly united in effort. They were inspired, not by any selfish consideration of personal reward or pre-eminence, but by one general God-honouring motive—the glory of His Name and the salvation of the people. The only rivalry that was among them was a provoking of one another unto love and good works. We cannot be truly united in the great work of God unless all merely sectarian and personal interests sink out of sight in the one intense desire for the building up of that cause which alone can bring honour and glory to God our Saviour. The struggle of the churches is often more like the confusion of Babel than the conviction of Pentecost. "We are workers together with Him" (2 Cor. 6. 1).

V. This Work was Successful. The word "repaired" occurs thirty-four times. Each builder repaired—made anew and finished—that piece of work given him to do. They were all successful in their work, although all did not do, perhaps, the same amount of work. In the temperament and manner of these workers there would, doubtless, be great diversity; but in their object and purpose there was great unanimity. Baruch seems to have been quite an enthusiast for the work, he is distinguished as "earnestly repairing the other piece" (v. 20). Then those who had houses "repaired every one over against his own house" (v. 28); and Meshullam "repaired over against his chamber" (v. 30). Earnestness is good, but it is only as wild fire in the service of the Lord, if we are not prepared to begin at home. Building for God should begin at the Jerusalem of our own door. Joshua said: "As for me and my house, we will serve the Lord." To say, "the prophet has no honour in his own country," is no excuse for a Christian worker's failure at home. Our influence for Jesus Christ abroad will be pretty much like what it is at home. The Holy Spirit will never put a premium on hypocrisy. These workers succeeded because they would not be discouraged, although "their nobles put not their necks to the work of the Lord" (v. 5). There are "independent gentry" in the spiritual, as well as in the social sense—those who have such a large stock of self-respect that they cannot bend their necks to the work of the Lord. They may give a collection or a suggestion, but they will not stoop to personal service Like many church professors, they are frozen with respectability. But those whose hearts God hath touched have also got God-touched hands, so they press on with the work, and the God of Heaven, He prospers. "Therefore, my beloved brethren, be ye steadfast, immovable, always abounding in the work of the Lord, for as much as ye know that your labour is not in vain in the Lord."

It may be interesting to note that the names of the first and last workers mentioned are suggestive of Jesus Christ as the Alpha and Omega of this great spiritual work. Eliashib (God the Restorer) (v. 1), and Malchiah (God is King) (v. 31). Between the rising of the High Priest and the coming of the King the work was done.

PERSEVERANCE IN THE MIDST OF OPPOSITION.

NEHEMIAH 4. 1-11.

"Alas! how light a cause may move
  Dissension between hearts that love—
  Hearts that the world in vain had tried,
  And sorrow but more closely tied;
  That stood the storm when waves were rough,
  Yet, in a sunny hour, fall off
  Like ships that have gone down at sea,
  When Heaven was all tranquillity."—*Moor*.

THE more powerfully the young oak is bent before the blast, the more deeply does it strike its roots into the stiff, stubborn soil beneath. Although persecution is not something to be coveted, yet it is not to be shunned or lightly esteemed. "Blessed are ye when men shall revile you...falsely for My sake; rejoice and be exceeding glad, for great is your reward in Heaven" (Matt. 5. 11, 12). Everything that sends the roots of our spiritual life deeper down into the will of God will make us more steadfast and fruitful for Him. We shall note—

I. The Nature of the Opposition. There was the—

1. TANTALIZING ARROWS OF SCORN. Their quiver seemed to be full of them. They sneered at their character. "What do these feeble Jews?" (v. 2). They were feeble in number, and, in the eyes of their wealthy opponents, they were feeble in resources; but they saw not the helping hand of God which was with them. They sneered at their motives. "Will they fortify themselves?" "Will they sacrifice?" As much as to say, "How can they succeed in saving themselves? How will they ever set up a worship that will secure the presence and help of God?" The Lord knoweth them that are His. They sneered at their enthusiasm. "Will they make an end in a day?" They are going at the work as if they were going to finish it in a day. The lukewarm Christian is not likely to be mocked at by the easy-going worldling. They sneered at the task attempted. "Will they revive the stones out of the heaps of the rubbish?" Their aims are too lofty; they attempt too much. They sneered at the work done. "Even that which they build, if a fox go up, he shall break down their stone wall" (v. 3). Such are the criticisms with which all faithful workers for God are assailed; but the building goes on, for such labour is not in vain in the Lord; for He scorneth the scorners, but giveth grace unto the lowly (Prov. 3. 34). Then came—

2. WICKED CONSPIRACY OF THE ENEMY. "When the breaches began to be stopped, then they were very wroth, and conspired all of them together to fight and to hinder it" (vv. 7, 8). But in vain do these fowlers spread their

net before the eyes of the God of Heaven. They said,
"They shall not know, neither see, till we come among them
and slay them" (v. 11). But God knew, and God saw, and
it was with Him, and not with these "feeble Jews," that
they had to do. It was like the conspiracy of thorns
against the devouring fire. Though hand join in hand, the
wicked shall not triumph nor escape punishment. All the
united forces of hell cannot impede the progress of those
who trust in God, and courageously do His will.

3. DISCOURAGEMENT OF DOUBTING FRIENDS. "Judah
said, The strength of the bearers of burdens is decayed, and
there is much rubbish: so that we are not able to build the
wall" (v. 10). Opposition is bad enough when it comes
from without, but it is a worse heartburn when it comes
from those who have hitherto been our friends and helpers.
Judah got discouraged because he lost sight of God, and
kept looking at the adversaries, the weakness of the burden-
bearers, and the much rubbish that lay in the way, and,
having lost faith himself, he sought to discourage others in
the work, saying, "We are not able to build the wall." A
discouraged man is a useless man in the work of the Lord;
he is worse than useless—he is a positive hindrance. "Be
strong and of a good courage: be not afraid, neither be
dismayed, for the Lord thy God is with thee" (Josh. 1. 9).

II. **The Steadfast Character of the Workers.** They
had—

1. A MIND TO WORK (v. 6). They had no mind to
sit moping over their difficulties, or to spend their time
in mere talk or fault-finding. The love of God constrained
them.

> "I will not work my soul to save,
>   For that the Lord hath done;
> But I will work like any slave,
>   For the sake of God's dear Son."

They not only had a mind to work, but they had a mind

also to have their work "joined together." Instead of joining the work together, some have a mind to work alone, while others seem to think that all the work should be done by themselves.

2. A HEART TO PRAY. "Nevertheless, we made our prayers unto God" (v. 9). A working mind should always be accompanied with a praying heart. Those who believe that "God is a Refuge" will most certainly flee to Him in a time of storm. Those who have no heart to pray will soon have no mind to work. We are called, not only to "put on the whole armour of God," but also to "pray always with all prayer" (Eph. 6. 11-18). Work for God must be done in the Spirit of God. It is through prayer that strength is imparted for service.

3. AN EYE TO WATCH. "We set a watch against them day and night" (v. 9). Watching and praying are frequently linked together in the Scriptures of truth (see Matt. 26. 41; Mark 13. 33; Eph. 6. 18; 1 Peter 4. 7). It was not necessary that these watchmen should occupy their time in following all the movements of their adversaries, it was enough that they watched the interests of their God-given work. It is sad to see many of the Lord's servants so busy studying the pull-down tactics of the enemy that they neglect to build up. Watch and pray, that ye enter not into this temptation.

WORK AND WEAPONS.
NEHEMIAH 4. 12-23.

"Faith's meanest deed more favour bears
Where hearts and wills are weighed,
Than brightest transports, choicest prayers,
Which bloom their hour and fade."—*Newman.*

MAN was not made to mourn, but to work (Gen. 2. 15) and, as Houghton says, "Man must toil for good, or he shall toil for ill." Man is a toiler, either for God or against Him. He that is not for Me, said our Lord, is against Me. In attempting to do some definite work for God, it is good to "count the cost," but in counting the cost, let us take heed, that we count on Him who is able to bear the cost. We must measure our difficulties, and our needs, with the strength and resources of Him whose we are, and whom we serve. There are some suggestive thoughts for workers here.

I. The Workers' Position. "Therefore in the lower places, and on the higher places, I even set the people after their families with their swords" (v. 13). We may not like the lower places, because there we are more exposed to the wrath of the enemy and the workers themselves may need to go out of sight. We would much prefer the "higher places" in Christian work, where we could see and be seen. Slum work is never so pleasant to some as preaching in a pulpit or on a platform. These workers had grace enough to go where they were sent, and to do their part gladly, knowing that each piece of work was a needful part of the great whole. The order was "after their families." How beautiful to see whole families united in furthering the work of the Lord.

II. The Workers' Privilege. "Be not afraid... remember the Lord, and fight (pray) for your brethren, your sons, and your daughters, your wives, and your houses" (v. 14). Those devil-driven adversaries will never be able to make this man afraid, whose mind is stayed on that God who is "great and terrible." These warrior-toilers were not asked to fight for themselves, but for their brethren, etc. But well they knew that in seeking the good of their households they were securing their own salvation. This fighting for our sons and daughters, wives and houses must be done in faith. Fight the good fight of faith. The promise is to you and to your children "Believe on the Lord Jesus Christ and thou shalt be saved, and thy house" (Acts 16. 31). Remember the Lord; remember His power and His promise, and pray for your brethren, etc. The more we think of Him the more will we think of others.

III. **The Workers' Encouragement.** "God brought their counsel to nought" (v. 15). The enemy had entered into a secret conspiracy to fight against Jerusalem, and to hinder the work (v. 8). They had planned to fall upon them unawares, but God "disappointed the devices of the crafty, so that their hands could not perform their enterprise" (Job. 5. 12). How was this victory won? It was won through prayer (v. 4). They cried unto God, and He "turned their reproach upon their own head." Those who live in communion with God are not easily taken by surprise. The weapons that are formed against such shall not prosper. Take no thought for your life: your Father knoweth.. From the closet of prayer you can bombard and bring to confusion all the forces of hell. When Samuel cried unto the Lord, the Lord thundered upon the Philistines (1 Sam. 7. 10). Who shall stand when He appeareth.

IV. **The Workers' Weapons.** "For the builders, every one had his sword girded by his side" (v. 18). Yet while every worker had his recognised weapon, there were different ways in which they were held. Some had their weapons held by others, while they did the work (v. 16). Some wrought with the one hand, and held the weapon with the other (v. 17). Others wrought with their swords girded at their sides. Work and warfare are the characteristics of the Christian life. They are in danger of working in vain who neglect the sword of the Spirit, which is the Word of God. The other danger is to be so taken up with the weapons that we neglect the work. The servants of Christ must be aggressive as well as defensive. Blessed be the opposition that makes us cling more firmly to the sword of the Spirit, for our weapons are not carnal, but spiritual and mighty. If God be for us, who can be against us (Rom. 8. 31). Put on the whole armour of God, that ye may be able to stand. Sword-girded workers are everywhere needed in these present times. Are you one?

V. The Workers' Warning. "In what place ye hear the sound of the trumpet, resort ye thither" (v. 20). While working and watching they were to hold themselves in readiness for a gathering together at any moment at the call of the trumpet. As the work of building went on, and parts of the wall got built up, the workers became in some places separated from one another, and so felt the need of listening for the trumpet call. Be ye also ready, for in such an hour as ye think not, "the Lord shall descend from Heaven...with the trump of God...and we shall be caught up together" (1 Thess. 4. 16, 17). Blessed are they who work, and watch, and wait for the heavenly call.

VI The Workers' Devotion. These men were so thoroughly devoted to the work that they willingly practised self-denial for its good. We dare not pretend to be consecrated to the work of the Lord unless we are prepared to sacrifice personal ease and comfort for His sake. Their whole-heartedness is seen in their working long hours. "From the rising of the morning till the stars appeared" (v. 21). They were no mere hirelings, yawning for the hour when they might drop their tools and make for home and their own private pursuits. Those who long to get out of the work of Christ are unfit for it. It is one thing to be weary in the work, it is another to be weary of it. Their zeal was also seen in their "lodging within Jerusalem" for the good of the cause. This implied separation from all those who were without. They willingly sacrificed this liberty for the bondage of service. Those who dwell with the King for His work are the most likely to be successful in pleasing Him. Then, again, they kept themselves in constant readiness for the work. "None of us put off our clothes" (v. 23). The building of the wall was not a matter of convenience, but of life. "This one thing I do" (Phil. 3. 3), was the all-absorbing motive. Be followers of them. Be fervent in spirit, serving the Lord.

A FIGHT WITH SELFISHNESS.
NEHEMIAH 5. 1-13.

"Not by looking within, but by living without
    This centre of self, shall a man grow wise.
  Let us, leaving ourselves, then, go boldly about,
    And take part in the business of earth and skies."—*Lytton.*

CARLYLE has said, "Alway there is a black spot in our sunshine, it is...the shadow of ourselves." A shadow of selfishness—as black as midnight—appears before us here, in the first five verses of this chapter. Great distress had come into the city. The enemy had succeeded in intercepting the food supplies, and, alas, the wealthier portion of the people began to take advantage of their poorer brethren, by enriching themselves to their terrible cost. Lands, vineyards, houses, and even sons and daughters, were mortgaged, or exchanged for bread (vv. 1-5). Things got so unbearable that a "great cry" was raised by the people. The behaviour of Nehemiah during this painful crisis gives us a further revelation of the greatness and stability of his character—features which ought to characterise every one called of God into His service. These features are—

I. **Uprightness.** "I was very angry when I heard their cry" (v. 6). It is only the truly righteous soul that can be truly angry at unrighteousness. This is not that "anger without a cause" which is in danger of judgment (Matt. 5. 22), but the holy anger which is akin to the

"wrath of the Lamb." Alas, that there should be so many
of God's servants whose convictions don't seem to be pure
enough or deep enough to move them with indignation at
the merciless greed of some religious professors. These
men were "brethren" (v. 1), but they showed no brotherly
love.

II. **Courage.** "Then I...rebuked the nobles and
the rulers" (v. 7). Courage in the Name of God is absolutely necessary in those called to take the lead in His
work (Josh. 1. 6, 7). Nobles and rulers, moneyed and
influential men, are often allowed to escape deserved
reproof just because they have happened to be born and
brought up in more favourable circumstances than others.
The tyranny of the moneyed class is only equalled by the
envy of the poorer class. The servant of Christ must not
strive either for personal advantage or the praise of men,
but in the name of his Master he must fearlessly speak out
the truth as manifested in His Life, and Word, and Work.
"I am the Truth."

III. **Unselfishness.** "We, after our ability, have
redeemed our brethren the Jews which were sold unto the
heathen; and will ye even sell your brethren?" (v. 8).
Nehemiah had sought, as far as his means would allow, to
redeem to liberty those who had been sold unto the heathen,
but these selfish nobles and rulers had sought to get gain
by selling their brethren. Love to others under heathenish
influences, and a willingness to give according to ability—
both of time and means—for their salvation, are the unfailing characteristics of all those who sincerely serve the Lord
Jesus Christ. The Cross of Christ has not yet been clearly
seen, if selfishness has not yet received its death-blow
(Gal. 2. 20). Think of the ability of faith and love.

IV. **Holy Jealousy.** "It is not good that ye do:
ought ye not to walk in the fear of God because of the

reproach of the heathen?" (v. 9). When God's people
do not walk in His fear they bring reproach upon His holy
Name (Rom. 2. 24). It is a melancholy fact that many of
Christ's servants are more jealous about the honour of their
own name than His. When men defame us, does it cut us
more deeply to the heart than when we hear them casting
reproach upon the Name of our Lord Jesus Christ? Are
all our vital interests so interwoven with the Name
and work of our Lord and Saviour that when He is
touched we are touched, and that those who honour Him
are honoured by us?

V. Thoroughness. Nehemiah was neither luke-warm
nor half-hearted. Whatsoever he did, he did it heartily
and completely, as unto the Lord. Like Boaz, he is not
content until he has "finished the thing." Thoroughness,
to be perfectly sound, must be governed by the purest
motives, and acting in the clear light of the Divine will,
otherwise it may be but the wild fire of fleshly enthusiasm.
The thoroughness of Nehemiah's character comes out here
in his demand for restoration. "Restore, I pray you, to
them, this day, their lands," etc. (v. 11). And after he
had received their promise to do so, see how he significantly
"shook his lap," warning them against unfaithfulness to
their vows (v. 13). Such whole-hearted effort was crowned
with success, for "all the congregation said, Amen, and
praised the Lord, and did according to the promise." How
will men believe what we say, as Christ's ambassadors, if
we do not fearlessly declare the whole counsel of God,
keeping back nothing. All the demands of God must be
reiterated by His servants, or the message delivered will be
destitute of that fine, keen edge which makes it effectual in
the hearts of those who hear it. The gospel of restoration
has two aspects: (1) The restoring of the soul unto God;
(2) the restoring of ill-gotten gain to others (Lev. 6. 4;
Luke 19. 8).

NEW TRIALS.
NEHEMIAH 6. 1-9.

"Only those are crowned and sainted,
Who, with grief, have been acquainted."
—Longfellow.

WHEN Carlyle was shown a "Comic History of England,"
he naively asked when they would have a comic Bible? To
him history was a sacred thing. To the Christian the
Providence of God should be as sacred as the Word of God.
But the enemy, in one shape or other, will even seek to
devour those who are enthusiastic for the work of God.
Two new temptations present themselves to Nehemiah.
There was what might be called—

I. The Compromise Temptation. "Come, let us
meet together in the plain of Ono" (v. 2). This wily
temptation came when they heard that the wall was built,
and that "there was no breach left" (v. 1). While the
building went on they ridiculed and threatened, but now
that success had come they attempt to lure them down to
their level, that some compromise might be made. Satan
knows how to play the fox, when it does not suit him to
roar as a lion. We are not ignorant of his devices. When
the enemy speaks fair you may be sure that there are
seven abominations in his heart (Prov. 26. 25). Notice
how Nehemiah met this temptation.

1. HE KNEW HIS OWN MIND. "I cannot come down"
(v. 3). He could not even say "I will think of it." As one
who was entirely devoted to the work of the Lord, his whole
soul revolted at such a proposal. His feelings were akin to
those of Peter and John when they said, "We cannot
but speak the things which we have seen and heard"
(Acts 4. 20).

2. HE KNEW HIS WORK. "I am doing a great work."
All work for God is great when judged by its eternal results

Every thing must be great that has God in it. He was doing a great work, he was not dreaming about it. They are not easily tempted who are found so doing.

3. HE KNEW THE DANGER OF COMING DOWN. "Why should the work cease, whilst I leave it, and come down to you" (at that time the doors had not yet been set up upon the gates, v. 1). It is more honourable to work than to talk about it. It is at the sacrifice of our usefulness in the service of God that we "come down" to the plain of mere worldly wisdom. This same temptation came to our Lord while hanging on the Cross. Was He not doing a great work there, when they cried to Him, "Come down from the Cross and we will believe?" Although Nehemiah was assailed in this subtle fashion "four times," yet just as often did the shield of faith save him. Be steadfast and immovable in the work of the Lord.

II. **The Evil-rumour Temptation.** The fifth attempt to ensnare this man of God and ruin his work was made in the form of a false and slandering report. They declared that his purpose was to rebel against the king, and to make himself king in Judah, and to appoint prophets to preach of him in Jerusalem (vv. 5-7). In short they charged him with pride and self-seeking. This is no new thing. Men, who are themselves selfish, can never understand the motives of those who seek only the glory of God. When the ungodly find that they cannot baffle the Christian worker they will not scruple to misrepresent his motives. Note how Nehemiah met this scurrilous attack. He met it with—

1. A FAITHFUL REBUKE. "There are no such things done as thou sayest, but thou feignest them out of thine own heart" (v. 8). He not only denies the charge, but points out also the source of all the mischief, "thine own heart." The heart is deceitful above all things. It was a strong

sharp thrust, but he knew that the seat of disease was deep down. The man who would be faithful to God cannot always speak smooth things. Mealy-mouthed ministers will never accomplish much for the Kingdom of God. The faithful servant of Christ must reprove and rebuke, as well as exhort.

2. AN URGENT PRAYER. "Now therefore, O God, strengthen my hands" (v. 9). We never have more need to pray than when we have been shooting the arrows of conviction at the hearts of our King's enemies. Our appeals to men should be instantly followed with an appeal to God.

(1) *The Need.* "Strengthen my hands." He wanted strong hands to carry out the purposes of God in his life. Hands that "hang down" in weakness are useless hands. The spider taketh hold with her hands, so does the man of faith.

(2) *The Urgency.* "Now therefore." Now, because of my present need; therefore, because of the strength and wrath of the enemy. My God shall supply all your need. He can perfect His strength in your weakness; therefore "wait on the Lord" (Isa. 40. 31).

SUCCESS.
NEHEMIAH 6. 10-16.

"Easy indeed it were to reach
A mansion in the courts above,
If swelling words and fluent speech
Might serve instead of faith and love. "—*Cowper.*

ONE of the profound sayings of Mazzini was, "Action is the Word of God; thought is but His shadow." Deeds will always speak louder than words. The runner is not crowned unless he strive lawfully. The trials and temptations of Nehemiah were to him what the refiner's fire is to the silver, or the lapidary's wheel to the diamond. The lustre of his character was purified and brightened through the ordeal of suffering. The trial of your faith is more precious than gold. But Nehemiah's warfare is not yet over. Here we have—

I. Another Temptation to Evil. This last attempt to ensnare this man of God seems to have been the most subtle of all. Shemaiah, who had the name of a prophet, tempted Nehemiah to come with him into some secret chamber within the temple, and to shut themselves up, saying that his enemies were coming in the night to slay him (v. 10). When the snare is laid by the Ahithophels it is all the more dangerous, it is the wolf in sheep's clothing. The poison of error is more difficult to detect when administered by a professed religious teacher, who is secretly in league with the enemies of God. The Devil's last dodge is to appear as an angel of light.

II. Another Steadfast Resistance. Nehemiah said, "Should such a man as I flee?...I will not go" (v. 11). As far as he presently knew, it may have been all true what Shemaiah said, but he felt in his heart that it would be for him a God-dishonouring act to seek his own personal safety at the sacrifice of his God-given work. "Should such a man as I flee?" I, who am in the hand of God, doing His will, and who am as safe on the wall of service as within the closed doors of ease and idleness? "I will not go." God Himself is my refuge and strength, not His earthly house. If He fails me, His temple can afford me no security. It is good for us to remember who we are, and whom we serve, in the hour of temptation and danger. Why should the sons and servants of God be driven about with every wind of doctrine? Personal influence for the cause of Jesus Christ is often sacrificed on the altar of cowardly fear. "Dare to be a Daniel." There is no armour provided for the back.

III. Another Defeat for the Enemy. "And lo, I perceived that God had not sent him: therefore was he hired that I should be afraid...that they might reproach me" (vv. 12, 13). The dastardly motives of Shemaiah have been discovered. The sheep skin has fallen from the wolf, the hireling has been found out. It is not easy to deceive a man filled with the Spirit of God. The object was to fill Nehemiah with the fear of man, and so paralyse him for the work of God. The behaviour of this sneaking and deceitful prophet is not more reprehensible than that of some modern critics, who, in the garb of friendship, seek to paralyse the efforts of Christ's servants by inspiring them with fear and distrust. But the Church is wakening up, and will soon be saying, like Nehemiah, "Lo, I perceive that God has not sent them." Be sure your sin will find you out. No weapon formed against the work of God can prosper. "What time I am afraid I will trust in Thee" (Psa. 56. 3).

IV. Another Appeal unto God. "My God, think Thou upon Tobiah...and the rest of the prophets, that would have put me in fear" (v. 14). There is no recrimination, no attempt at revenge; he knows that his judgment was with his God, so he hands over his enemies to Him to have their case considered. "Think Thou upon them." Our Lord Himself had those who sought to cast him down from His excellency, and the disciple is not greater than his Lord. When Paul referred to Alexander the coppersmith, who did him much evil, he said, "The Lord reward him according to his works" (2 Tim. 4. 14). In circumstances like these Christ has left us His example, "Who when He was reviled, reviled not again;...but committed Himself to Him that judgeth righteously" (1 Peter 2. 23). Them that are without, God will judge (1 Cor. 5. 13).

V. Another Triumph for Faith. "So the wall was finished,...and they were much cast down in their own eyes, for they perceived that this work was wrought of God" (vv. 15, 16). Like the Lord Jesus Christ, Nehemiah could say, "I have finished the work Thou gavest Me to do" (John 17. 4). When there is steadfast faith in God, strength and victory will be given for every God-given task, although the way may be "through much affliction and reproach." That which fills the mouth of God's children with laughter and their tongue with singing (Psa. 126. 2, 3), makes the eyes of their enemies to be "cast down." It is a humbling discovery for them when they perceive "that the work was wrought of God," and that in their jealousy and blindness they have been fighting against Him. Such a startling discovery every Christ-rejecter will surely make sooner or later. Yes, the eyes of the haughty will yet be "cast down," and their faces deeply dyed in crimson shame when they perceive what God hath done for His faithful followers. This is the victory that overcometh the world, even our faith.

WORD AND WORK.
Nehemiah 8.

"O Word of God incarnate!
O Wisdom from on high!
O Truth unchanged, unchanging!
O Light of our dark sky!
We praise Thee for the radiance
That from the hallowed page,
A lantern to our footsteps,
Shines on from age to age."—*W. How.*

In this chapter we have a very refreshing change in the programme, in the form of an urgent appeal to the Word of the Lord as revealed in "the book of the law of Moses." There is something like the breath of a revival in it, in that it is the people themselves who cry out for it (v. 1). There is a beautiful fitness of things in this, inasmuch as the Word of God should always be associated with the work

of God. The sword and the trowel were both needed.
The word of edification must follow the work of salvation.
The whole scene is most impressive and suggestive. We
shall look at—

I. The Preacher. "They spake unto Ezra the scribe
to bring the book" (v. 1). Ezra was known as a ready
scribe in the law of Moses (Ezra 7. 6). Being also a priest,
he was well qualified as an exponent of the Scriptures. As
a priest, he was the recipient of grace; as a scribe, he was
familiar with the truth. Grace and truth came by Jesus
Christ, and in a measure must come by every preacher of
the Gospel who has the Divine call.

II. The Place of Meeting. "Before the street"
(v. 3). He read the Book in the open square, in front of
the street that was before the watergate. He stood upon
"a pulpit of wood" (v. 4). Thus the first pulpit mentioned was built in a public square for open-air work. In
the secret closet, or the market square, where Jesus is, 'tis
Heaven there. The Christ-possessed boat of Peter on the
lake was a holier place than the God-forsaken temple at
Jerusalem.

III. The Hearers.

1. They were NUMEROUS. "Both men and women:
all that could hear with understanding" (v. 2). The
congregation literally hungered for the Word of God.
What a delightful privilege to minister to such a
people.

2. They were ATTENTIVE. "From morning until mid-
day...all the people were attentive to the book" (v. 3).
They were more interested in the book than the preacher.
They sought not the man, but the message.

3. They were REVERENT. "When he opened the book...
all the people stood up" (v. 5). For Israel to "stand up"

was virtually to declare their willingness to hear and obey. To stand up before God is no new method of testifying to our readiness to believe Him.

4. They were RESPONSIVE. "All the people answered, Amen, with lifting up their hands: and they bowed their heads, and worshipped the Lord" (v. 6). They responded to the demands of God's word by bowing their heads and offering Him the adoration of their hearts. It is a solemn thing to hear the Word of the Lord and refuse to yield to its claims. Be ye doers of the Word.

IV. The Preacher's Manner.

1. HE BEGAN BY BLESSING THE LORD (v. 6). He was deeply conscious of the greatness of the occasion, the greatness of God, the greatness of the message, the great need of the people, and his own great responsibility.

2. HE STUCK TO THE BOOK. "He read in the book, in the law of God" (v. 8). He well knew that what the people needed, was not his thoughts, but the thoughts of God as written in that book. My thoughts are not your thoughts saith the Lord.

3. HE SPOKE DISTINCTLY (v. 8). There was no silly attempt at intoning for the sake of musical effect. He spoke straight out, clear and incisive. As R. L. Stevenson said, "The Bible should be read freshly as a book, not dreamingly as the Bible."

4. HE EXPLAINED THE TEXT. "They read distinctly and gave the sense." This was no formal heartless reading of the word. The soul of the man was greatly exercised, so that the real meaning of the words might be seen. There would not be so many senseless hearers, if all preachers were as faithful as Ezra to the Word of God.

5. HE ENFORCED THE TRUTH. "He caused them to understand." His business was to make them to understand what the mind of the Lord was. It is not enough that they heard it, they must, as responsible beings, be able, by the exercise of their own minds, to grasp intelligently the thoughts of God concerning themselves. He that hath My word, let him speak My word faithfully. What is the chaff to the wheat? saith the Lord (Jer. 23. 28).

V. The Effect Produced.

1. THEY WEPT. "All the people wept when they heard the words of the law" (v. 9). Only reading the word! Yes, but such reading as brought conviction to the heart, and the tears of penitence to the eyes. When the Word of God, which is the sword of the Spirit, is believed, it proves itself "quick and powerful, sharper than any two-edged sword."

2. THEY REJOICED. "And all the people went their way . . . to make great mirth, because they had understood the words" (v. 12). The Word at first may pierce the heart and melt down the will, but it is to the end that we might rejoice in Him (v. 10, *last clause*). Mourning because of sin must precede the joy of salvation.

3. THEY MINISTERED. They were to "eat the fat and drink the sweet, and send portions unto them for whom nothing is prepared" (v. 10). And they gladly did so (v. 12). By the grace of God, we may now eat the fat and drink the sweet, but surely the love of Christ should constrain us to remember those who are as yet outside the Kingdom of God, and for whom "nothing is prepared." "Freely ye have received, freely give" (Matt. 10. 8). Give to them that love of God which has been so freely given to you.

A CALL TO PRAISE.

NEHEMIAH 9. 1-25.

"Some murmur when their sky is clear
And wholly bright to view,
If one small speck of dark appear
In their great Heaven of blue.
And some with thankful love are filled,
If but one streak of light—
One ray of God's good mercy—gild
The darkness of their night."—*Trench.*

THIS chapter opens with the great day of fasting and humiliation. The seed of Israel had broken their unholy alliance with the strangers, and now made public confession of their sins. For three hours the Book of the Law was read, and for other three hours they confessed and worshipped. Now the call comes to "Stand up and bless the Lord their God for ever and ever" (v. 5). They had been reading and hearing of the great things God had done for their fathers, until their souls were stirred up from their silent depths to bless Him who was almighty to save and to keep. In this review of the past there are some powerful reasons given why they should "stand up and bless the Lord." Because He is the—

I. **God of Creation.** "Thou hast made Heaven, the Heaven of Heavens, with all their host," etc. (v. 6). The Heavens declare the glory of God, the glory of His greatness, His wisdom, and power. The earth showeth forth His handiwork, in the variety and perfection exhibited in nature. The Heavens and the earth are the visible expressions and proofs of the Eternal Mind, and should call forth praise and adoration. They would also praise Him because He is the—

II. **God of Grace.** "Thou art the Lord who didst choose Abram, and broughtest Him forth...and gave him the name Abraham...and madest a covenant with

him" (vv. 7, 8). By faith Abraham went out, but by
grace was he chosen. By grace are ye saved. The grace
that came to Abraham through the call of God, comes to us
all in the Gospel of Jesus Christ. All who accept this call
will, like Abraham, be led forth into a new sphere, will
receive a new name, and will enter into a new life by
covenant promise—the life of faith. They desire to praise
Him because He is the—

III. **God who Answers Prayer.** "Thou didst see
the afflictions of our fathers...and heardest their cry"
(v. 9). He sees the afflictions of His people in the Egypt
of this world, and hears their cry when they come to
the Red Sea of agonising trial. His ear never becomes
heavy through weariness; He is the Rewarder of them
that diligently seek Him. Stand up and bless the Lord
for this. He is also the—

IV. **God of Deliverances.** He "shewedst signs and
wonders upon Pharaoh...and didst divide the sea, so
that they went through on dry land...and led them in
the day by a cloudy pillar, and in the night by a pillar
of fire" (vv. 10-12). He saved them from their strong
enemy, and led them forth by a new way. Every movement of the pillar was a fresh deliverance on their behalf.
The Cross of our Lord Jesus Christ was the instrument
by which all our enemies have been overthrown, and the
Holy Spirit is our Guiding Pillar and daily Deliverer
from the bondage of darkness and the wearisomeness of
the wilderness pilgrimage. Stand up and bless the Lord
your God for this. Moreover, He is the—

V. **God of Revelation.** "Thou camest down...and
spakest with them from Heaven, and gavest them right
judgments and true laws, good statutes and commandments" (v. 13). Every good and perfect gift cometh
down from the Father of Lights. We ought to be thankful

to God that He hath given to us statutes that are right, in which the heart can rejoice, and a commandment that is pure, enlightening the eyes (Psa. 19. 8, 9). No man, by the process of searching, can find out God as He has been pleased to reveal Himself in His Word, and through His Son. It needs God to make known God. Let us bless Him that He has so made Himself known, that we, by faith, can rejoice in Him with enlightened eyes. Further, He is the—

VI. God who Supplies all our Need. He "gavest them bread from Heaven, and water out of the rock... and promised them that they should possess the land" (v. 15). A provision that covered their present and future needs. The hunger of those who pilgrimage with God can only be satisfied with "bread from Heaven;" the thirst of such can only be quenched with water from the "Smitten Rock," and their future prospect can be brightened only by His "sure Word of promise." My God shall supply all your need according to His riches in glory by Christ Jesus. Stand up and bless Him for this, and, lastly, for this other great fact, that He is the—

VII. God of Long-suffering Mercy. "Yet Thou in Thy manifold mercies forsook them not in the wilderness" (v. 19). See how they tempted God. They were disobedient, "refused to obey." They were forgetful, "neither were mindful of Thy wonders." They were rebellious, "appointed a captain to return to their bondage" They were idolatrous, "they made a molten calf" (vv. 16-18). Yet, in His manifold mercies, He was "a God ready to pardon, gracious and merciful, slow to anger, and of great kindness" (v. 17). Instead of answering their ingratitude and unbelief with judgment, He added mercy to mercy, by "giving them also of His Spirit to instruct them" (v. 20), so that they could testify, after forty years, that as far as the grace and goodness of God were concerned, "they lacked nothing" (v. 21). As they "read in the book of the law," on that twenty-fourth day of the month, of the marvellous goodness of their God in the past, their hearts began to burn within them, and no wonder. Why are our hearts so irresponsive to all the manifestations of His wonder-working grace toward us in Jesus Christ? Shall we not stand up this day, at the remembrance of His love, and bless His gracious Name for ever and ever?

A CALL TO PURITY OF LIFE.
NEHEMIAH 13.

"To see the face of God, this makes the joy of Heaven!
The purer then the eye, the more joy will be given."—*Trench.*

NEHEMIAH had left Jerusalem, and gone back to the royal court at Babylon (v. 6). Perhaps in fulfilment of the promise made to the king before he was sent to build the wall (see chap. 2. 6). How long he had been away is difficult to say, but on returning he found things in a very grievous condition. Backsliding had set in, and a powerful tendency to compromise with evil. Many had become lovers of money more than lovers of God. At once this single-eyed man of God raised his voice against them and their unseemly doings, and sought to bring them back to a life of conformity to the Word and will of God. What their hindrances were to a life of purity and power are very much the hindrances with which we have to do. What was the nature of them? Notice their—

I. Relationship to the Mixed Multitude. "When they heard the law, they separated from Israel all the mixed multitude" (v. 3). The law forbade the mixing of the people of God with the nations that knew not God, so as to lose their identity. When the mixed multitude went up out of Egypt with the host of Israel this did in no way mar their character as a people separated unto God, but it was different when they went with the mixed multitude. Our relationship, as Christians to the world, is that of Christ's—in it, but not of it. The men of the world are indeed a "mixed multitude," and one of the chief dangers of the followers of Jesus Christ is to get so closely associated with them and their ways as to lose their testimony for Him (2 Cor. 6. 17).

II. Relationship to False Professors. "Eliashib the priest...was allied unto Tobiah...and he prepared him a chamber in the courts of the house of God" (vv. 4-9). Tobiah had the name of a saint (goodness of Jehovah), although he had the nature of a godless sinner. It was a startling discovery Nehemiah made in coming back to Jerusalem to find that his old enemy who had mocked them while building (chap. 4. 3) was now comfortably quartered in one of the large chambers which should have been used as a store-room for the house of God (v. 5). He had no portion nor right in Jerusalem (chap. 2. 20). But there are men like Tobiah who are mean enough to take all the personal comfort they can get out of the house of God, while they in heart deny God, and sneer at His servants. It was surely an unholy alliance between Eliashib the priest and Tobiah the Ammonite; such an alliance as often leads the overseers of the house of God into God-dishonouring compromises with the worldly-minded. Nehemiah would tolerate nothing that disgraced the holy Name, and hindered that testimony for which the house existed. So he "cast forth all the household stuff of Tobiah," and occupied the chamber with the things of God (v. 8, 9). Tobiah's household effects may have been very good and beautiful stuff, but they were as filthiness in the holy place (2 Chron. 29. 5), because they were still Tobiah's and not God's.

III Relationship to the House of God. Another source of danger to the purity and power of the Christian life is to allow self-interest to overrule the claims of

God's house. "Why is the house of God forsaken?"
he asks. It is a reproach to God that His house should be
forsaken (vv. 10, 11). The Levites and singers appointed
for the work of God's house had fled, "every one to his
field," because their portions had not been given them. To
withhold the tithes and offerings needed to maintain an
honourable testimony to His Name is equivalent to robbing
God (Mal. 3. 8). The house of God was not meant for an
ornament, but as a witness. Alas! that it should be so, of
many places claiming to be houses of God; they are more
ornamental than useful in the way of bringing men to God.
But the labourer, not the ornamental loiterer, is worthy
of his hire. Although there is a close connection in
Malachi 3. 10 between tithes and spiritual blessing, yet the
Church in Laodicea had seemingly plenty of "meat in the
house," while still in a state of spiritual destitution. There
must not only be the gifts, but purity of motives in giving.
Whatsoever ye do, do it heartily, as unto the Lord.

IV. Relationship to the Day of Rest. Nehemiah
contended with the nobles for permitting this buying,
and selling, and transferring goods on the Sabbath day
(vv. 15-22). It was an infringement of the law of God
(Lev. 23. 32). The Sabbaths were God's. He gave
them "to be a sign between Me and them, that they might
know that I am the Lord that sanctify them" (Ezek. 20. 12)
Indifference to the sanctity of God's day of rest could only
be interpreted as an expression of their disregard for the
God who gave it. The Lord's day now (first day of the
week), given us as a sign of His resurrection, is regarded by
many in very different ways. It is still the day of rest, and is
manifestly the gift of God, sanctified by Him in the raising of
His Son from the dead. Neglecting this day of rest, and not
honouring it as of God, has been the fruitful source of much
backsliding on the part of God's people. He that regardeth
the day as unto the Lord will certainly be blessed in so doing.

V. Marriage Relationship. "In those days Jews had married wives of Ashdod...and their children spake nalf the speech of Ashdod and could not speak in the Jews' language" (vv. 23-25). The fruit of this unholy alliance was a marred and mongrel testimony. The children were not to blame for this defect. The tree is known by its fruit. Getting unequally yoked with un-believers has marred the lives of many of God's children. Even Solomon was led into sin through this course (v. 26). Those who would "marry in the Lord" must do their courting in the Lord. The Christian man who sets his affections on an "outlandish woman," or the Christian woman who allows her affections to be captivated by an outlandish man are proving the outlandishness of their own hearts to the Lord Jesus Christ. If any man would live godly, he must suffer even the persecution of a grieved and godless sweetheart. Neither are Christian fathers or mothers to give their daughters to men who are unbelievers, no matter what their social standing might be (v. 25). Paul's arguments against such unions are unanswerable. "What communion hath light with darkness?...What agreement hath the temple of God with idols? Ye are the temple of the living God....Wherefore be ye separate" (2 Cor. 6. 14-18).

"How sweet the mutual yoke of man and wife,
    When holy fires maintain love's heavenly life."

VASHTI, THE SELF-WILLED, REJECTED.
ESTHER 1.

"Oh let Thy sacred will
    All Thy delight in me fulfil!
    Let not me think an action mine own way;
    But as Thy love shall sway,
    Resigning up the rudder to Thy skill."—*Herbert*.

THE book of Esther belongs to the times of Ezra and Nehemiah, and was probably written by Mordecai (chap. 9. 20). As has been often noted, the Name of God does not occur, and is never referred to in it. But although His Name is not found, His hand is everywhere visible. It may be fitly called, "The book of the providence of God." In this brief history we have a striking confirmation and fulfilment of that principle taught in Romans 8. 28: "All things work together for good...to them who are the called according to His purpose." Each of the leading persons in the book presents a separate type of character, under the unconscious but over-ruling providence of God. Men and women are free to act as they may, and while responsible for their actions, there lies behind all the great purpose of God to manifest Himself. The events in the book are thrilling: Vashti, the queen, is deposed; Esther, the orphan, is crowned; Mordecai, the despised, is honoured; and Haman, the boaster, is hanged. We shall consider first the downfall of Queen Vashti.

I. Her Name. Vashti means beauty. The king desired to show the princes her beauty, "for she was fair to look upon" (v. 11). Physical as well as moral beauty is always attractive, but mere outward comeliness has frequently proved a temptation and a snare. It is a dangerous gift when there is no corresponding comeliness of spirit. It is no uncommon thing to find the most beautiful spirit in a rough and uncomely body.

II. Her Position. She was the queen of Ahasuerus, the greatest king on the earth. His name means "majestic prince." What an honour to be the sharer of the glory and riches of such a king. Ahasuerus in some respects may represent Him who is the King of kings and Lord of lords. Especially in the greatness of his influence and in the generosity of his character in making a great feast for all his princes and for all his people (vv. 3-5). And like the great Gospel feast there was no compulsion. Every one was to choose for himself as to how much or how little

he was to take (v. 8). A greater than Ahasuerus is here
and it is our privilege to belong to Him. Queen Vashti
was not more beautiful in the eyes of her king than those
are in the eyes of the King of kings, in whom the "beauty
of the Lord" has been put. Being made partakers of the
Divine nature we become children and heirs together with
Him.

III. **Her Opportunity:** "The king commanded Vashti
to come before him with the royal crown, to show the
people and the princes her beauty" (vv. 10, 11). We
are not so much concerned just now with the customs of
this heathen court, with the seemliness or unseemliness of
this command, but with the principles that lie underneath.
Vashti held her position as queen by virtue of the king's
choice and favour, just as we, by the grace of God, have
been called and exalted. This command to appear before
the people with the crown royal—the gift of the king—to
show them her beauty, and so please the king, was giving
her an opportunity of doing a most acceptable service. It
was her duty as well as her privilege to obey. Is there not
a similar opportunity offered us, as the royal house of the
King of Heaven? Should not that beauty which the Lord
our God hath put upon us be shown forth for the honour
of His great Name? Let your light—the light of your
life—so shine before men. This is an opportunity that we
will not always have.

IV. **Her Rebellion.** "But the queen refused to come
at the king's commandment" (v. 12). The call was very
urgent, for seven chamberlains had been deputed to carry
it out, but she deliberately refused to obey. The reason
probably was that as she, too, had "made a feast for the
women in the royal house which belonged to the king"
(v. 9), she did not wish to break up her present enjoyment
for the sake of pleasing the king in such a small matter.
How often the acts of our disobedience to God have their

roots down in our self-made plans and our determination to
carry them out. We have prepared a feast for ourselves and
others, and things are going on beautifully when some
definite call from the King comes, but we judge it unworthy
of our attention meanwhile, and disobey, utterly unconscious of the terrible fruits that will certainly follow.
One refusal to obey may cast us out of the fellowship
of the King.

V. Her Example. "This deed of the queen shall
come abroad to all women, so that they shall despise their
husbands in their eyes" (v. 17). "Acts speak louder
than words." Vashti, being queen, was compassed about
with a great cloud of witnesses, so that her actions had far-
reaching results. This is an aspect of the Christian life
that cannot be too carefully considered. We, like her,
walk in high places, and one false step may be to others a
license to sin. "No man liveth unto himself" (Rom. 14. 7).
This is true, especially of the servant of God. As wives are
to be subject to their own husbands, so must we be subject
to Christ (Eph. 5. 22-24).

VI. Her Rejection. "Vashti came no more before
king Ahasuerus" (vv. 19-21). He made Esther queen
instead of Vashti" (chap. 2. 17). Her disobedience led to
entire separation from the fellowship of the king. Doubtless she little imagined that this simple refusal would result
in such disastrous consequences. A thought, an act, and a
crown lost. How long she lived to mourn over her folly we
know not, but surely her days would be spent in shame
and bitterness of soul. For this same reason (disobedience)
many get out of fellowship with the Lord Jesus Christ.
There is sin in the heart, and the Lord will not hear. There
has been failure through preferring our own will to the
will of our Lord, and now there is no liberty of access.
The failure will be all the more grievous if another has
been called of Him to take our place and our crown. Hold

that fast which thou hast as a servant, that no man take
thy crown (Rev. 3. 11). It is possible, through lack of
self-subjection, even to preach to others, and yet, as a
servant, become a castaway (1 Cor. 9. 27).

ESTHER, THE HUMBLE, EXALTED.
ESTHER 2, etc.

"Obedience is nobler than freedom. What's free?
The vexed straw on the wind, the frothed spume on the sea;
The great ocean itself, as it rolls and it swells,
In the bonds of a boundless obedience dwells. "—*Lytton.*

ESTHER means "star." Star-like characters are sure to be
seen and recognised. Light is self-assertive. The deposition
of Vashti is followed by a most exciting search for a queen.
It was a search for given qualities. It was not "Whosoever
will may come." In this case the number was very elect.
We are thankful that candidates for Heaven are not sought
for on this principle. Not the beautiful, but sinners, Jesus
came to call. Some of the notes in the song of Mary might
well have been sung by Esther. "He hath regarded the
low estate of His handmaiden....He that is mighty hath
done to me great things" (Luke 1. 48, 49). Observe—

I. **Her Condition.** "She had neither father nor
mother," but was brought up by Mordecai, her aged cousin
(chap. 2. 7). No one seemed further away, by birth and
circumstances, from being a queen than she was. But in
the mysterious providence of God the most unlikely things
do happen. No one seemed more unlikely to become a
servant of Jesus Christ than Saul of Tarsus. Poverty, or
ignorance, or guilt are no barriers to the infinite grace
of God.

II. **Her Call.** "Esther was brought into the kings'
house" (v. 8). She is now conscious that she has been
called as a candidate for a crown. Not many had such a

chance brought within their reach, but still she was just
one among others.   In this race only one could receive the
prize.   It is very different with the call that comes to us
through the Gospel of Christ.   Every one who receives this
call may also receive the crown of life and eternal honour.
All that have been brought into our "King's house" will
be made to rejoice in His great and gracious presence.

III. **Her Character.**   That she was exceeding gracious
and trustworthy is apparent from the fact that she pleased
the keeper of the women more than the others (v. 9),
and that she was true to Mordecai's instructions in not
revealing her nationality.   Her implicit obedience to her
guardian is a noteworthy feature of her humble and submissive spirit (v. 20).   This may seem a small matter,
but it is just such a matter that God in His providence
never overlooks.   It is what we are in the secret of our
own souls that shows itself when the time of strain and
testing comes.   "As a man thinketh in his heart, so is he."
It is in the good and honest heart that the seed of the
kingdom springs up into God-glorifying fruitfulness.

IV. **Her Choice.**   "When the turn of Esther was
come to go in unto the king, she required nothing but
what Hegai, the king's chamberlain, appointed" (v. 15).
Certain necessary things were appointed to be given to
each of those candidates for queenship, but any other thing
they might wish for the beautifying of their person, or that
might help to commend them to the king was not to be
denied them.   The others evidently required many other
things to perfect their preparation, but it is noted of Esther
that she "required nothing."   She chose to be satisfied with
those things appointed by the king.   She left herself
entirely in the hands of him who had the work of preparation committed to him.   Her own thoughts or devices find
no place here.   So let us submit ourselves to the Holy

Spirit, whose office it is to sanctify us, and fit and prepare us for the presence of the King. It will fare all the better with us if, like Esther, we "require nothing" but what He has appointed, satisfied with the garment of His righteousness, even of His only.

V. Her Crown. "The king loved Esther...and she obtained grace in his sight,...so he set the royal crown upon her head" (v. 17). Her humility and faith are now rewarded by a public manifestation of the king's favour—crowned with glory and honour, although she did nothing but obey. The way to the throne was open for her whenever the king loved her. What a privilege to be loved by a king, by the King of Heaven. The love of God opens the way for us into the heart and home of God. The crown is the symbol of honour and power. Pentecost was the crowning day for the early disciples, when the tongue of fire rested on each of them, and they all received the Royal authority of Heaven, becoming partners with the King of Glory and sharers of His Kingdom on earth. To find His "favour" is to find His crown.

VI. Her Courage. "I will go unto the king, which is not according to law, and if I perish, I perish" (chap. 4. 16). A testing-time had now come, when all the power and authority she possessed were needed for the salvation of those who were condemned to die. Haman had succeeded in getting the sentence of death passed upon all Jews; Mordecai pleads with Esther as their only hope, but the law forbade anyone approaching the king, on pain of death, without an invitation. Nevertheless, Esther consecrates her life to this great object, and casts herself into the breach. It was a bold step. But although the law was against her, she knew that the heart of the king was for her. This also is our encouragement in giving ourselves for the salvation of others. If, like Esther, we have come into honour and power by the grace of our king, it is also "for such a time as this," a time of salvation for others. All the authority and power we have received is absolutely needed for this great work. The law of the flesh will always be against us in approaching the King as soul savers. Let us, like Esther, give ourselves entirely to it. "If I perish" in a work like this, then it is a blessed and worthy object for which to die. But she did not perish. "None perish that trust in Him."

VII. Her Conquest. She obtained favour: the golden sceptre was held out to her. Then the king said unto her, "What wilt thou, Queen Esther, and what is thy request?" etc. (chap. 5. 1-3). She then identifies herself with the Jews, and, pleads for her own and their lives (chap. 7. 3, 4). Her request is abundantly answered; the enemy is overcome, and her people are saved. She sees of the travail of her soul and is satisfied. This great achievement reminds us of a greater than Esther, who, when the law was against us, cast Himself down in the presence of God on that awful spot called Calvary, saying, as it were, "If I perish, I perish." But God raised Him again, and made Him a Prince and a Saviour. The way to such conquests is self-surrender. If we are to be the saviours of others it can only be by the sacrifice of ourselves to this end. To this end have we been called into His kingdom. "Receiving the end of your faith, the salvation of souls" (1 Peter 1. 9, Gk.).

MORDECAI, THE FAITHFUL, REWARDED.
ESTHER 2-10.

> "Be strong, be good, be pure!
>   The right only shall endure."—*Longfellow.*

> "All God does, if rightly understood,
>   Shall work thy final good."—*Keble.*

THIS "little man," as the name Mordecai indicates, had been carried away from Jerusalem with the captivity.

Little did he or his captors know what an important part he was destined to play in the kingdom of Babylon.

"God moves in a mysterious way,
His wonders to perform."

Little also did he imagine, when he agreed to adopt his orphan cousin, that she would yet be queen in Babylon. This book of the providence of God is true to its character, being full of surprises. We shall fix our attention now on the career of Mordecai. He was—

I. **Merciful.** It was a very merciful act to take the girl Esther, who was an orphan, and adopt her as his own daughter (chap. 2. 7). This may seem a very ordinary thing, but the sequence was extraordinary. It seemed the right thing for him to do, and he did it. That is where the point lies. He opened his heart as well as his home for her, and the blessing that is promised to the merciful came to him (Matt. 5. 7).

II. **Faithful.** Two of the king's chamberlains had plotted to kill the king. The thing was known to Mordecai and he boldly revealed the dastardly design to Esther, who told the king in his name (chap. 2. 22, 23). If one would be true to themselves and to righteousness they must be prepared, if need be, to do things that may bring others into shame and condemnation. There are those who, if they don't plot against the King of Heaven, they do it against His people and His cause. Well, if the thing is known to you there is no need for you fighting against them. Tell the King about it, who, for His own sake, will surely deal with the offenders. Be faithful to the interests of your Lord and King, and, by the good hand of God your reward will come openly.

III. **Consistent.** "But Mordecai bowed not to Haman, nor did him reverence...for he was a Jew" (chap. 3. 2-4). He refused to prostrate himself, and give to the haughty

Haman that homage which is due only to God. By this act of resistance he declared his faith in and reverence for God. Mordecai was a man in whose eyes a vile person is contemned, but who honoured them that fear the Lord (Psa. 15. 4). A man's faith is of no value if it does not affect his daily life. How can a man say that he believes in God if he is not ready to obey God rather than men (Acts 5. 29). Those whose lives are governed by the fear of God will not be found doing just as others do, even for "peace sake." It may seem to some "men-pleasers" but a trifle, yet if he had yielded on this point he might never have been lifted up to the place of national honour that was afterwards his.

IV. Despised. "Then was Haman full of wrath" (chap. 3. 5); and when he learned that Mordecai was a Jew he "scorned to lay hands on him alone," and sought to destroy "all the Jews" (chap. 3. 6). But after laying his plans for the destruction of the Jews he was persuaded by his wife to hang Mordecai on a gallows fifty cubits high (chap. 5. 14). All this wrath and proposed blood-shedding because one man had courage and conviction enough not to violate his conscience and deny his God. Is the game worth the candle? No, saith the man who walks by sight, and not by faith. But what saith the Lord by His wonder-working providence? If any man will live Godly he must suffer persecution, because he will be guided and controlled by motives and principles that have no place in the affairs of the selfish and ungodly. This is where the shoe pinches, unless it is a good fit. The man of God will never feel comfortable in the shoes of a man of the world, and not to be in the world's fashion is in itself a cause of offence. "But blessed are ye when men shall revile you for My Name's sake;" great is your reward in the heavenlies.

V. Tested. "He rent his clothes...and went into the city, and cried with a loud and bitter cry" (chap. 4. 1).

The death sentence had gone forth against him and all his people. It was a most terrible experience. His sackcloth and agony awakened the compassion and inquiry of the queen (chap. 4. 4, 5). He was sorely cast down, but not destroyed, for his faith in God was unfailing. "If thou holdest thy peace," he said to Esther, "then shall deliverance arise to the Jews from another place" (chap. 4. 14). It was a tremendous strain that was upon him. Who was to make intercession for his helpless countrymen if he did not? If he held his peace now perhaps some other might arise, and this would be to his great shame. He left no stone unturned, but his faith was in the unfailing providence of God. The trial of your faith may be painful, but it is precious when found unto the praise and honour of God (1 Peter 1. 7). Nothing is impossible with God.

VI. Honoured. God begun to work deliverance for Mordecai by giving the king a restless night (chap. 6. 1). The national records are read, and the report of Mordecai specially noted, and the desire is bogotten in the heart of the king to reward his timely warning (chap. 6. 3, 4). Who would have thought that, within one week, the man who had erected a gallows to hang this stiffnecked Jew who refused to bow to him, would be led forth by that same man, seated on "the king's horse, adorned with royal apparel, and the crown upon his head, as the man whom the king delighteth to honour." That same week he had on his finger the ring of authority worn by Haman, his enemy. It does not take God long to work a perfect transformation act, and turn His servants' tears and wailings into songs and praises. Not only is he saved himself, but exalted to a position of glory and power that he might be the means of saving others (chap. 8. 7, 8). When any one is brought by God into a position of privilege and into a condition of power it is that great and needful things may be done by them. "I will bless thee and make thee a blessing" (Heb. 6. 14).

HAMAN, THE PROUD, DESTROYED.
ESTHER 3-7.

"The lawless wish, the unaverted eye,
　　Are as a taint upon the breeze
To lure foul spirits; haughty brows and high
　Are signals to invite them nigh,
　　Whose onset ever saints await on bended knees. "—*Keble*.

IT has been said that "pride destroys or misleads more souls
than deliberate wickedness." The history of Haman is a
verification of that saying of the wise man: "Pride goeth
before destruction, and an haughty spirit before a fall"
(Prov. 16. 18). His Name means "magnificent," but his
chequered career proves that his nature was ignominious.
We see him—

I. **Promoted.** "King Ahasuerus promoted Haman,
and advanced him, and set his seat above all the princes
that were with him" (chap. 3. 1). The greater our privilege, the more terrible will be our downfall if we fail to
walk humbly with our God. Capernaum was exalted to the
highest point of privilege, but through the blindness of
unbelief fell to the deepest depths of dishonour and shame.
"Let him that thinketh he standeth take heed lest he fall."
Through grace, every Christian has been promoted by the
King of Heaven, and has his seat above all the princes of
the earth. Let us see that we walk worthy of such an
high calling.

II. **Easily Offended.** "When Haman saw that
Mordecai bowed not, nor did him reverence, then was
Haman full of wrath" (chap. 3. 5). A man of his position
and dignity might easily have afforded to overlook the
seeming disrespect of the poor Jew; but no, his haughty
pride was wounded. The more authority he got the more
overbearing and tyrranical he became. Is not this how
spiritual pride works? Do we think that all men are going
to honour us because we have been promoted by the king?

To be easily offended because we are not honoured by certain men is an evidence of pride; it is a sign that we are seeking our own glory, when anger or wrath finds a place in our hearts against any one who fails to respect us as perhaps we think they should. The servant is not greater than his Lord. It is sometimes said, "He is a good man, but very touchy." Touchiness may be another name for selfishness.

III. **Boastful.** "Haman told them (his friends) of the glory of his riches,...and how the king had advanced him above the princes and servants of the king" (chap. 5. 11). He glories in his riches, his possessions, and his position. He exalts himself because he has been advanced above the other princes and servants of the king. The men of the world who have their portion in this life have little need to boast, for such riches can soon grow wings and fly away. "Treasures of wickedness profit nothing" (Prov. 10. 2). Paul says that "Proud boasters are inventors of evil things" (Rom. 1. 30). And such was Haman. All unholy boasting is the fruit of impure motives. Our spiritual promotion is "not by works, lest any man should boast" (Eph. 2. 9).

IV. **Revengeful.** "The thing pleased Haman, and he caused the gallows to be made for Mordecai" (chap. 5. 14). There was still a "fly in the ointment" of Haman's glory, pomp, and pride: "All this availeth me nothing so long as I see Mordecai the Jew sitting at the king's gate" (chap. 5. 13). The greatness of a soul is seen in its readiness to overlook personal insults and injuries, but this man's little selfish soul could not bear it. He made no attempt to win Mordecai's favour by kindness or patience, but greedily thirsts for his Jewish blood. The feeling of revenge, or even of grudge, against another is as much opposed to true Christian experience as death is to life. It is not for us to

avenge ourselves, but to commit all to the Lord, who hath
said: "Vengeance is mine, I will repay" (Rom. 12. 19).

V. Self-Confident. When the king said unto him,
"What shall be done unto the man whom the king delighteth to honour? Haman thought in his heart, To whom
would the king delight to do honour more than myself"
(6. 6). In the pride and self-sufficiency of his heart he
could see no one more fit or deserving special honour than
himself. When any one comes to this, the cup of their
iniquity is just about full, and their humiliation and downfall is at hand. The principle of "suffer me first" manifests
itself in many different forms, and never more loathesome
than when it appears in the words or acts of a Christian
worker. The law for the children of God is: "In honour,
preferring one another" (Rom. 12. 10).

VI. Disappointed. "Then the king said to Haman,
Make haste, and take the apparel and the horse, as thou
hast said, and do even so to Mordecai the Jew" (6. 10).
It was a very humbling revelation to Haman that that hated
Jew, for whom he had prepared the gallows, was to be honoured by the king as one more deserving than himself. God
has His own way of making appointments for them that
mourn in Zion, in giving them beauty for ashes, the oil of
joy for mourning, and the garment of praise for the spirit of
heaviness (Isa. 61. 3). He knows how to turn our mourning into dancing, and when to put off our sackcloth and gird
us with praise (Psa. 30. 11). In vain does Haman spread
the net before the eye of Him whose wisdom and power
governs the interests of His people. All the haughty in
heart will certainly be brought to shame and confusion:
sooner or later will the hopes of the hypocrite be cut off.
The man must be in a demoniac state of soul when the
honour and exaltation of another brings such overwhelming
grief and disappointment. Envy is cruel as the grave.

VII. Doomed. "So they hanged Haman on the gallows that he had prepared for Mordecai" (7. 10). He made a pit, and digged it, and is fallen into the ditch which he made (Psa. 7. 15). The wicked is snared in the work of his own hands (Psa. 9. 15). The wages of sin is death. In the den of lions Daniel did not get a scar, but when his enemies were cast in they "break all their bones in pieces or ever they came to the bottom of the den." The gallows of judgment that came to Haman was just as high as the murderous purpose that filled his heart. With what measure ye mete, it shall be measured unto you again. He that humbleth himself shall be exalted, but he that exalteth himself shall be abased. The God of grace is also the God of judgment.

DO IT HEARTILY.

WHEN Sir Thomas Lawrence was asked how he bestowed such consummate care upon a certain picture intended for a semi-barbarous foreign court, he replied: "I cannot help it; I do the best I can, unable through a tyrant feeling to do anything else." It would be well for all the servants of Jesus Christ, whose work is to be exhibited at the court of Heaven, if they had something of this "tyrant feeling" that cannot be half-hearted, but must always do their very best. "Whatsoever ye do, do it heartily as unto the Lord."

FITTED FOR BOTH WORLDS.

THERE is a curious fish, says Agassiz, in his "Journey in Brazil," called "Anableps," which have four eyes; or, rather, eyes which are divided into an upper and lower half, by which they can see equally well in air or water. It is no difficulty for them to look into both worlds, when they have received by nature the capacity for it. All who have been born from above have received the capacity to see the kingdom of God; but this does not in any way unfit them for the duties of this lower world.

EXPOSITORY OUTLINES
NEW TESTAMENT.

CHRIST, THE LIFE AND LIGHT OF MEN.
JOHN 1. 1-5.

"He who from the Father forth was sent,
  Came the true Light, light to our hearts to bring,
  The Word of God—the telling of His thoughts;
  The Light of God—the making visible;
  The far-transcending glory brought
  In human form with man to dwell."—*Macdonald.*

THE Gospel of John has been well called "the Gospel of
Eternity," for it is the Gospel of God. John was a specially
prepared vessel for this very honourable ministry. He had
been from his youth a beloved apostle. "His head had
rested on the Lord's breast, he had stood beside the Cross,
had witnessed the Ascension, had cherished till her death
the Mother of the Lord, had seen the Jewish dispensation
closed and the Holy City overthrown, and to him the
beatific visions of the Apocalypse had been granted." The
great purpose of this Gospel is very fittingly expressed in
chapter 20. 31. "These have been written that ye may
believe that Jesus is the Christ, the Son of God, and that
believing ye may have life in His Name." All the key-
words of his Gospel are found in this verse. The opening
words of this chapter are among the most profound ever
penned by the hand of man. They reveal a three-fold
relationship of the Lord Jesus Christ in His—

I. **Relationship to God.** He is called the Word,
the "Logos." Christ Himself is the uttered speech and
thought of God. He is the visible expression of the

invisible God. "For the life which was with the Father was manifested unto us" (1 John 1. 2). This Word was in the beginning. "The Lord possessed Me in the beginning of His ways...I was daily His delight" (Prov. 8. 22-30). The Word was with God. Yea, more, the Word was God. Man's finite mind cannot grasp the mystery of the Trinity, but the devout believer can bow and adore. That He who was in the form of God, and thought it not robbery to be equal with God, should make Himself of no reputation, taking upon Him the form of a servant, and dying on a Cross for the sin of the world, is a mystery of grace that can only be fathomed by the mystery of the Trinity.

II. **Relationship to Creation**. "All things were made by Him, and without Him was not any thing made that was made" (v. 3). Paul taught the same doctrine, "God...created all things by Jesus Christ" (Eph. 3. 9) It pleased God to bring the old creation into being through the instrumentality of His Son; it has also pleased Him that the new creation should be "in Christ Jesus." By Him He made the worlds (Heb. 1. 2), and by Him He seeks also to redeem this world lost in sin. He by whom God made all things has also made peace by the Blood of His Cross. The Lord Jesus Christ as the Word of God holds the same position towards the new creation as He did to the old. "Without Him was not any thing made." Without Him God did nothing, so without Him we can do nothing. All things were created by Him and for Him, and by Him all things consist or hold together. He is the centre and support of all, as well as the Maker. "Thou art worthy, O Lord, to receive glory, and honour, and power; for Thou hast created all things, and for Thy pleasure they are and were created" (Rev. 4. 11). If all things were created for His pleasure, surely He shall see of the travail of His soul and be satisfied.

III. **Relationship to Men**. "In Him was life, and

the life was the light of men." Why is the Life spoken
of as the light of men, and not of creation? He has made
the Light of the material universe, but He is the Light of
men. Man is something distinct from and superior to other
created things. He is a personality that needs the Divine
Personality to meet his every want. "In Him was life."
The source of life was in Him, and God, in giving us His
Son hath given to us eternal life (1 John 5. 11). The life
manifested in Christ Jesus is the true light which should
lighten every man coming into the world. I am come
that they might have life. Christ as the Word of God is
that living bread which came down from Heaven, that a
man may eat and not die. Man shall not live by bread
alone, but by every word of God.

Then observe—

1. What this LIGHT is—"The life was the light."

2. Where this light SHINES—"The light shineth in
darkness." Christ as the Light did not shine on the darkness of the world, but in the darkness. He was made flesh,
and dwelt among us. His own words are, "I am come a
light into the world" (John 12. 46). The purpose of the
light is to overcome the darkness. The centre of this
darkness is the human heart. The God who commanded
light to shine out of darkness is He who hath shined in our
hearts, to give the light of the knowledge of God (2 Cor. 4. 6).

3. The EFFECT of its shining—"The darkness compre-
hended it not." Two words are used in the Revised
Version—one in the text and the other in the margin—
which if taken separately bring out the twofold result
of this shining of the true light.

(1) The darkness *apprehended* it not. The darkness of
wilful unbelief remained unconscious of the dawning of
this new day—"they knew not the time of their visitation"
(Luke 19. 42-44).

(2) The darkness *overcame* it not (R.V., *margin*). Thank God, that in the case of many the darkness of sin and fear was not able to overcome or resist the bright shining of His truth. No matter how dense the darkness is, it cannot in any way overcome the purity or purpose of the light. The light shines on, but men may condemn themselves by loving the darkness rather than the light (John 3. 19).

HOW TO BECOME CHILDREN.
JOHN 1. 6-13.

> "Thou would'st like wretched man be made
>   In everything but sin,
> That we like Thee might become,
>   As we unlike have been."—*Stennet.*

"THERE was a man sent from God, whose name was John: the same came for a witness." The "True Light" was heralded by a special messenger from Heaven. "Sent from God...for a witness." That is a perfect life which fulfils the purpose of God, although it may be both solitary and brief. It is not necessary that a man should live long, but if his life is not to be a failure it is necessary that he should live to the glory of God. As soon as we become "children of God" by being born anew from above, we enter into that relationship with Him that makes it possible for us to become like John, "a man sent from God...for a witness." Then, how can we become children of God? The answer here is short and simple, "As many as receive Him, to them gives He the right to become children of God" (v. 12, R.V.). No man has the right to be called a child of God who has not received Him. "God hath made of one blood all nations," but the blood of nations is not the same as the Blood of Christ. Great emphasis is here put upon the Him whom we are to receive. The act of receiving avails only because it brings us into contact with the One.

I. **Who Made the World** (v. 10). The world

was made by Him. He who made the world can easily
remake a human soul. His creative power was manifested,
while in the world, by His miraculous works, such as
feeding the thousands with a few loaves, and stilling the
tempest and the raging waves.

II. **Who was in the World** (v. 10). Him who
made the world, and who humbled Himself to be born
into the world in the likeness of sinful flesh, that He might
get into personal touch with man's sins and sorrows. In
the world but not of it, among sinners but entirely separated
from them, in the world as the visible representative of the
invisible God.

III. **Who is the True Light** (v. 9). This is the
only light that can possibly "lighten every man coming
into the world," because this true light is the life of men.
Him who is eternally perfect, with all the perfections of
eternity. . He is the "true Light," the "true Vine," the
"true Bread." He is "the Truth." To receive Him is to
receive the light of life.

IV. **Who was Rejected by His Own.** "The
world knew Him not, and His own received Him not"
(vv. 10, 11). They knew Him as the Son of Joseph, but
as the Son of God they refused to acknowledge Him
Although they lived and moved and had their being in
Him, yet they knew Him not. They received with eager
ness His daily bounties, but Him they received not. No
one could convince Him of sin. No one could find a fault
in Him. Yet His own received Him not. The fact that
He was first rejected, then accepted by His own kinsfolk
is another proof of the divinity of His character. He did
the works that none other man could do, and so attested
His claims. As many as receive Him must be prepared to
suffer reproach with Him.

V. **Who has Authority to Make us Children**

of God. "As many as received Him, to them gave He the right to become children of God" (v. 12, R.V.). This prerogative is His alone. No church privilege or laying on of hands can give any one the right to become a son of God. The Spirit of adoption is the gift of God (Rom. 8. 15). There is no other way whereby we can become the children of God but through "faith in Christ Jesus" (Gal. 3. 26). Christ came as the sent one of God, to redeem us, that we might receive the adoption of sons (Gal. 4. 4, 5). He has the right to adopt because He had the power to redeem. As many as receive Him receive redemption from sin and guilt.

VI. Who has Power to Regenerate the Soul. "Which were born, not of blood, nor of the will of the flesh, nor of the will of man, but of God" (v. 13). To become a son of God implies regeneration by the Spirit of God. It is not a natural birth—"not of blood." It cannot be produced by any amount of fleshly energy—"nor of the will of the flesh." Neither can it come by the force of intellectual effort—"nor of the will of man." It is of God, and is God's immediate answer to our faith in His Son Jesus Christ. As many as receive Him are born of God. How shall I put thee among the children? "Receive Him."

THE WORD MADE FLESH.
JOHN 1. 14-18.

"Who did leave His Father's throne
To assume thy flesh and bone—
Had He life or had He none?
If He had not lived for thee
Thou hadst died most wretchedly,
And two deaths had been thy fee."—*Herbert.*

"THE life of man," says Westcott, "is the knowledge of God. But this knowledge lives and moves. It is not a dead thing, embalmed once for all in phrases." The Word

was made flesh, and dwelt among us. This is holy ground.
Let us approach as Moses did the burning bush. Here we
see a—

I. Mysterious Incarnation. "The Word was made
flesh." He who was "with God," and who "was God,"
has suddenly appeared in the likeness of sinful flesh. How
would Elijah have felt if that "still small voice" that
spoke so clearly to his heart had mysteriously appeared in
the form of flesh and bone? Christ as the Word could not
be seen, and the flesh as such could not be heard, but the
"Word made flesh" could be both seen and heard. The
flesh without the living Word has no message or virtue in
it for the sins and sores of this needy world. The union of
the Word and the flesh is as much a mystery as the unity
of the Trinity. Great is the mystery of godliness: God
manifest in the flesh. It was all of grace that Christ took
on Him the seed of Abraham instead of the nature of angels.
The mystery of the Incarnation is the mystery of grace.

II. Profound Humiliation. "And dwelt among us."
It was not a hurried greeting, like an angel's visit. It
was the voluntary adoption of Himself into the family of
humanity. God, who dwelt in the miraculous "pillar of
cloud," and tabernacled with Israel in the wilderness, has
now humbled Himself to take the common form of sinful
men, and dwell among them. What a stoop, the image of
God taking the likeness of sinful flesh.

III. Divine Manifestation. "No man hath seen God
at any time: the only begotten Son, . . . He hath declared
Him" (v. 18). He who was "in the bosom of the Father"
was well fitted to make such an declaration. In the
life of Jesus Christ the character of the "King eternal,
immortal, and invisible, . . . whom no man hath seen or
can see," hath been graciously manifested. As "no one
knoweth the Son save the Father, so neither doth any one

know the Father save the Son, and he to whomsoever the Son willeth to reveal Him" (Matt. 11. 27). It takes God the Father to fully apprehend the greatness of the character of God the Son. It takes God the Son to give a perfect declaration of God the Father, and it takes God the Holy Ghost to make man capable of receiving and enjoying such a manifestation. What a revelation is this? "I have manifested Thy Name unto the men which Thou gavest Me out of the world" (John 17. 6).

IV. **Provided Salvation.** "The Word was made flesh, and dwelt among us . . . full of Grace and Truth" (v. 14). "Grace and Truth came by Jesus Christ" (v. 17). The grace of Jesus Christ is the winsomeness and kindness of God, and He is "FULL" of it. The grace of God which bringeth salvation to all men, hath appeared in the person of His Son. But this grace has not come at the sacrifice of truth, for it is "grace and truth" that here meet together. It is in Him that righteousness and peace kiss each other, like two pure minded lovers (Psa. 85. 10). Although salvation comes to us as a ministry of grace, it is at the same time "the ministration of righteousness," through Christ Jesus (2 Cor. 3. 9). In Him God is just in justifying the unjust who believe in Jesus Christ His Son. We should ever remember that it is the grace of the infinite and eternal GOD that has come to us by Jesus Christ.

V. **Blessed Testimony.** "We beheld His glory, . . . and of His fullness we all received" (vv. 14-16, R.V.) A wonderful vision—"His glory." A wonderful possession —"Of His fullness." They saw His glory on the mount of transformation. But this outward manifestation was only the visible expression of the inward glory of His grace, in coming forth to suffer at Jerusalem for the sin of the world. It is a great sight to behold the glory of God in the face of Jesus Christ, the glory of the only begotten of the Father. Those whose eyes are opened thus to see His

glory have hearts prepared to receive of His fullness.   His
fullness is the fullness of Divine riches, which are unsearchable.   It was after that Joseph's brethren beheld his glory
that they were privileged to receive of His fullness.   It was
after the disciples had seen the glory of His resurrection
that they received of the fullness of the Pentecostal gift.   It
is when we have seen the glory of His grace that we seek
after the fullness of His salvation.   The glory of Christ is
the glory of GRACE.   Who can fathom it?   Who has ever
yet seen the horizon of its glory?   This is a glory that can
yet be seen.   This is a fullness of which we may yet receive.
Have you seen His glory?   Are you being satisfied with
His fullness?

JOHN'S TESTIMONY OF CHRIST.
JOHN 1. 29-34.

> "Who follows in His train?
> Who best can drink His cup of woe
>   Triumphant over pain;
> Who patient bears His cross below,
>   He follows in His train."—*Heber.*

"COMING events cast their shadows before them." The
coming of the solitary and suffering Christ was foreshadowed
by the appearing of the solitary and suffering Baptist.
John's confession of himself prepared the way for his
testimony of his Lord: "I am not the Christ;" "I am not
Elias." "I am the voice of Him who is the Word of God,"
crying, "Make straight the way of the Lord" (vv. 19-23).
It is needful that we should know ourselves if we would
bear a true testimony for Christ.   He who said, "I can do
all things through Christ, which strengthened me," also
said, "In me, that is, in my flesh, dwelleth no good thing."
In these verses John tells us seven things about the Lord
Jesus Christ, unto which we may well give heed.   Observe
that—

I. **He is the Lamb of God** (v. 29). God's chosen Lamb to bear away the sin of the world, to which all the sacrifices of the old dispensation pointed. It was then "a lamb for an house," it is now a Lamb for a world (1 John 2. 2). The Lamb of God was God's manifestation of his own meekness and submissiveness to the awful necessity of Divine suffering for the atonement of sin. This is the Lamb who, in the purpose of God, was "slain from the foundation of the world" (Rev. 13. 8). If it was needful that "your lamb shall be without blemish," it is certainly so of His. The Blood of Christ shed upon the Cross is a token to the whole world of God's willingness to "pass over," in forgiving grace, all who believe in Him (Exod. 12; 1 John 4. 10).

II. **He was Before Me** (v. 30). Yes, a long time before John, for He is "before all things." Although John was conscious that he was the forerunner of Christ, he was conscious also of the deeper truth that Christ was before him, as a father is before his son. John's ministry was of God's appointment, but only because of the greater ministry of His Son. It is easy for us to believe that Christ was before us, but how easy it also is for us to forget that we are called to be His servants, by virtue of this fact.

III. **He is Preferred Before Me** (v. 30). "A man which is become before me (R.V.). In all things He must have the pre-eminence. The Lamb of God must ever stand in the front of all our purposes, as He does in the forefront of all God's plans and purposes. When a servant of Christ becomes more anxious to get himself than his Master into the place of eminence before the people, he has begun to play the traitor. God prefers His Son above all His servants, therefore let not the servant insult Him by preferring himself.

IV. He would be Made Manifest to Israel (v. 31).
The Paschal lamb was laid up on the tenth day of the
month, and manifested on the fourteenth (Exod. 12).
There were three stages in the manifestation of the Lamb
of God: (1) His Baptism; (2) His Transfiguration; (3) His
Crucifixion. In the first we have the proof of His Divine
mission; in the second we have a revelation of His
blameless character as a Lamb; in the third we have
the accomplishment of His substitutionary work as a
sinoffering.

V. He is the Anointed One. "I saw the Spirit descending from Heaven like a dove, and it abode upon Him"
(v. 32). The dove-like Spirit came from an "opened
Heaven," and was accompanied with the assuring voice:
"Thou art My beloved Son" (Matt. 3; Luke 3). Him
did God the Father seal unto that day of redemption,
accomplished on Calvary's Cross. With the Holy Spirit
there came the Divine attesting voice. Whenever the holy
anointing comes, the voice of God must be distinctly heard.
With Pentecost came the tongues of fire. Every baptism
of the Holy Spirit will be followed with the testimony of
God. "Ye shall be witnesses unto me when the power of
the Holy Ghost is come upon you" (Acts 1. 8).

VI. He is the Baptiser with the Holy Ghost. "Upon
whom thou shalt see the Spirit descending...the same
is He which baptiseth with the Holy Ghost" (v. 33).
John bears emphatic witness to the two great aspects of
Christ's work: (1) He shall take away sin; (2) He shall
baptise with the Holy Ghost. The one is the correlative
of the other. We have the same ground for expecting
Christ to baptise us with the Holy Ghost as that He should
take away our sins. Surely these are two distinct experiences, and ought to be definitely enjoyed by each believer
in Jesus. Pentecost is the counterpart of Calvary.

VII. **He is the Son of God.** "I have seen and have borne witness that this is the Son of God" (v. 34, R.V.). As the Lamb, He put away sin by the sacrifice of Himself; as the Son, He is almighty to save. John was a man sent from God, that He might bear witness that He is the Son of God, so that Israel, as a nation, may recognise Him as the promised Messiah. It was as "the Son of God" that Satan tempted Him in the wilderness. Because He is the Son of God, with power, He is well able to fulfil every promise He has made. "If ye believe not that I am He, ye shall die in your sins" (John 8. 24).

THE FIRST DISCIPLES.
JOHN 1. 35-42.

The perfect way is hard to flesh,
It is not hard to love:
If thou wert sick for want of God,
How swiftly wouldst thou move.

Be docile to thine unseen Guide;
Love *Him* as *He* loves thee;
Faith and obedience are enough,
And thou a saint shalt be. "—*Faber*.

"IT is safer to obey than to govern," although our own foolish hearts would rather lead than follow. There is something like a halo of glory about these two men, who first ventured to "follow Jesus." It is easy to follow Jesus in a crowd, but in almost every company or family there is need for some one with courage enough to take the initiative, and step out for Christ, and as an example to others. These early disciples became followers of Jesus in much the same way in which disciples are made now. How was that? There was—

I. **A Simple Testimony.** "John stood and, looking upon Jesus as He walked, he said, Behold the Lamb of God" (vv. 35, 36). The preacher was "John." His attitude was, "looking upon Jesus." His subject was "The Lamb of God." His manner was earnest—he "stood," concentrating his whole soul upon the message. He was also practical—"Behold." See him now. It was a short message, but it was a word spoken in season, full of power, and was immediately fruitful.

II. **An Act of Faith.** "The two disciples heard him speak, and they followed Jesus" (v. 37). Faith cometh by hearing, and hearing by the word of God. They heard and they followed. They had been following John, but now, on the testimony of John himself, they leave the servant of Christ and follow his Master. John's desire should be the desire of every herald of the Lord Jesus Christ. "He must increase, I must decrease" (John 3. 30). He preached not himself, but Christ the Lamb of God, and so they believed. Their faith was evidenced by their following. It may have cost them much to turn their backs upon their late beloved master, but the sacrifice is readily made for the fellowship of Him who can put away sin. There was no time to delay. The choice had to be made at once, for Jesus "walked," and would soon be out of sight.

III. **A Heart-Searching Question.** "Jesus turned and said unto them, What seek ye?" (v. 38). Jesus will test the motives of those who follow Him before He commits Himself to them. What seek ye? Do you expect worldly honour and preference by following Me? Is it some earthly gift from Me, or is it ME ye seek? I am the way, the Truth, and the Life. In following me are you seeking the Way to God, the Truth of God, and the Life of God? What seek ye? Let this question search our own hearts. As professed disciples of Christ, what are the secret motives that animate our Christian life? Are we more anxious to be honoured by Christ than to honour Him? "If any man would follow Me, 'et him deny himself" (Matt. 16. 24).

IV. An Anxious Inquiry. "They said unto Him, Master, where dwellest Thou?" (v. 38). Perhaps they feel that the Master's question is difficult to answer in full, and if they knew where He abode they might go and have a lengthened interview with Him, so that they could calmly unburden their whole hearts unto Him. This answer reveals the deep sincerity of their souls. They wish to know HIM as the Lamb of God which taketh away the sin of the world. Where dwellest thou? He dwells (spiritually) in the bosom of the Father (v. 18). and those who would abide with Him will also dwell in God.

V. A Gracious Invitation. "He saith unto them, Come and see." They gladly accepted His invitation, and "came and saw where He dwelt, and abode with Him" (v. 39). This was a blessed and memorable experience, and so John mentions the very hour of the day—"the tenth hour." "Come and see." What grace and privilege those sweet words convey to their anxious souls. It is the opening of a wide and effectual door into fullness of blessing. How sad for them if they had failed to enter in. Is not this same privilege ours, in a deeper sense? "Come unto Me, all ye who labour and are heavy laden, and I will give you rest" (Matt. 11. 28). Believe, and thou shalt see.

VI. A Willing Service. "Andrew findeth his own brother Simon, . . . and he brought him to Jesus" (vv. 40-42). That quiet time of close fellowship with Jesus results in immediate fruit-bearing. "They that wait on the Lord shall renew their strength." Companying with Christ leads to clearness of views and boldness of action. He could say, "We have found the Messias." They had sought and found, so their testimony is clear and persuasive. Their work for Him began after they had been with Him. "This is My beloved Son, hear Him" (Matt.

17. 5.), then serve Him.   Quiet Andrew did a great work when he brought the boisterous Peter to Jesus.   Can we be truly following Christ if our lives are not constraining others to follow Him?   Herein is my Father glorified, that ye bear much fruit: so shall ye be My disciples" (John 15. 8).

NATHANAEL'S CONVERSION.
JOHN 1. 43-51.

> "My Master, they have wronged Thee and Thy love!
> They only told me I should find the path
> A *via Dolorosa* all the way!
> Narrow indeed it is...Oh, why
> Should they misrepresent Thy words, and make
> 'Narrow' synonymous with 'very hard?'
> For Thou divinest wisdom, Thou hast said
> Thy ways are ways of pleasantness, and all
> Thy paths are peace."—*F. R. Havergal.*

THERE was a great difference between the manner of the conversion of Nathanael and that of Saul, but the inward change was much the same.   See how it came about, for he

I. Heard.   "Philip saith unto him, We have found Him of whom Moses and the prophets did write, Jesus of Nazareth" (v. 45).   He heard the joyful tidings from one who had himself been found of the Christ, and satisfied with Him.   Philip's Gospel was not an *it*, but a HIM—Him in whom the hope of Israel lay; Him who answers all the predictions of Moses and the prophets, and meets all the needs of a human soul and a perishing world.   He heard— but how shall men hear without a preacher? and how shall they preach except they be sent.   All who have found Him are surely able to witness for Him.

II. Questioned.   "Nathanael said unto him, Can there any good thing come out of Nazareth?" (v. 46).   Although Jesus was born in Bethlehem, He was brought up in Nazareth, that He might be called a Nazarene (Matt. 2. 23)

Nazareth was an insignificant and, perhaps, an infamous town. How could the greatest of all prophets come from such an unlikely place? Like Nicodemus, he was disposed to ask, "How can these things be?" Philip was not inclined to dispute the matter with his thoughtful inquirer, but simply answered, "Come and see." It is wonderful how difficulties melt away when the troubled one gets face to face with the Son of God. The misty clouds of doubt cannot stand when He appeareth, for His words are soul-healing and enlightening beams. It is truly heavenly logic to meet the "How's" of an inquirer after Christ with the "Comes" of the Gospel. How can a man know that Christ is able and willing to save? Come and see.

III. **Proved.** Nathanael came to Jesus, and when Jesus saw him coming He said of Him, "Behold an Israelite indeed;" and Nathanael said unto Him, "Whence knowest Thou me?" (vv. 47, 48). Jesus at once manifested Himself to this honest seeker as the gracious and merciful heart-searcher. "Before Philip called thee, I saw thee." Nathanael has found that "good thing" which did not come out of Nazareth, but out of Heaven. He came and saw for Himself the wisdom and power of God manifested in Jesus the Christ. This guileless seeker very quickly became a joyful finder. It is when the seed falls into an honest heart that it brings forth fruit.

IV. **Believed.** "Because I said unto thee, I saw thee under the fig tree, believest thou?" (v. 50). The inference is clear that he did believe. What else could he do? The evidence of His Messiahship had been over-whelmingly convicting, as the demonstration made had been entirely with himself. Christ's Divinity was proven by His operating upon His own heart and conscience—not by any outward display of miracle. Moral miracles are the monuments which still attest His Divine power and

Godhead.   The best way to prove the Divinity and
saving power of Jesus Christ is to submit yourself to
Him, then you will get a witness within that cannot
be silenced.

V. Confessed. "He answered and said, Rabbi, Thou
art the Son of God, Thou art the King of Israel" (v. 49).
He believed with his heart, now he makes confession
with his mouth. The confession was fearless and full.
As the "Son of God" He was mighty to save; as the
"King of Israel" entire submission was His due. If we
acknowledge Him as Saviour we should also submit to
Him as King, for He is both Saviour and Lord. The
confession Thomas made was: "My Lord and my God!"
Many in those days, as now, believed on Him, who were
afraid to confess Him (John 12. 42, 43). Remember that
it is those who confess Him before men that He will confess
before His Father in Heaven (Matt. 10. 32).

VI. Was Encouraged. "Thou shalt see greater things
than these,...ye shall see Heaven open," etc. (vv. 50, 51).
There is always an "open Heaven" and a blessed "hereafter" for those who so confess Him. It is a glorious
and soul-satisfying vision to see an "open Heaven and
the messengers of God ascending and descending upon
the Son of Man." This is the ladder which Jacob saw.
There is no other way of communication between a sin-
cursed earth and an "open Heaven" but by Him. "I am
the Way, no one can come unto the Father but by Me."
He is the Mediator between God and men, the Man Christ
Jesus. Only "angels of God" can do business in this way;
the unclean shall not walk therein. Only those whose
delight it is to fulfil the purposes of His will can ascend and
descend upon this holy way. Have we seen this vision, and
are we being encouraged and strengthened in our daily life
by it?

THE FIRST SIGN.

JOHN 2. 1-11.

"In holy books we read how God hath spoken
   To holy men in many different ways;
But hath the present world no sign or token?
   Is God quite silent in these latter days?

The Word were but a blank, a hollow sound,
   If He that spake it were not speaking still,
If all the light and all the shade around
   Were aught but issues of the Almighty will. "—*Coleridge*.

"THIS beginning of His signs did Jesus in Cana of Galilee, and manifested His glory" (v. 11, R.V.). Perhaps this was one of the "greater things" which Jesus promised that Nathanael should see (chap. 1. 50). The "glory" of Jesus, the carpenter, had not yet been seen. There may be some significance in the fact that the first manifestation of "His glory" was on the "third day" of His appearing unto Israel, as the "third day" was to be the day of His greatest sign of all—the resurrection. We shall note the—

I. **Occasion of this Sign.** "A marriage in Cana." Marriage is, or at least ought to be, a united effort to perfect mutual happiness. But this marriage party did not seek this great blessing without the presence of the Lord, so "Jesus was called and His disciples;" and Jesus went, for He does desire to give His blessing to every lawful attempt after holiness and happiness. Every occasion is holy when Jesus Christ is there, and every holy season is a happy one. Jesus being there, there soon arose that need which He alone could meet: "there was no wine." Something awanting; yes, something for Jesus to do. Wherever He is there must needs be something done that will "manifest His glory." No efforts of men after true happiness can be successful without His gift of infinite grace. His wine is needed to fully satisfy the heart of man. "Thou hast kept the good wine until now." Those who drink of His "wine" are fully conscious that it is the very best that can be got on earth (Isa. 55. 1, 2). Christless pleasures are lifeless, and soon wither.

II. **Meaning of this Sign.** It was the manifestation of the—

1. GLORY OF HIS ALL-SUFFICIENT GRACE. The first word uttered by Jesus on this great occasion was significant: "Fill." Oh! how characteristic this is of the liberality of His gracious heart. "Fill the water pots." He who is "full of grace" (chap. 1. 14) delights to give fullness of blessing. Less than 130 gallons might have sufficed, but this was to be a manifestation of His grace, so He gives "exceeding abundantly" above all their expectations. Every water jar was filled. He gives as much as we have room for. Open the mouth of thy expectation wide, and He will fill it.

2. GLORY OF HIS TRANSFORMING POWER. "The water was made wine." The first miracle of Moses, by whom the law was given, was to turn water into blood; the first miracle of Him, by whom grace and truth came, was to turn water into wine. The blood speaks of judgment, the wine of fullness of joy. The commonest mercy in life can, by Him, be changed into the richest of blessings. Not only common mercies, but common men, like Peter and John, can He transform by His wonder-working power into vessels made meet for the Master's use. Every soul converted to God has been as definitely and as successfully operated upon by the Lord Jesus Christ as when He turned the water into wine. The performing of this sign was the evidencing of His ability to make all things new. Believe ye that I am able to do this? Present yourselves unto God, that ye may be "transformed by the renewing of your mind" (Rom. 12. 1, 2).

3. GLORY OF HIS SUPERLATIVE CHARACTER. "Thou hast

kept the good wine until now" (v. 10). The last state is better than the first. The converted life is better than the purest of unconverted lives, as wine is richer than water. Christ could do nothing else but give "the best," as His words and works are true manifestations of His real character. Christ alone is the Maker of that wine which brings gladness without sorrow. All other wines manufactured by others to cheer the heart of man are but deceptive imitations. Christ gives the best, the best joy, the best peace, the best hope, the best promises, the best friendship, the best reward. Godliness is profitable for the life that now is, as well as that which is to come. If your life has not been changed by the power of Jesus Christ, the best is yet in store for you. O taste and see that the Lord is good. Good as His wine is now, there is yet something better kept for us, when we shall gather at the "marriage of the Lamb" (Rev. 19. 7). Thou hast kept the best until now.

CLEANSING THE TEMPLE.
JOHN 2. 13-19.

"Are we not holy? Do not start!
It is God's sacred will
To call us temples set apart
His Holy Ghost may fill."—*A. Procter.*

THERE is a striking contrast between the scene at the marriage in Cana of Galilee (v. 1) and that at the passover in the temple of Jerusalem. At the one Christ was an invited guest, at the other He was an unwelcomed stranger, although the temple was His "Father's house." In the one He wrought a miracle of grace, in the other a miracle of judgment. To honour Him is to be blessed, to dishonour Him is to be condemned. The temple is a figure both of the Lord's body and of ours (v. 21 and 1 Cor. 6. 19). In the light of this we shall examine this miracle of cleansing.

I. **The True Character of the Temple.** The Lord
calls it "My Father's house" (v. 16). It was identified
with the Name of God, and was to be a witness for Him.
In it God revealed Himself, and man communed and worshipped. It was the earthly house of the heavenly and
eternal King. But now, "know ye not that your body
is the temple of the Holy Ghost, which is in you." Ye are
the temple of the living God, as God hath said, "I will
dwell in them" (2 Cor. 6. 19). After the temple at
Jerusalem was "left desolate" by the rejection of Christ,
the Holy Ghost came down at Pentecost and took possession
of one hundred and twenty temples, so that they became
witnesses for the Lord Jesus Christ (Acts 1. 8).

II. **How the Temple was Defiled.** It was defiled
by those who professed to be the friends of the temple,
who used their religion as a cloak, that they might secure
worldly gain for themselves. They had a zeal for the House
of God, because this brought them personal profit, but they
had no zeal for God Himself, or the honour of His Name.
It is possible to have a zeal for the House of God (the
Church) and yet be defiling the temple of the Holy Ghost all
the time. If any man defile this temple, him (as a witness)
shall God destroy. There is a religious zeal that is unholy
and polluting in the sight of God; it is a zeal kindled on
the vain altar of self-love, and fed with the fuel of selfish
and worldly ambitions. That Christian life is utterly
defiled that is governed by such sordid and debasing
motives. To be more concerned about the body, or the
forms and ordinances of the Church, than the purpose of
the Holy Ghost in the body or Church, is to introduce a
kind of traffic into the holy courts that pollutes and brings
dishonour upon the House and Name of God. All worldly-
mindedness and self-seeking brings moral defilement into
that body which is the temple of the Holy Ghost.

III. **How Christ is Treated in a Defiled Temple.**

"The zeal of thine House hath eaten Me up." They were so zealous about the things of the House that the Lord of the House Himself was to them as One who had been devoured and put out of sight. He had not place in all their appointments, no say in anything they did. He was treated as if He had absolutely no claim neither on them nor on the affairs of the House. This is the place the Almighty Redeemer gets in the lives of those who, for gain and honour among men, have allowed the love of the world to eat up their Christlikeness, or those who are so zealous for the things of religion that they have neither time nor desire for real fellowship with Christ Himself. They have a form of godliness, but they deny Him who is the power. O ye zealots for the externals of the Church, what are you doing with Christ?

IV. **How the Temple was Cleansed.** It was cleansed by the incoming of the Master Himself. It would have been a very long while before these sellers and money-changers moved in this direction. His presence means purity. The intruders, with their defiling traffic, were "driven out." There is no other remedy for those Christ-dishonouring thoughts and motives, which have been ruling Him out of His own House, and setting up a business in His Name for the honour and glory of self. Who of these wretched usurpers shall be able to stand when He appeareth for He is like a refiner's fire, He shall sit upon the throne of the heart as a refiner and purifier of silver (Mal. 3. 1-3). The scourge may be needed, but in the hands of this merciful Purifier it is a scourge of "small cords." It must be a great grief to His heart to see a soul redeemed by His own Blood, that it might become a temple of God, turned into a mere "house of merchandise." Ye are not your own, for ye are bought with a price, therefore glorify God in your body and your spirit which are His. Give Christ His rightful place in the temple of the heart, and those selfish

and defiling motives, which are like so many unholy
traffickers, will quickly be driven out of the life.

V. The Sign of His Authority as a Cleanser. After
this "Vanity Fair" had been cleared out of the temple
courts, the Jews asked Him, "What sign shewest Thou
unto us, seeing that Thou doest these things" (v. 18).
The fact that He was able to drive them all out by the
power of His own word and will—for it was not by mere
physical force—might have been proof enough of His
Divine authority, but He answered, "Destroy this temple
(body), and in three days I will raise it up, not build it up
(vv. 19-22). His power to rise from the dead is then
the evidence of His power to cleanse the temple for the
glory of the Father. Is He able now to purge the heart
and cleanse the life from every polluting thing? His
resurrection is the answer, the sign. This evil generation,
or this dispensation of evil, shall have no other sign given
to it, but the sign of Jonas the prophet (Matt. 12. 39, 40).

THE NEW BIRTH.
JOHN 3. 1-9.

"Open thy bosom, set thy meshes wide,
And let in manhood—let in happiness
Amid the boundless theatre of thought—
From nothing up to God—which makes a man.
                                              —*Young.*

FROM nothing but darkness and death, up to the light
and life of God, is the experience of all who have been born
from above. In seeking to understand this most searching
truth, as brought before us in these verses, we would
endeavour to point out that it is—

I. Taught by the Wisest of Men. The signs which
Jesus wrought proved Him to be "a teacher come from
God." Right through all His public life we see Him

as "a man approved of God, by miracles and wonders."
"Never man spake like this man," was the testimony even
of His enemies. It was He who is the Wisdom of God that
said, "Ye must be born again!" There is no escape from
this. Christ said it, and Christ means it.

II. **A Necessity to the Kingdom of God.** "Except
a man be born anew, he cannot see the kingdom of God"
(R.V.), "cannot enter into" (v. 5). By nature we are
born spiritually blind, and so cannot see into that sphere
where God alone is King; and Satan has so blinded the
mind that it is morally impossible for such to enter into
it. Any birth or life that is after the will of the flesh is
unfit for the Kingdom of God (John 1. 13). Everything
that sinful man touches is defiled, and nothing that defileth
shall enter into this heavenly kingdom. This new kingdom
in Christ Jesus can only be peopled by a new creation after
His own likeness (2 Cor. 5. 17). The Kingdom of God is
not meat and drink, it does not consist of mere carnal
pleasures, which any unrenewed man can enjoy, but it is
righteousness of heart, peace with God, and joy in the Holy
Ghost, which no unregenerated one can possibly enjoy. He
must be born from above before he can enter into the
possessions of those things which are above. The pure in
heart shall see God.

III. **A Mystery to the Natural Man.** How can
a man be born when he is old?" Nicodemus, being
still a mere natural man, was not able to receive this great
spiritual truth; it was foolishness unto him, because he had
not that faculty by which he could discern spiritual things
(1 Cor. 2. 14). But he was not condemned for the lack of
an understanding of it. It is those who love the darkness
rather than the light that bring themselves into the condemnation (v. 19). Nicodemus loved the light of truth,
and was an earnest seeker after it. It is the darkness of
unbelief that does not comprehend the true light that now

shineth (John 1. 5). Although a man cannot reason out the
mysteries of the new birth, that does not make it any the
less needful. He is not asked to explain it, but he is asked
to acknowledge his personal need of it. If it were possible
for a man to be born again after the flesh fifty times
over, that would in no way alter the case; he still needs
to be born from above if he is to enter into the kingdom
of God.

IV. The Work of the Holy Spirit. "The wind
bloweth where it listeth...so is every one that is born
of the Spirit" (v. 8). It is the Spirit that quickeneth,
the flesh profiteth nothing in the work of regeneration
(John 6. 63). "That which is born of the flesh is flesh."
Who can bring a clean thing out of an unclean? That
which is born of the Spirit is spirit, or is spiritual. By
no law of evolution or effort of man can that which is flesh
bring forth that which is spirit. Only that which is
begotten by the Holy Spirit of God is fit to enter into the
Kingdom of God. The second birth, like the second Adam,
is from Heaven (1 Cor. 15. 47), and is conceived in the
heart by the Holy Ghost. The works of the flesh are in
fearful contrast with the fruit of the Spirit (Gal. 5. 16-25).
He that soweth to the flesh can only reap corruption. The
Spirit is sovereign, and, like the wind, moves where He
willeth; thou hearest the voice thereof but canst not tell,
etc. (R.V.). There is much about the Spirit's manner of
working that we cannot tell, but to hear His voice, and to
obey His will, is to pass from death into life; for to be
spiritually-minded is life and peace (Rom. 8. 6). The
sword of the Spirit is the Word of God, the incorruptible
seed which liveth and abideth for ever, and by which we
are born again, as soon as that Word is received by faith.
Of His own will begat He us with that Word of Truth which
brings new life and hope to the believing heart by creating
a vital and eternal union with the Son of God.

THE WAY INTO LIFE.

JOHN 3. 14-21.

"Art builds on sand: the works of pride
And human passion change and fall;
But that which shares the life of God,
With Him surviveth all."—*Whittier.*

"How can these things be?" said Nicodemus, in answer
to Christ's most searching statements regarding the
"new birth." The verses indicated above may be taken
as our Lord's full and perfect explanation of how a
man can be "born again" even when he is old. As
such they are of vital significance to every man. They
contain the—

I. **Revelation of a Great Need.** "As Moses lifted
up the serpent in the wilderness, even so must the Son
of Man be lifted up" (v. 14). There was great need for
Moses lifting up the serpent in the wilderness, because
it was God's remedy for a serpent-poisoned people. So
must the Son of Man be lifted up for a sin-poisoned world.
The lifting up of the serpent was to attract the eye of the
perishing, that they might look and live. There was none
other Name under Heaven given among men whereby they
could be saved (Acts 4. 12).

II. **Revelation of Great Love.** "God so loved the
world that He gave His only-begotten Son" (v. 16). If
ye love them that love you, what thanks have ye, do not
even the Gentiles the same? This is not like the love of
God, for, while we were yet sinners, Christ died for us
(Eph. 2. 4). The depth and intensity of God's love can
only be measured by the unworthiness of the objects, and
the greatness of the Gift. He might have so loved the
world as to speak through His Son, but He so loved as to
give His Son, and in giving Him—as the "only-begotten
of the Father, full of grace and truth"—He gave to the

world a perfect remedy for all its sins and sorrows (Rom. 8. 32). Herein is love, love in the perfection of its nature, and in the greatest possible manifestation of its power.

III. **Revelation of Great Suffering.** Intense suffering is surely implied in the fact of God giving up His Son unto the death for us all, and in that the Son yielded Himself to be lifted up upon the Cross for the sins of the world (John 8. 28). The way of life for fallen man is through the soul agony both of the Father and of the Son. Sin is such a fearful thing that even God Himself cannot deal with it but at the expense of terrible personal suffering. When Nicodemus, puzzled with the doctrine of the "new birth," asked the Lord Jesus Christ, "How can these things be?" his question reached further and deeper than he could possibly conceive of. How can a sinner be transformed into a saint? Through the sufferings of God, through the giving up of His Son, and the shedding of His Blood (Acts 20. 28).

IV. **Revelation of a Great Purpose.** "That whosoever believeth in Him should not perish." "That the world through Him might be saved" (vv. 16, 17). This purpose of salvation is first individual, then world-wide, when the kingdoms of this world shall become the Kingdom of our Lord and of His Christ. The "lifting up" of the Son of Man was the unlocking of the door of hope for a guilty world; it was the breaking forth of the sin-cleansing stream from the opened fountain of almighty grace (Zech. 13. 1). The saving purpose of God is the crowning purpose of the Bible, it towers high above all others, and casts its hallowing shadow over them all. Only "through Him" can salvation come.

V. **Revelation of a Great Privilege.** Salvation,

through being made a new creature, is the greatest possible blessing that the God of infinite love can bestow upon sinful men, and yet He offers it upon the easiest possible terms— "Whosoever believeth in Him." This great salvation is threefold:

1. Deliverance from PRESENT CONDEMNATION (v. 18).

2. Deliverance from FUTURE DESTRUCTION (v. 16).

3. Assurance of present and ETERNAL LIFE (vv. 15-16). Note that it is "he that believeth on Him" that is not condemned. There is no justification before God through believing in our works or our ways, nor in the Church or the Creed. It is our God-given privilege to trust Him whom He hath sent. Behold, now is the accepted time.

VI. The Revelation of a Great Responsibility. "This is the condemnation, that light is come into the world, and men loved darkness rather than light" (vv 19-21). The Son of God has come as the Light and Life of men. Those who love the darkness of spiritual death, rather than the light of spiritual life, will not come to the light, lest their foolish and sinful deeds should be reproved; but he that loves and desires the truth will come to the light as Nicodemus did, even if he should come in the darkness, that his life and deeds may be adjusted with God. He had an honest heart. It is the attitude of the heart toward Christ, as the Light of life, that leads to justification or condemnation. To love the darkness of an unregenerate state, is to prove ourselves unfit for the Kingdom of God. To love the light, as revealed in Christ, is to be more anxious to be right with God than with the opinions of men, or with the thoughts of our own deceitful hearts (Psa. 139. 23-24). The true Light now shineth! Are we hating it, or coming to it? This hating, and this coming, is a continual process.

JOHN'S LAST TESTIMONY.

JOHN 3. 25-36.

"My son forsake thyself, and thou shalt find Me!
Lord, how often shall I resign myself, and
Wherein shall I forsake myself? Always, yea,
Every hour: as well in small things as in great."

—*Thos. a Kempis.*

JOHN'S disciples were evidently grieved at the growing
popularity of Jesus (v. 26).   They were, like some modern
disciples, more the followers of a man than witnesses
for God.   Sectarianism, which is just another form of
selfishness, always blinds the eyes to the greatness of
Christ's mission, and to the real relationship of His
servants to Himself.   But the Spirit-taught man of the
desert knew better than be offended.   "He must increase,
but I must decrease" (v. 30).   These last words of the
Baptist, spoken in justification of the growing power of
Jesus Christ, are full of deep significance.   They teach
us—that

I. **All Christian Success comes from God.**   "A man
can receive nothing, except it be given him from heaven"
(v. 27).   John is, of course, referring here to the pre-
eminence given to Christ as the Son of Man.   "This is
my beloved Son in whom I am well pleased."   The secret
of all success in Christian, that is, in spiritual work,
lies in the favour of God.   Every good gift and perfect
boon is from above (James 1. 17, R.V.).   The lifting-up
that is not of God, is doomed to a terrible disappointment.

II. **The True Friends of Christ Rejoice in His
Exaltation.**   "The friends of the bridegroom rejoice
greatly . . . this my joy therefore is fulfilled" (vv. 29-30).
He that hath the bride (the Church) is the bridegroom
(Christ).   She is chosen through His grace and redeemed
by His blood.   John, as the friend of the bridegroom,
finds his joy fulfilled in that which honours HIM, and

brings gladness to his heart. This indeed is true friendship. Did not our Lord say of His disciples, "I have called you friends?" (John 15. 15). Have we John's mark of friendship? Do we rejoice because of His voice? Is the cup of our joy filled full because Christ is being honoured, even when we ourselves are being more and more dishonoured in the eyes of men? If our hearts are right with Him, there will be fullness of joy at the increase of Christ and the decrease of self.

III. **He that Cometh from Above is Above All** (v. 31). This is emphatically true of Jesus Christ. The source of His existence and the character of His life is from above, and is above all. But this is also true of every one that is born from above—born of God. They are in character and destiny "above all" that is of the world, the flesh, and the Devil. Their affections are set on things above, and they live above the doubts, the darkness, and the uncertainties of the world, and the Christ-dishonouring ways of ungodly men. We must come from above before we can attack successfully all the forces of evil that are from beneath (Eph. 6. 12, 13).

IV. **To Receive Christ's Testimony is to Honour God.** "He that receiveth His testimony hath set to His seal that God is true" (vv. 33, 34). "He whom God hath sent speaketh the words of God." Not to believe Him and the record given of Him is to make God a liar (1 John 5. 10). What was the testimony of Jesus Christ? He declared that "He came not to be ministered unto, but to minister, and to give His life a ransom for many" (Mark 10. 45). He came as a servant to reveal the words and will of God, and as a Redeemer to give Himself a sacrifice for sin. To receive His testimony by believing it, and acting on the authority of it, is to set the seal of the whole life upon the truth of God. We have never accepted

the word of His salvation until we have really set the seal
of our personal trust upon it.   Let God be true.

**V. The Father hath Honoured the Son in Every-
thing.**   "The Father loveth the Son, and hath given
all things into His hand" (v. 35).   To think of the Saviour
of sinners being so loved and honoured by the eternal God
and Father is enough to fill every believing heart with
unutterable praise and everlasting adoration.   "The Father
hath shewed Him all things that Himself doeth, and hath
committed all judgment unto the Son" (John 5. 20-22).
"Jesus knew that the Father had given all things into His
hands" (John 13. 3).   "Thou hast given Him power over
all flesh" (John 17. 2).   "Thou hast put all things under
His feet...He left nothing that is not put under Him"
(Heb. 2. 8).   "All power is given unto Me in Heaven
and in earth" (Matt. 28. 18).   "Of the increase of His
government and peace there shall be no end" (Isa. 9. 7).
"In Him dwelleth all the fullness of the Godhead bodily"
(Col. 2. 9).

**VI. To Believe on the Son is to have Everlasting
Life** (v. 36).   This mighty, God-honoured, all-embracing
Name is the only name "given among men whereby
we must be saved."   There cannot be another such a
One that has "power over all flesh to give eternal life"
(John 17. 2).   Eternal life is the gift of Him who has
"power over all."   Did He not say, "If ye believe not that
I am He, ye shall die in your sins?" (John 8. 24).   That
He gives eternal life and peace to all who believe in Him is
to us the proof of His eternal power and Godhead.

**VII. To Disbelieve the Son is to Abide under the
Wrath of God.**   "He that believeth not the Son shall
not see life; but the wrath of God abideth on him."   At
the Cross of Christ the wrath of God is revealed from
Heaven against all ungodliness and unrighteousness of

men, who hold the truth in unrighteousness (Rom. 1. 18). Those who know the Gospel, but have not submitted to the Son, are guilty of holding the truth in unrighteousness. God can by no means clear those who are guilty of rejecting the atoning Blood of His Lamb. Outside this Ark of Refuge is to be still beneath the dark cloud of judgment. Jesus only can deliver from the wrath to come (1 Tim. 1. 10). Hear ye Him.

THE LIVING WATER.
JOHN 4. 7-14.

THESE words of Jesus Christ about the "Living Water, spoken as they were to the sinful Samaritan, are deeper and more lasting than the well of Jacob. This well is unfathomable! This Water is everlasting!

I. **The Nature of It.** Our Lord calls it "Living Water" (v. 10). It is living in the sense that it is life-giving. That which Christ gives is not something to keep us alive, but something to make us alive. This water of "grace and truth," which came by Jesus Christ (vv. 1-17), is the water which saves and satisfies (Eph. 2. 8). It is not given merely to refresh, but to regenerate. The elements of eternal light and life are in it.

II. **The Source of It.** "Thou wouldest have asked of Him, and He would have given thee." He Himself is the disposer of this living water. Unto Him has been "given power over all flesh, that He should give eternal life" (John 17. 2). "This is the pure river of water of life, clear as crystal, proceeding out of the throne of God, and of the Lamb" (Rev. 22. 1). The original source of this grace and truth is the gracious heart of the eternal God, and has been manifested to us in the life and sufferings of the Lamb.

III. **The Efficacy of It.**

1 IT QUENCHES THIRST. "Whosoever shall drink of the

water that I shall give him, shall never thirst" (v. 14). They never thirst for the muddy waters of sin who have drank, and keep drinking, of the water that Christ gives. They shall never thirst for any other drink, neither in this life not in the life which is to come. "They shall not thirst for ever" (Newberry).

2. IT BECOMES A SPRING WITHIN. "The water that I shall give him shall become in him a spring of water" (v. 14, Newberry). The idea here is that, when any one drinks this water, or, in other words, receives this grace and truth offered in Christ, there is opened up within that one a fountain of new life and blessedness—a secondary source, within the heart, of perennial joy and satisfaction. Every saved soul is a citadel of God, and although constantly besieged by the sins and sorrows of earth, they have an unfailing source of supply within. This fountain flows on for ever, springing up into the ocean of eternal life and praise, in the presence of God and the Lamb.

IV. **The Conditions of It.** "If thou knewest the gift of God, thou wouldest have asked of Him" (v. 10). The conditions are knowing and asking. As soon as we know what the Christ has to give us, this knowledge should surely lead to asking and receiving. How will sinners ask of Him the greatest of all gifts, if they do not know that the gift of God is eternal life? They were blessed who knew the joyful sound of the jubilee trumpet, because they believed and received their liberty through it. If thou knewest the gift of God thou wouldest not frequent those streams which have their source in this sin-poisoned world, and which can never reach down to the thirst of a human spirit. This is eternal life to know Him. Ask and ye shall receive.

V. **The Freeness of It.** "Whosoever drinketh of this water" (v. 14). "Whosoever will, let him take the water

of life freely" (Rev. 22. 17). Christ Himself, as the
Fountain of Living Water, is the Gift of God to a world
perishing with a thirst that is unquenchable apart from
Him. Whosoever, is the choice word of the infinite grace
of God. It was among the first and the last words used in
connection with the redemption that is in Christ Jesus
(John 3. 15, 16; Rev. 22. 17). Does your soul thirst for
these waters as the hart panteth after the water brooks?
Then here is your hope: "Ho, every one that thirsteth,
come ye" (Isa. 55. 1). It was on the last and greatest
day of the feast that Jesus stood and cried, "If any man
thirst, let him come unto Me and drink."

THE WOMAN OF SAMARIA.
John 4. 1-30.

"A love that gives and takes—that seeth faults,
Not with flaw-seeking eyes like needle-points,
But loving, kindly, ever looks them down
With the overcoming faith of meek forgiveness."—*Lowell.*

"He must needs go through Samaria." There was a must
needs for every word Christ spoke, and for every act that
He did. Those Jews, which had "no dealings with the
Samaritans," usually avoided going through Samaria when
journeying from Judea to Galilee; but Christ's love for
sinners constrained Him to go that way. He lived not to
please Himself, but to seek and to save the lost. In this
He has left us an example that we should follow His steps.
Meanwhile let us centre our thoughts on the woman.
See her as—

I. **A Flagrant Sinner.** It is quite clear from verse
18 that this woman lived in a condition of shameless
immorality. She seems to have been the chief among this
class of sinners. But Jesus knew when and where to find
her. It is no mere chance-work to come into contact with
the Son of God. He knoweth the way that we take.

II. **An Awakened Questioner.** "How is it that Thou...askest of me?" etc. (v. 9). As soon as she comes into His presence her curiosity is aroused. Whoever could come into touch with Christ without being moved in one way or another. Yet some dare to pronounce Him nothing more than human. This Samaritan knew that He was a Jew, although the Jews, in their hate, declared that He was a Samaritan (John 8. 48). It is interesting to note that it was the un-Jewish largeheartedness of Christ that first awakened her interest in Him. This is His chief characteristic as the Saviour of sinners.

III. **A Carnal Reasoner.** Jesus answered the woman's inquiry with a revelation of Himself, as the Giver of "living water." He sought to make her conscious of her need of the "Gift of God" (v. 10). Her answer shows that she was in total darkness as to spiritual things. "Sir," she said, "Thou hast nothing to draw with, and the well is deep" (v. 11). As if this life-giving water was to come out of Jacob's well. But she was not more blind than Nicodemus was when he said, "How can a man be born when he is old?" Through sin, the descent of man from God is so great that, without a miracle of grace he cannot receive the things of the Spirit of God (1 Cor. 2. 14). Carnal reason has never yet understood the Word of God.

IV. **A Bewildered Trifler.** "Sir, give me this water that I thirst not, neither come hither to draw" (v. 15). She has now got a faint glimmering that He is not speaking of the water in the well of Jacob; but she has the idea that the water He gives is but a substitute for that which was in Sychar's Well. So her quick, flippant answer is: Oh, that would be very convenient; just give it me that I may be saved the pain of thirst, and the trouble of carrying it from the well. Her curiosity seems now turned into a sort of half-puzzled spirit of ridicule. As yet she is unfit to receive the Kingdom of God by faith. The deep things of God are never revealed to a frivolous soul. The plough of conviction must be driven deeper down. The seed of the Word must have an honest heart.

V. A Religious Inquirer. The Lord met her flippant reply with these stinging words: "Go, call your husband" (vv. 16-20). This led up to the confession: "Sir, I perceive that Thou art a prophet." All lightness and frivolousness seems now to vanish, and in downright earnestness she asks Him to settle for her that vexed question as to "where men ought to worship." The mental and moral process through which this woman passed is in beautiful harmony with the teaching of all the New Testament, and with present-day Christian experience. The question now with this anxious soul is: Where should I worship? How am I to be put right with God? What must I do to be saved?

VI. An Earnest Listener. Now that the conversation had so wonderfully turned upon the most vital point for a sin-smitten seeking soul, with what eagerness would she drink in the message of light and life from her Saviour's lips. What a message this is (vv. 21-24). "Woman, believe Me...worship the Father in spirit and in truth...God is a Spirit." This was a new revelation to her, and was the death-blow to all her prejudice, self-righteousness, and sectarianism. It was also the opening of a new door of hope for her, in bringing salvation within her reach there and then. "I know that Messias cometh," she said. "When He is come, He will tell us all things." Jesus saith unto her, "I that speak unto thee am He." What a transforming revelation this was!

VII. A Fearless Testifier. She went and said to the men of the city, "Come, see a man which told me all things that ever I did: is not this the Christ?" (vv. 28-30). Yes, this is the Christ, who tells us plainly what we are, and what we need, and who offers to supply that need without money or price (v. 10).　She was not ashamed to own Him, as the revealer of her sins, and the Anointed One of God; and her earnest, faithful testimony was blessed to the salvation of many (v. 39).　She had no commission, but the expulsive power of a new revelation became in her irresistible.　We speak that we do know, and testify that we have seen.　The love of Christ constraineth us.

FAITH: ITS NATURE AND REWARD.
JOHN 4. 46-54.

"He, bounteous of thy faith, for not misspent
Is confidence unto the Father lent;
Thy need is sown and rooted for His rain . . .
Trust on! One day, beyond all thought of praise,
A sunny joy will crown thee with its rays:
Nor other than thy need, thy recompense. "—*MacDonald.*

SOME of God's brightest blessings come to us clothed in the dark weeds of mourning.　If this nobleman's heart had not been moved through the sickness of his son, he never would have known the healing power of Jesus Christ through faith.　Blessed is that sorrow which constrains us to go believingly to the Son of God.

I. An Earnest Request.　"When he heard that Jesus was come...he went and besought Him that He would come down and heal his son" (v. 47).　He heard, he went, he besought.　This is the workings of an honest heart. His request that Christ would "come down" shows faith in the power of His presence, but perhaps a lack of faith in His promise.　The Lord would teach the nobleman and us that His Word is as good as Himself.　"The words that I speak unto you are spirit and life. "　They have the same character as Himself.

II. A Gentle Rebuke.　"Jesus said unto him, Except ye see signs and wonders, ye will not believe" (v. 48).

"The Jews require a sign" (1 Cor. 1. 22). In this reply, Christ was saying to the nobleman, as it were, Are you not prepared to believe Me just now without seeing signs and wonders wrought by Me? You are prepared to believe that I am the Messiah if I come down and heal your son, who is at the point of death. "Ye will not believe except ye see." There is a faith that is more noble than this. "Believe and thou shalt see." What better are they of our own day, who will not believe except they feel. A lame faith is always on the look out for the crutches of "signs and wonders."

III. **A Definite Promise.** When the nobleman had said, in effect: Signs or no signs, in Thy mercy, "come down ere my child die," then the Lord offered to his faith the word of healing, "Go thy way, thy son liveth" (vv. 49, 50). In giving him His Word He was giving him the "bread of life" both for himself and his son. "Man shall not live by bread alone, but by every word that proceedeth out of the mouth of God." "Faith cometh by hearing, and hearing by the Word of God."

IV. **A Believing Act.** "The man believed the Word ...and went his way" (v. 50). Now that he is prepared to believe Christ, without seeing signs, he is satisfied with His Word of promise, and so went his way, asking for nothing else. He had the blessedness of the man who had not seen, and yet had believed (John 20. 29). This is the faith that crowns the Christ with glory and honour. The faith that saves is a faith that acts confidently. To have faith in Christ for anything promised, that is yet unseen, is to have the evidence that that thing is in reality for you (Heb. 11. 1). "He that believeth on the Son hath." We walk by faith, not by sight. What vital importance our Lord always associates with His words. They are "spirit and life." A man is either blessed or doomed, according to his attitude toward them. To believe His

testimony is to set to our seal that God is true (John 3. 33 .
To disbelieve this record is to make God a liar (1 John 5. 10)

V. A Confirming Evidence. "As he was going
down, his servants met him, saying, Thy son liveth...
when?...yesterday at the seventh hour. So the father
knew that it was at the self same hour in the which Jesus
said unto him, Thy son liveth" (vv. 51-53). Is such
faith not always confirmed by the providence of God?
Had Joshua not to confess, at the end of his eventful life,
that "not one thing had failed of all that the Lord had
promised?" (Josh. 23. 14). Believe and thou shalt see, for
in the "self same hour" in which the almighty Redeemer
says that expected thing shall be done, it will be done.
Those who go in faith, and at His bidding, as this nobleman did, will surely find that He is faithful who hath
promised. The assurance of salvation must as certainly
follow the act of faith.

THE IMPOTENT MAN.
JOHN 5. 1-15.

"The Blessed One—
He read the tear-stained book of poor men's souls."
—*Kingsley.*

THIS pool called Bethesda, "House of Mercy," seems to
have been the Jerusalem hospital. The fourth verse is left
out of the text in the Revised Version. The water was
evidently subject to intermittent bubbling, and perhaps
possessed many healing virtues. But it is not with those
who went into the pool that we have to do, but with the
man who did not get in, and yet was healed. Observe his—

I. Sorrowful Condition. "He had an infirmity thirty
and eight years" (v. 5). This infirmity was probably
the result of his sin (v. 14). Like sin itself, it was an
old-standing disease. As far as his own ability, or any

mere human power was concerned, he was past hope. This house of mercy was his last shift. The mercy of God is the sinners' only hope.

II. Humble Position. This "certain man was there." Where? There—among the "blind, halt, withered, waiting." He was not ashamed to take his place among the helpless and the needy. If he had refused to take this self-humbling step he never would have been healed. Pride and shame keep many a one away from the saving touch of Christ. To many God is still saying, "How long will ye refuse to humble yourselves?" It was when the wretched publican took his place as a sinner that he was justified (Luke 18. 13).

III. Fruitless Effort. "While I am coming, another steppeth down before me" (v. 7). He had taken his place among the "impotent folk." Now he is doing the best he can; but his best only ends in failure and disappointment. There are a great many "others," seen and unseen, within and without, that are ready to step down before a soul seeking salvation. This the broken law of God is sure to do. Salvation is not of works, lest any man should boast. His repeated failure makes him more prepared for the saving grace of Jesus Christ.

IV. Merciful Deliverer. "When Jesus saw him lie, and knew...He saith unto him, Wilt thou be made whole?" (v. 6). He knoweth the path of those whose spirits have become overwhelmed (Psa. 142. 3). This poor man was waiting for a more convenient season, but that was not what he needed. He needed one to save him where he was, and as he was, and that Christ offered to do. Wilt thou be made whole, where you are, just now? When he answered, "Sir, I have no man," etc., it was clear that he did not know to whom he was speaking, for those who are saved by Christ need no other man. Wilt thou that I should make thee whole?

V. Personal Call. "Rise, take up thy bed and walk"

(v. 8). This call must surely have come to him with
startling suddenness. He had not walked for "thirty and
eight years." But there is always that inexplicable
something about the Person and Word of the Lord
Jesus Christ that awakens the confident expectation of
the diseased and the downcast. It was utterly useless for
any other man to say, "Rise and walk." It would only
be solemn mockery, but coming from His lips the words
were "spirit and life."

VI. Sudden Change. "And immediately the man
was made whole" (v. 9). He believed the word of the
Lord, acted on the authority of it, and found in his happy
experience that he had received the blessing for which
he so much longed. He got it, not by working, striving,'
or struggling, but by simply believing. The change
wrought in him was both sudden and complete: "immediately...made whole." The cure itself was a mystery,
but the fact of it was a certainty—perfect and God-like.

VII. Fearless Testimony. "The man departed,
and told the Jews that it was Jesus which had made him
whole" (v. 15). Having met the Lord in the temple
(v. 14), he now confesses Him before men, and before
such men as were bitterly opposed to Him. "With the
heart man believeth, and with the mouth confession is
made unto salvation" (Rom. 10. 10). By grace are we
saved through faith, but faith is manifested before men by
works (James 2. 18). Some refuse to confess Christ because
they love the praise of men more than the praise of God
(John 12. 42, 43). To deny Him before men is to be denied
by Him before the Father in Heaven (Matt. 10. 32, 33).

I AND MY FATHER.
John 5. 17-43.

The Gospel of John is the "Holy of Holies" in the tabernacle of the New Testament. John could no more invent

the things taught in this book than he could make a ladder that would reach unto Heaven. John's Gospel is the Gospel of "the Father and the Son," or the Son's relationship to the Father. With the exception of Matthew 11. 27, this great theme is almost never touched by the other evangelists. This is "holy ground." Let us approach it, as it were, with humble and unshod feet. From Christ's own lips we learn that—

I. He was Loved by the Father. "The Father loveth the Son, and sheweth Him all things that Himself doeth" (v. 20). One of the proofs of this love is that He "sheweth Him all things that Himself doeth." The Father loveth the Son, and hath given all things into His hand (John 3. 35). It is the manner of our gracious God to manifest His love by giving (John 3. 16).

II. He was Sent by the Father. "The Father Himself hath sent Me" (v. 37). Christ, as the Son, "proceeded forth, and came from God," but not of Himself, as independent of the Father's desire and purpose (chap. 8. 42). "When the fullness of the time came, God sent forth His Son" (Gal. 4. 4, R.V.). What a comfort this thought must have been to Him "in sorrow's lone hour." All Christ's servants are so sent (John 17. 18).

III. He Came in His Father's Name. "I am come in My Father's Name" (v. 43). He came as the Father's representative among men, and because of this "they received Him not." Men whose lives are opposed to God are always ready to receive those who come in their own name (Acts 5. 36, 37). To come in His Father's Name implied that He also came in His Father's nature (chap. 14. 10).

IV. He Seeks to do the Will of His Father. "I can of myself do nothing...I seek not mine own will, but the will of the Father which hath sent Me" (v. 30). His

own will was so entirely submitted to the will of His
Father that He could, or would, do nothing in the strength
of it.   His whole delight was to do the will of God, because
His law was within His heart (Psa. 40. 7, 8).   His meat,
the strength of His life, was to do the will of Him that
sent Him (chap. 4. 34).   With Him it was, "Not as I
will, but as Thou wilt," at any cost (Matt. 26. 39).

V. He Followeth His Father's Example. "My
Father worketh even until now, and I work.   The Son
can do...what He seeth the Father doing" (vv. 17-19,
R. V.).   The Father knows no Sabbath in seeking the
salvation of the lost, neither does the Son (v. 16).   The
eyes of the Son, as a servant, were continually towards
the Father, as His Master.   The Father was Christ's
example, even as Christ is ours.

**VI. He Possesses the Father's Prerogative of
Life.** "As the Father hath life in Himself, so hath He
given to the Son to have life in Himself" (v. 26).   The
Father, who hath the life in Himself that is entirely
independent of all circumstances, hath bequeathed the like
inheritance to the Son, so the Son could say, "As I live by
the Father, so he that eateth Me, even he shall live by Me"
(chap. 6. 57).   Christ, our Life.

VII. He Quickeneth whom the Father Will. "As
the Father raiseth up the dead...even so the Son quickeneth
whom He will" (v. 21).   Christ is "the resurrection and
the life."   All that the Father hath given Him, through
faith in His Name, are made alive from the dead.   Neither
the Father nor the Son will be disappointed with the final
results of the great redemption.

VIII. He Judgeth in the Father's Stead. "The
Father judgeth no man, but hath committed all judgment
unto the Son" (v. 22).   He hath given Him authority
to execute judgment, because He is the Son of Man (v. 27)

Because Christ condescended to take upon Him "the likeness of man," God hath appointed Him the Judge of all mankind (Acts 10. 42). Either in grace or in judgment every knee shall bow in the Name of Jesus (Phil. 2. 10). All the affairs of the kingdom of grace have been delegated to Him who gave Himself a ransom for all (1 Tim. 2. 6; Acts 17. 30).

IX. **He Claims Equality with the Father.** "All may honour the Son, even as they honour the Father (v. 23, R.V.). He that honoureth not the Son, honoureth not the Father. He that hateth Me, hateth My Father also (John 15. 23). I and My Father are one. Whosoever denieth the Son, the same hath not the Father (1 John 2. 23). The life, the character, and work of Jesus Christ were so vitally connected with the life, the character, and work of the Father that, in the estimation of both, they were one. Kiss the Son, and you will find your soul's refuge in the bosom of the Father.

CHRIST AND THE HUNGRY MULTITUDE.
John 6. 1-14.

"Wouldst thou go forth to bless? Be sure of thine own ground!
Fix well thy centre first, then draw thy circles round."—*Trench.*

A LIFE centred in God as the basis of operation must be a success, for no enemy will ever be able to break through and cut off this connection. Christ's attitude toward the multitude, as before us here, furnishes us with the principles of all true missionary enterprise. Thousands had followed Him to the other side of the lake, because "they saw the miracles which He did." But Christ's anxiety was to satisfy their need, not to entertain them with wonder-working. He knew that they were hungry, just as He still knows that there are multitudes whose chief necessity is for the Bread of Life. Observe how this is done: He

I. **Desires that they should be Fed.** "Whence shall
we buy bread, that these may eat?" (v. 5). His will
is that they should be satisfied, and He so wills because He
has compassion on the multitude (Matt. 14. 41). The
infinite tenderness of His heart towards the needy constrains
Him to seek their good. He willeth not the death of any.
The deepest yearning of His soul is that the hungry crowd
should have the Bread of Life offered them, and that "these
may eat."

II. **Knows where the supply is to come from.** "He
Himself knew what He would do" (v. 6). No one is
needed to advise Him who is the "Wisdom of God."
He knew what He would do, not what He would try to do.
He never makes a demand without being prepared to
supply all that is requisite for the carrying out of His
will. The Lord's purposes are not mere experiments, they
are accomplished facts in His mind. He knew what He
would do when He set His face like a flint to go up to
Jerusalem. He also knew what He would do when He said,
"All power is given unto Me, . . . go ye therefore."
His servants may be often tried and proven, but, looking to
Him, there can be no defeat.

III. **Seeks the Thoughtful Interest of His Followers.**
"Whence shall we buy bread" (v. 5). He knew Himself
what He would do, but He desires that the minds and
hearts of His disciples should be exercised about this great
and needful business of feeding the hungry multitude.
In using this form of the pronoun, we, He was declaring
a community of interests between Him and His followers.
The true missionary spirit has its source and the secret of
its abiding freshness in the constant realisation of this great
fact. Is Christ not saying to His Church to-day, "Whence
shall we find bread, money, men, that the hungry millions
in heathendom may eat and live?" What is the answer?
"Lord, Thou knowest." Pray ye the Lord of the harvest.

IV. Makes use of Little Gifts. "There is a lad here with five barley loaves and two small fishes; but what are they among so many?" (v. 9). "Jesus took the loaves" (v. 11). They were not too small for Him. He who created the Heavens and the earth knows the true worth of a little thing, when put into His hand. God hath chosen weak things . . . and things which are despised . . . that no flesh should glory in His presence (1 Cor. 1. 27-29). "Follow Me," He says, "and I will make you fishers of men." These little things have their value increased immensely by being at His disposal; so is it with every life committed to Him.

V. Himself is all-sufficient for this Emergency. "He gave thanks and distributed . . . to them . . . as much as they would" (v. 11). The source of supply was in Himself, not in what was merely given to Him. It is because of His infinite power and fullness that He is able to use weak things in the manifestation of His riches and glory. He puts the treasure in an earthen vessel that the excellency of the power may be seen to be of God. "Commit thy way unto the Lord, trust also in Him, and He shall bring it to pass" (Psa. 37. 5).

VI. Feeds the Hungry through His own Disciples. "He distributed to the disciples, and the disciples to them that were set down" (v. 11). Of themselves they could do nothing to meet the necessity of the eager crowd, but, through Him, they could do all that was needed. Our sufficiency is of the Lord. We, like the disciples of old, are greatly privileged in having this heavenly bread committed to us, but, like them, we would be verily guilty if we stored it up, instead of delivering it to the starving multitude for whom it is intended. Freely ye have received, freely give: and give it to those in the back row of heathenism as freely as ye give to those in the front row of the homeland. The manna that was "laid up" instead of used, bred worms and stank. Those given to self-seeking will surely be visited with the worms of pride, discontent, and envy; their Christian character will have an unsavoury breath about it. Give, and it shall be given unto you, good measure, pressed down, and running over.

VII. Provides Enough for All. "As much as they would" (v. 11). "They gathered and filled twelve baskets (or wallets) with the fragments" (v. 13). There was abundance in the provision of Christ for every one of them. If any lacked or went away without being perfectly satisfied, the blame was their own. Christ Himself, who is "the Bread of Life," is all-sufficient to satisfy the hunger of all who come to Him (v. 35). In Himself there is bread enough and to spare for the unfed millions who are still spending their money for that which is not bread (see 1 John 2. 2). This standing order of the Lord Jesus Christ, "Give ye them to eat," is being but very partially and timidly obeyed. There is no danger of His resources failing, therefore, as His disciples, let us show our faith in Him by the diligent use of those "goods" which He hath committed unto us for the furtherance of His kingdom and the glory of His Name (Matt. 25. 14).

JESUS IN THE SHIP;

OR, INSTANT SALVATION.

JOHN 6. 16-21.

"Immanuel! God with us in His meekness;
  Immanuel? God with us in His might
To bind our wounds, to gift with strength our weakness,
  To bring us, *redeemed*, to the home of light."—*Morgan*.

WHEN Jesus had given the multitude this sign, that He was the "Bread of Life," by feeding them, He had to withdraw to the "mountain Himself alone," as He perceived that their intention was to take Him by force and make Him a king. His crowning day had not yet come. He well knew that they would yet take Him by force and crown Him with the thorns of derision. The disciples waited till even, but as Jesus did not come, and as it was getting late, they entered their boat and made for the other side. The whole scene is full of suggestive meaning. We note—

I. A Conscious Need. Their condition was most painful. "It was now dark, and Jesus was not come to them, and the sea arose by reason of a great wind" (vv. 17, 18). A threefold sorrow was theirs: darkness, danger, desertion. Neither the darkness nor the tempest need trouble us if only that wonderful all-comforting Presence is with us. Their sorrowful state resembles that of many now: in darkness, in danger, and Christless, but, worst of all, quite unconscious of their sad condition.

II. A Great Discovery. "They see Jesus walking on the sea, and drawing nigh unto the ship" (v. 19). This is the greatest discovery the sinful, sorrowful soul of man can make. Jesus, the merciful, in the midst of the darkness: Jesus, the mighty, treading the threatening waves of death beneath His feet; Jesus, the divine, "drawing nigh" unto the distressed. The Christ will surely find His way to those who feel their helplessness, and who long for Him. He knows where the troubled seeking heart is, and how best to reveal Himself to such. He comes to seek and to save the lost.

III. A Comforting Message. "It is I, be not afraid" (v. 20). It is the prerogative of the Lord Jesus Christ to save from fear. No other creature under Heaven could utter these words without incurring ridicule. This is the language of a conqueror. It is I, be not afraid of the darkness, for I am the Light; be not afraid of death, for I am the Life; be not afraid of your sins, for I am thy Salvation; be not afraid of hell, or of judgment, for I am He who was dead and is alive again for evermore, and have the keys of death and hades. "It is I, be not afraid;" cast all your care upon Me, for I am thy Creator, thy Redeemer and Friend. Into these few words you may read the "Gospel of the grace of God."

IV. A Willing Reception. "Then they willingly received Him into the ship" (v. 21). They gladly accepted His offer of Himself. What an opportunity this was at such a time! We cannot imagine them refusing the salvation that was offered them in Himself. Yet this is what multitudes are doing every day. It was Him they received, they could not receive His Word and reject Him. Christ and His Word will stand or fall together. They took Him into their ship in distress, and, blessed be His Name, He was quite ready to go. O heart, distressed with doubt and fear, take the Saviour in!

V. An Immediate Result. "Immediately the ship was at the land whither they went" (v. 21). This langauge clearly indicates that a miracle of grace was wrought. They were instantaneously saved from their dangerous position, and had the desire of their hearts fully met, by suddenly arriving at their longed-for haven. The receiving of Christ into the heart is always accompanied with deliverance and rest. There is nothing too hard for Him. The saving of His people is the great purpose of His mission. When the disciples got to about the middle of the lake they seemed to be dead beat, but what they could not do Jesus immediately did when He got an entrance into their ship. Not by works of righteousness which we have done, but according to His mercy He saved us. Instant salvation is the gift of Him who alone can save to the uttermost.

THE IMPERISHABLE MEAT.
JOHN 6. 26-29.

"Knowledge is a barren tree, and bare bereft of God."—*Morris.*
"Though I have all knowledge, and have not love, I am nothing."
—*Paul.*

MANY had been following the Lord, but He who looketh upon the heart rebuked them for their mean and selfish motives in doing so. "Ye seek Me, not because ye saw the miracles, but because ye did eat of the loaves and were filled." To look upon Christ as merely a loaf-providing Saviour was to dishonour Him, and deceive their own souls. Christ did not come to feed men, but to save men. It is not always necessary that a man should live, but it is necessary that he should be saved. He gave them loaves, but He is the Bread of Life. The words of our Lord here are very searching. They reveal a—

, I. **Disappointing Work.** "Labour not for the meat which perisheth." This does not mean that a man should not work for his daily bread, for "he that will not work should not eat." The meat that is worth working for should fulfil the true characteristics and purposes of food, it should meet and satisfy the cravings of hunger. Therefore, do not spend the whole energy of your being labouring for a perishable meat that will never satisfy an imperishable soul. "Wherefore spend your money for that which is not bread, and your labour for that which satisfieth not?" (Isa. 55. 2). Give up the disappointing business of attempting to satisfy your soul with earthly goods (Luke 12. 19).

II. **A Satisfying Work.** "Labour...for that meat which abideth unto eternal life" (R.V.). You cannot too earnestly seek this meat, for it is—

1. SUITABLE. Suitable to your eternal spirit, because the elements of eternity are in it. Christ Himself is that meat : seek Him. "I am the Living Bread : if any man eat of this

Bread, he shall live for ever" (v. 51). The teaching and the work of Jesus Christ are sufficient to meet the whole need of man for time and eternity. Bread is not more suitable to the hungry, or water to the thirsty, than Christ is to the real deep needs of men.

2. SEASONABLE. This imperishable meat never grows stale. Time can work no change on this. It is the incorruptible provision of the incorruptible God for the incorruptible soul of man. It is as fresh to-day as when it was baken on Calvary, and taken out of the oven of the grave on the resurrection morning. It is seasonable in the early morning of life, at midday, and in the twilight of old age. It is in season every day of the week and every month of the year. In church or in market, in palace or in cot, in prosperity or adversity this heaven-sent food is always fit for use.

3. SATISFYING. It is "that meat which endureth." "He that cometh to Me shall never hunger" (v. 35). Those who eat of this Bread will not seek satisfaction from any other source. Those who are walking in the sunshine have little regard for candles. The pilgrim, who has a fountain of water springing up within his own soul, will not be strongly tempted to stoop at the muddy pools by the dusty highway. This bread is guaranteed to satisfy every eater, for "Him hath God the Father sealed" (v. 27). God will never put His "hall-mark" upon a counterfeit. That life must be absolutely pure before it can receive His stamp. "This is My beloved Son, in whom I am well pleased." There is none like Christ to satisfy.

III. **How this Work is to be Done.** The question is asked, "What shall we do that we might work the works of God?" The answer is plain and striking: "This is the work of God, that ye believe on Him whom He hath sent" (v. 29). Then, to labour for this meat is the labour of faith, for this meat is the gift of God (v. 27). Faith must work its way to the Person of Christ. Men's faces are usually turned to the world in their search for the bread of satisfaction, but with what fruitless labour? The work of God is not merely that ye believe, but that ye believe "on Him whom He hath sent." The object of your faith must be Him, as the Sent One of God: sent to seek and save the lost. "This is His commandment, that ye should believe on the Name of His Son, Jesus Christ" (1 John 3. 23). The work and will of God has not yet been done in you, unless you have "believed on Him."

THE TRUE BREAD.
JOHN 6. 30-40.

"Unlike philosophy, the Gospel has an ideal life to offer, and not to a few only, but to all."—*Jowett*.

THE Jews, in the blindness of their hearts, still clamoured for a sign from Christ, that He was that "meat which endureth unto everlasting life," after He had already fed them with miraculous bread. None are so ill to convince as those who have made up their minds that they will not be convinced. Moses, they said, "gave our fathers bread from Heaven to eat: what dost Thou work?" It is one of the glories of the Gospel that such questionings often lead to fuller revelations of the mysteries of Christ's character. It was so here. Jesus now shows Himself as that Bread from Heaven, of which the manna was a type. Observe the—

I. **Source of this Bread.** "My Father giveth you the true Bread from Heaven" (v. 32). It was not Moses who gave you that bread from Heaven, but My Father who now sends Me as His provision for your sinful souls. "I am from above," He said. Every aspect of Christ's character, every act and word all prove that He was from

Heaven. This world could not possibly produce such a unique Personality. His parents, His surroundings, or, in fact, anything outside of Himself was utterly powerless to manufacture such Bread as this. "I came down from Heaven" (v. 38).

II. **Form of this Bread.** "I am." Christ does not give this Bread, but He is the Bread. "I am the Bread of Life" (v. 35). "This is the Bread which the Lord hath given you to eat," was said of the manna (Exod. 16. 15), and is absolutely true of Him who is the gift of God. Surely the form in which this bread is served to a perishing world is very attractive. What could be more inviting to a weary, hungry soul? He is altogether lovely, and to the hungry heart He is always and everywhere precious. "My flesh is meat indeed" (see Heb. 10. 19, 20).

III. **Nature of this Bread.** It is called (1) the true Bread (v. 32). The true Bread is that which fully meets and perfectly satisfies all the needs of man. The vain philosophies of worldly wisdom can never do this. None but Christ can satisfy. None other Name has the virtues in it needed for the healing of the sores and sorrows of a sin-smitten soul. He is the true Bread because He satisfies every part of the deep and complex character of man. (2) The Bread of God (v. 33). Not only does Jesus Christ meet all the hunger of man's heart after God, but He meets all the hunger of God's heart after man. "This is My beloved Son, in whom I am well pleased." Let us adore Him who can both satisfy the heart of God and man (Prov. 8. 22-30). He is also called (3) The Bread of Life (v. 35). He is the living and the life-giving Bread, so, to come into personal contact with Him by faith is to receive the life eternal.

IV. **Purpose of this Bread.** To give "life unto the world." The world of unspiritual humanity has many things attractive and useful without Christ, but it has not life. The world needs the Light and Life of Christ before it can become pleasing unto God. The world is hungry at heart for the true Light and the true Bread of satisfaction, but, in unbelief, it will not look beyond itself for these infinite blessings. Whatever men may think or say, God deals with this world as a blind and dead thing, and so in mercy sent His Son as its Light and Life

V. Way this Bread is to be Taken. Two simple words are here used to express this act of appropriation. "He that cometh to Me shall never hunger; and he that believeth on Me shall never thirst. " To come to Christ, or to believe on Him, is that definite exercise of soul toward Him which makes Jesus Christ and all that He is our own (v. 35). Then after the soul has received Him by faith it must go on day by day appropriating Him as its daily food. Living by faith in the Son of God. They that wait on the Lord shall renew their strength. Eat, O friends and let your soul delight itself in fatness. Except ye eat the flesh of the Son of Man, ye have no life in you.

THE PROHIBITED AND THE INVITED.
JOHN 7. 32-39.

"God, being so great, great gifts most willingly imparts;
But we continue poor that have such narrow hearts. "—*Trench.*

AT this great temple feast Jesus twice cried. The first was the cry of rebuke (v. 28), the second was the cry of pity and compassion (v. 37). To them, as to many now, Jesus Christ was a great mystery. They knew Him, yet they knew Him not. They could not reconcile the "carpenter's son" with the Son of God. But, nevertheless, Jesus fearlessly declares His unique relationship to the Father, and the purpose of His coming into the world

(v. 29). It was to those "officers" sent by the Pharisees and chief priests to take Him, that this hard, searching statement was made, which we might call—

I. **The Prohibition.** "Ye shall seek Me, and shall not find Me, and where I am ye cannot come" (v. 34). He did not say here, "Where I go, ye cannot come," but "Where I am ye cannot come." This could not refer to His bodily presence, for they were now standing together within the precincts of the temple, but to His moral and spiritual attitude toward the Father. Two questions arise here: (1) Where was Jesus that they could not come; and (2) How could they not come where He was.

1. WHERE THEY COULD NOT COME. "Where I am ye cannot come." Then where was He? He was living in the presence of God. He was filled with the love of God. He was rejoicing in the will of God. He was guided by the Spirit of God. He was kept by the power of God. In Spirit this was where He was, and this is where they could not come.

2. WHY THEY COULD NOT COME. Because of their ignorance. They knew not the Father (v. 28). Because of their pride. They were self-satisfied. Because of their unbelief. They believed not Him as the true witness from God. So that, in their present condition of mind and heart it was morally impossible for them to come where He was. The lesson for us is very obvious, for the principle at work here is eternal and unchangeable. We cannot come to where Christ is, without possessing the Christ-like nature. Into His holiness, peace, and power, we cannot come, unless we forsake our own thoughts and ways, and yield ourselves entirely in obedience to His Word and will. "Where I am ye cannot come," unless ye come the way that I came, by being "born of God" and baptised of the Holy Spirit.

II. **The Invitation.** "If any man thirst let him come unto Me" (v. 37). In your pride and unbelief "ye cannot come," but if you are thirsting for a deeper, truer, holier life, then here is your great opportunity. "Come unto Me and drink." To drink of His truth and Spirit is to come where He is. The self-satisfied cannot come, the thirsty may.

1. THE INVITED. It is the thirsty who are invited to drink. The invitation is to Himself: "Come unto Me." It is not, "Come to the temple, or to the Church, or to any particular form of worship." Apart from Him, every other source is polluted, every other cistern broken. It is not the gifts of Christ thirsty souls need, so much as Christ Himself. To drink of Him is to receive of His fullness, which alone can quench and satisfy the thirst of a soul after righteousness and God. A thirst for the living God is capacity for Him. Jesus Christ is the only One who ever could honestly challenge the thirsty souls of men to prove Him as all-sufficient to meet their every need.

2. THE PROMISE. "He who believes in Me, from within him, as the Scriptures has said, rivers of living water shall flow" (v. 37, Weymouth's translation). When we have come into this place of fullness of blessing, then we have come to "where He is." When we believe on Him, as He believed on His Father, then from within us, as from within Him, there will flow rivers of living water, because the Holy Spirit will have free access into the inner life, and full control of the whole being. As good food received into a healthy stomach will manifest itself in vigorous, useful action by sending fresh rivers of life through the entire system, so will it be when the Spirit of Truth is received by an obedient heart. The fountains of the old life will be dried up, and another fountain opened within, which has its source in the Living God, and whose streams

are for the healing and salvation of others. "Ye shall not
find Me" (v. 34), said Christ to His fault-finders, for
fault-finders shall never find Him in all the true riches of
His glorious character. But "he that believeth on Him"
shall enter into the blessed fullness of that wondrous life.
Whosoever will, let him take the water of life freely
(Rev. 22. 17).

LAW AND GRACE.
JOHN 8. 1-11.

"Love seeketh not itself to please,
    Nor for itself hath any care;
    But for another gives its ease,
        And builds a Heaven in hell's despair. "—*Blake.*

"THE law commands us that such should be stoned; but
what sayest Thou?" Such was the problem thrust upon
Jesus Christ by those Scribes and Pharisees who sought to
tempt Him. The law of Moses was certainly more severe
than the law of the Romans. Knowing, as they did, the
gentleness and graciousness of our Lord, they perhaps
thought to compel Him to condemn Himself by opposing
the "command of Moses." This incident is intensely
critical and instructive, as it brings the claims of the law
and the workings of the grace of God face to face in concrete
form. We have here then—

I. **A Sinner under the Law.** That she was a sinner,
there was no denying of it, "taken in the very act." That
the law condemned her to be stoned to death was another
terrible fact that could not be denied (Lev. 20. 10). As far
as the law was concerned she was without hope. Where
there is guilt the law can do nothing else but condemn.
The wages of sin is death. Her accusers were also
clamouring for her death. But what about the adulterer?
According to the law the adulterer and the adulteress were

both to be put to death. Why were they so anxious to get Jesus to condemn her, while her companion in sin, or perhaps the seducer himself, had escaped? Man's guilty prejudice and wilful ignorance totally unfits him, not only from keeping God's law, but from administering bare justice to a fellow-creature with right motives. The accusers of a guilty sinner under the law are a terrible lot—the world, the flesh, and the devil.

II. A Sinner under Grace. The law and truth came by Moses, but grace and truth came by Jesus Christ. The law commands that she should be stoned; "but what sayest Thou?" Note the contrast—the law and Thou. The law is "holy, just, and good," and the law says "condemn;" but what sayest Thou? Canst Thou say "live" when the law says "die?" Christ's manner of treating this question throbs with vital interest to us, as it, in a measure, reveals His own character, in His attitude to the law, to the accusers and to the poor, guilty sinner. There was—

1. MYSTERY. In answer to this question, "What sayest Thou?" "He stooped down and wrote with His finger on the ground" (v. 6). He at first said nothing, but He did something. What He wrote no one can tell, but there must be some significance in the fact that at that moment He did stoop down and write. It was a unique position Christ was in. As He came to seek and save the lost, this question, although put so flippantly, would stir His holy soul to its deepest depths. "What sayest Thou?" He could not answer this question fully by saying; He could only do it by dying. His stooping down to write on the ground may be significant of His deep consciousness that spoken words alone could not suffice to convey His answer. He must stoop down to the grave, bearing the sinner's sins, before the guilty could be freely justified in the sight of God. He came...to give His life.

2. REVELATION. "So when they continued asking
Him, He said, He that is without sin among you, let
him first cast a stone at her" (v. 7). They saw the ugly
mote of uncleanness in the woman's eye, but not the beam
of hypocrisy in their own. They were looking only at
the woman's sin, but Jesus lifted Himself up and looked
at theirs. Their secret sins of unbelief and deceit are as
vile in His sight as the woman's sin. Thus the great New
Testament principle is introduced here. Jesus came to deal
with sin, not this or that sin, but sin as seen by the heart
searching eye of God. There are transgressors in thought
as well as in deed. Christ came not to set aside the law,
but to fulfil it. He Himself, who was "without sin," was
put to death by "wicked hands." The words of the Lord
Jesus here reveal something of the sinfulness of not having
love, even for a sinner caught in sin. With that grace which
has come to us in Christ Jesus, there has come also that
truth which is in God.

3. CONVICTION. "And they which heard, being convicted by their own conscience, went out one by one"
(v. 9). Instead of judging the woman, they find that, in
His presence they themselves are being judged. "He
taketh the wise in their own craftiness." "Judge not that
ye be not judged." They knew that Christ was full of
grace, but they overlooked the fact that this grace was
yoked with heart-searching truth. He could not cover up
the sin of hypocrisy. They "went out" because they had
not the courage or manliness enough to face their own sins,
even in the presence of the Saviour.

4. CONFIDENCE. "Jesus was left alone, and the woman
standing in the midst" (v. 9). The convicted accusers
fled, but the penitent woman stood her ground. They
could not condemn the woman when their own conscience
began to condemn themselves. If this woman's heart

had not been reached by the grace of the Lord Jesus Christ, she, too, would have taken this opportunity of going out after all her accusers had fled, but she willingly lingers in His presence. The love of Christ does not compel, but it constrains.

5. CONFESSION. "Jesus said unto her, Hath no man condemned thee?" She said, "No man, Lord" (vv. 10, 11). There was something more in this reply than mere courtesy: "No man, Sir." There was surely adoration: "Lord!" Had she not seen and heard enough to convince her that He was the searcher of hearts, and the Saviour of sinners. "No man, Lord." Where is the man that dare condemn in the Presence of our sin-forgiving Lord. Thank God, the Sinless One, is more approachable than self-righteous sinners.

6. SALVATION. "Neither do I condemn thee. Go thy way; from henceforth sin no more" (v. 11, R.V.). Christ came not to condemn, but to save (John 3. 17). She was saved from the condemnation of the law, from the accusations of men, and from the power of sin. She could do nothing to save herself but trust in Him who could save her to the uttermost. Who is He that condemneth? It is Christ that died. "Sin no more." A holy life is to be the evidence of sin forgiven.

CHRIST'S TESTIMONY CONCERNING HIMSELF.

JOHN 8. 12-30.

"God hath now sent His living Oracle
Into the world to teach His final will."—*Milton.*

THE questionings of those sceptical Pharisees constrained our Lord to say many things about Himself which otherwise might have been left unspoken. The Gospel of John would not have been so rich in Christology had these seemingly involuntary gleams of His personal glory not

been given. Those unbelieving Jews meant it to damage
His character, but God meant it for the fuller revelation of
His glorious nature. In these verses the Lord Jesus Christ
tells us seven things about Himself that are each full of
infinite meaning.

I. **He was Not of this World.** "I am from above;
I am not of this world" (v. 23). The wisdom, the character,
and the motives of Christ could not be the product of
"this world." The world by wisdom knew not God.
The parentage and all the environments of Christ's upbringing can in no wise explain Him. The only reasonable
explanation of His profoundly unique character and
mission is that given by Himself: "I am from above;" ye
are from beneath. The distance between Christ and
ordinary men is that which exists between Heaven and
earth, between this world and the presence of God's glory.
If any man love the world, the love of the Father is not
in him.

II. **He is the Light of the World.** "I am the Light
of the world, he that followeth Me shall not walk in
darkness, but shall have the light of life" (v. 12). There
is a very close affinity between life and light. The plant
that struggles for existence in a dark place will turn to
the faintest ray of light for life. So the soul that seeks
its life in the light of Jesus Christ will not abide in darkness, but will possess the light of life. The affinity between
light and life is not more close and vital than that between
faith and salvation. To receive the light of His truth is to
enter into the power of His life. The light that the world
needs is not in science, or art, or philospohy, but in Christ.
"I am the Light of the world." Alas, that men should
love the darkness of human reasonings better than the
light of divine life! (John 3. 19). Christ is the Light of the
world, all other lights are but the unsteady sparks of man's
kindling that cannot lead to God.

III. The Father was with Him. "I am not alone, but I and the Father that sent Me" (v. 16). The indomitable courage of the Man, Christ Jesus, may be partly accounted for by this fact—the conscious presence of the Father. "I am not alone." The only time He was alone was that brief, but awful, season when He cried on the Cross, "Why hast Thou forsaken Me?" This is the joyful testimony of the Son to the honour of the Father. "Not alone." The Man of Sorrows had a meat to eat that others knew not of. So may we if we follow in His steps. "Lo, I am with you alway" (Matt. 28. 20).

IV. He Spoke the Things which He had Learned from the Father. "I speak to the world those things which I have heard of Him" (v. 26). "As My Father hath taught Me, I speak these things" (v. 28). Christ came, not to do His own will, but the will of Him that sent Him. This is the Prophet whom God promised to raise up, and to put His words in His mouth (Deut. 18. 18). As the Servant of Jehovah, He was faithful unto death. For just before He went to the Cross He said, "All things that I have heard of My Father I have made known unto you" (John 15. 15). To reject the testimony of the Son, is to reject the Word of God the Father. To believe the Son is to believe the Father also. "I and My Father are One."

V. He Always Pleased the Father. "I do always those things that please Him" (v. 29). The Father Himself testifies to the truth of this. "This is My beloved Son in whom I am well pleased." This is one reason why our wayward souls can find repose in Jesus Christ. He who lived and died for us was always pleasing unto God. In Him was no sin, and we who believe are in Him, and accepted in God's Beloved. It is infinitely pleasing to us that our Substitute was infinitely pleasing to God. Thanks be unto Him for this heart-cheering testimony.

VI. To Know Him is to Know the Father. "If ye had known Me, ye should have known My Father also" (v. 19). The voice and compassion of the invisible God found audible and visible expression in the teaching and sufferings of Jesus Christ His Son (John 1. 18). No one can know the Lord Jesus Christ who does not see in Him the image of the Eternal Father. He was sent by Him, that through His suffering for us He might "bring us to God." He brings us into the knowledge of God, into the love and favour of God, and into the very likeness of God.

VII. To Disbelieve Him is to Die in Sin. "If ye believe not that I am He, ye shall die in your sins" (v. 24). This is a heart-searching ray of light from the Son of Righteousness. We dare not trifle with this clear unequivocal testimony of the Son of God. As He came to put away sin by the sacrifice of Himself, there is no escape from it, but by faith in Him. "He that believeth not the Son shall not see life" (John 3. 3). "If ye believe not that I am He." The emphasis here is not so much on what He says, as what He is. He is the sent One of the Father, speaking His words and doing His works, and, as such, He is the "Light of the world." To believe Him not is to live in darkness and to die in sin. By those words of the Father, spoken by Christ, shall the Christ rejecter be judged at last (John 12. 48). See that ye refuse not Him that speaketh from Heaven, for the Lord Jesus Christ has uttered God's last word in this great theme of eternal salvation (Heb. 12. 25).

CHRIST'S HEART-SEARCHING "IFS."
JOHN 8. 31-54.

> "Life is only bright when it proceedeth
> Towards a truer, deeper life above.
> Human love is sweetest when it leadeth
> To a more Divine and perfect love."—*A. Proctor.*

THE word "so" in John 3. 16 is a little one, but who has

ever yet been able to sound the depth of its meaning? It is like some of our Lord's "ifs" in this chapter, which are brimful of eternal significance. These are as hinges on which the life of the soul may swing in or out of fellowship with God. Let us examine them. There is—

I. **The "If" of Discipleship.** "If ye continue in My Word, then are ye My disciples indeed" (v. 31). True discipleship is the result of abiding in the truth, as revealed to us in Jesus Christ. Persecution is sure to arise because of this word, and many do get offended, and forsake it in theory or in practice (Matt. 13. 20, 21). To continue not in His Word is to become false-witnesses, and so to forfeit our fellowship with Him, for the soul of Jesus Christ can have no pleasure in the man that draws back from the clear light of His Word (Heb. 10. 38). Peter was a disciple indeed when he boldly preached the Christ whom he once denied.

II. **The "If" of Freedom.** "If the Son therefore make you free, ye shall be free indeed" (v. 36). The freedom which the Son of God gives is a freedom that can come from "none other Name under Heaven." It is freedom from the curse of the law (Gal. 3. 10); from the guilt of sin (Rom. 8. 33); from the power of sin (Rom. 6. 14); from the fear of death (Heb. 2. 15); and the fear of man (Acts 4. 18-20). It is the freedom of sons who have liberty of access into the Father's presence. It is possible to use a freedom that does not belong to us, but whom the Son makes free are free indeed.

III. **The "If" of Service.** "If ye were Abraham's children, ye would do the works of Abraham" (v. 39). "They which are of faith, the same are the children of Abraham" (Gal. 3. 7). The spiritual children of Abraham show their faith by their works, as he did. Abraham believed God, and his faith was evidenced by his works when he "went out not knowing whither he went," and

when he offered up his son Isaac. Those who are the true
children of the "Father of the faithful" will do works
worthy of their Father. Works of faith are the infallible
proofs of a true spiritual descent.

IV. The "If" of Sonship. "If God were your Father
ye would love Me" (v. 42). There is no way to the
Father but by the Son (John 14. 6). To know the Father,
as He is revealed to us in the Son, surely implies that we
will sincerely love the Son for so bringing us into such
a gracious knowledge of the Father. To call God Father,
and ignore the Son is to insult both Father and Son. The
evidence of our sonship with God is love to His Son. If
God is our Father in a true, practical sense, we will not
only supremely love the Lord Jesus Christ, but we will also
love every child of God, for "Every one that loveth Him
that begat, loveth Him also that is begotten of Him"
(1 John 5. 1).

V. The "If" of Responsibility. "If I say the truth,
why do ye not believe Me" (v. 46). He did speak the
truth, and live it, for no one was able to "convince Him of
sin." He spoke the truth about Himself, about His Father,
and about the needs and responsibilities of the people
(vv. 12-24). They could not deny the truthfulness of His
character, or the mercifulness of His mission, yet they
did not believe in Him, they did not commit themselves to
Him. "Why do ye not believe Me?" Who shall ever be
able to justify themselves in their unbelief? Oh, the infinite
madness of refusing to believe Him who is the living
embodiment of the Eternal Truth! The "why" will have
an awfully solemn ring about it, when the unbeliever meets
Him at the judgment throne.

VI. The "If" of Assurance. "If a man keep My
Word he shall never see death" (v. 51, R.V.). Eternal life
and salvation is in that Word. To keep it is to keep in the

antipodes of darkness and death. Death can have no power over that man whose life is hid with Christ in God. To keep His Word is to keep the message Christ brings, and to appropriate its offers to our own personal needs; it is to wrap ourselves in it as a garment, and to abide in it, and so keeping it, are kept by the power of God through faith. The promise is, "He shall never see death." He shall not only "never die" (John 11. 26), but never see death. Death is always a painful if not agonising sight. Of course, it does not mean the death of the body that we often see, but that awful death, the eternal penalty of sin and guilt (Rom. 6. 23), for which we are thankful that we shall never see. If it is such a blessing not to see it, what a horror it must be to be in it.

FROM DARKNESS TO LIGHT.
John 9.

"The Light everlasting
Unto the blind is not, but is born of the eye that has vision."
—*Longfellow.*

It is worthy of note that it was immediately after Jesus was about to be stoned out of His Father's house that He manifested His power as the "Light of the World," by giving a man sight who had been born blind (chap. 8. 59). The leading features of this chapter can be easily gathered up as we consider the story of this blind man. There was—

I. Blindness. "A man blind from his birth" (v. 1). But this blindness has all the mystery of the origin of sin hanging about it. It was not because he or his parents had sinned in any particularly grievous form that he was born blind, as some of the Jews seemed to teach (Luke 13. 2) but "that the works of God should be manifest in him." This man was born blind that the Son of God might have the opportunity of showing forth His divine power and mercy, and also that the wickedness of their own hearts might be revealed. Was not sin originally permitted to enter the world for the same reason—that the wonderful works of God's love and grace should be manifest in the incarnation and crucifixion of His Son? In the same way Lazarus was permitted to die, that the glory of God might be seen in raising him from the dead (John 11. 4). It is not so much with the mystery of sin and blindness that we have to do as with the fact.

II. **Deliverance.** The method of this man's salvation was about as strange and my terious as was the cause and origin of the disease. His eyes were anointed with clay made by a spittle, and then he was told to "Go, wash in the pool of Siloam" (vv. 6. 7). There was no virtue in the dust, nor in the spittle, nor in the clay formed, nor in the pool, nor in the washing to unseal the eyes of a man born blind, and to beget in him the gift of vision. All these were in themselves "weak things," but the eye-opening power lay in his obedience to the Word of Him who spoke as the "Light of the World." "He went his way therefore, and washed, and came seeing." The man was not responsible for being born blind, but he was responsible for accepting or rejecting the message of grace and salvation that had come to him by Jesus Christ. If he had despised the means, he would not have been obedient to the Word, and so would have remained in his darkness. The preaching of the Gospel may be like the dust, and the spittle, and the clay to some, but it is not with the preaching, as such, that men have to do, but with Christ's Word of command, that always accompanies such weak things: "Go, wash!" It is when we believe and obey Him, putting His Word to the test by an actual definite committal, that we "come seeing." There is now no excuse for spiritual blindness. "He that followeth Me shall not walk in darkness, but shall have the light of life" (chap. 8. 12).

III. Confession. When the neighbours asked him, "How were thine eyes opened?" (for they were thoroughly convinced that they were opened) his answer was simple and honest: "A man called Jesus made clay, anointed mine eyes, and said, Go wash; and I went, I washed, I received" (vv. 8-12). The blind man took no credit to himself in the matter, and is not ashamed to tell out all he knows about it, and that was not much. Like a new-born soul into the Kingdom of God's dear Son, he is so filled with joyous wonder that he is a mystery to himself. How these eyes must have sparkled with delight as he uttered these most significant words: "I went, and I washed, and I received sight." He could only tell of the means used; he could not explain how the miracle was wrought. That part belongs to Him who is the Light of the World. The change produced by the brightness of those once blind eyes was so great that they hardly knew him (v. 9).

IV. Assurance. "One thing I know, that, whereas I was blind, now I see" (v. 25). He could not, as yet, explain the character of Him who opened his eyes; he knew not whether he was a man who had sinned like others or not (v. 25); neither could he defend himself by argument against those philosophical, unbelieving Pharisees; but one thing he certainly did know, that a man called Jesus had opened his eyes. There are always those that are so perverse in their minds as to suppose that it must have been some other Jesus, and not Jesus Christ, who performed the wonder. There is no gainsaying the fact when a man's inner eyes have been opened, and when the old things of darkness are passed away, and all things are become new. This is the evidence that a man is in the light of Christ, and that he is a new creature (2 Cor. 2. 17). In this new power of vision he has the witness in himself. There is a joyful ring about this "I know." It is the confidence born of a blessed experience.

V. Testimony. Although he knew little about the
Man who opened his eyes, his faith in Him was very
great. When asked what he thought about Him, he
at once answered, "He is a prophet" (v. 17). The man
that could work such a miracle on a poor man, without
seeking any personal honour or recompense, must have
been sent by God. Again, after he had told them how
he had been healed, in the warmth of his enthusiasm he
added, "Will ye also be His disciples?" (v. 27). Meanwhile there was to him but one Man in all the world, and
that was the Man who opened his eyes. He was determined
to know nothing among them but Jesus who opened his
eyes. His creed was: "If this man were not of God, He
could not have done this great thing" (v. 33). It is a
sure sign that Jesus Christ has become a blessed Master to
that one who is most anxious that others should also become
His disciples. The Name of Jesus has little power in our
lives if it does not inspire us, fearlessly, to plead with
others to trust and follow Him.

VI. Persecution. "They reviled him" (v. 28). "They
cast him out" (v. 34). They could not bear his testimony,
so they reproached and mocked him. They could not
bear his company, so they cast him out of the synagogue.
He speedily gained the marks of a "blessed man" in
being "hated" and "separated." For our Lord Himself
hath said, "Blessed are ye when men shall hate you...
and separate you from their company...for the Son of
Man's sake" (Luke 6. 22). It is easier for the enemies
of the truth to revile than to refute. In casting out
the humble believer in Jesus, they cast away their own
credit as honest men. Any one of them would have been
as devoted to Jesus as he was if they had been born blind,
and in the same way received sight. But it seems almost
impossible for an ungodly man to think himself into the
Christian position and experience for a moment, so that he

might modify his judgment. As long as the veil of unbelief is over the heart, evidences are of little value.

VII. **Satisfaction.** After they had cast out the man, Jesus found him and talked with him, and revealed Himself to him, so that the man was constrained to acknowledge Him as Lord, and to "worship Him" (vv. 35-38). His being cast out brought him into closer contact with the Son of God, his Saviour. It was much better for Him to be outside with Christ than inside without Him. The Lord never fails to compensate, in some way or other, those who suffer for His sake (Isa. 66. 5). We infer that he was perfectly satisfied from the fact that he worshipped Him. He felt that the Lord had done so much for him that he could only fall down and adore Him for His mighty and matchless grace. This is something more than mere thanksgiving, something deeper than prayer; it is the most God-honouring act of which any creature in Heaven or in earth is capable. We cannot live without offering our desires unto God in prayer; but why are we so seldom overwhelmed with such a sense of His greatness and goodness that we can do nothing but bow and adore? Our service in Heaven will be that of adoration; why not practise it more now?

VIII. **Judgment.** "Jesus said, For judgment I am come into this world, that they which see not might see, and that they which see might be made blind" (vv. 39-41). Christ came not to condemn the world by an act of judgment, but, by His coming as the "Light of the World," could not avoid passing the sentence of death upon darkness and sin. Those words spoken by the Lord contain His own application of the spiritual meaning of the miracle, for all His miracles are typical of spiritual things. There are none so blind as those who don't wish to see. These Pharisees said, "We see," yet they saw not Jesus Christ as the "Light of the World," although He opened this blind man's eyes. They said, "We know that this man is a sinner" (v. 24), although that Man said, "Which of you convinceth Me of sin" (chap. 8. 46). Therefore, they were condemning themselves by preferring the darkness of ignorance and death to the light of knowledge and life. Those who are blind and know it (spiritually) shall soon have "no sin," for they will speedily turn to Him who has come to save sinners. But those who say, "We see," and abide in the light of those sparks of their own kindling, will find out their blindness when cast into the outer darkness of eternal doom. "Your sin remaineth" as long as you walk in your fancied light (v. 41). The opening of the blind man's eyes is a witness to Christ's power to impart that spiritual vision that saves from sin, and a warning to those who trust to the light of their own eyes, which lead into the ditch of everlasting darkness (1 Cor. 3. 18).

"ALL that proceeds not from spiritual regeneration, be it never so pure and brilliant in its glitter, is nothing towards salvation.—*Zeisius.*

"The grace of the Holy Ghost is free, not bound either to means, persons, or times."—*Majus.*

"Christianity consists not in secluding oneself and locking the room, and sitting with the prayer book behind the stove, else the Lord would not have talked with the Samaritan woman."—*Quesnel.*

"If God rested as the Jews would have men rest on the Sabbath, no sun would rise, no flower would blossom."—*Broune.*

"The Lord feeds and nourishes those who truly gather around Him."—*Schleiermachu.*

"The earthly mind always miscalculates."—*Schultz.*

"The power to draw men is greater than the power to punish."—*Heubner.*

BIBLE READINGS.

THE CROSS OF OUR LORD JESUS CHRIST.

No. 1.—THE WORD OF THE CROSS.*

"Here—in the ruin of my years—Master, I thank Thee
    through my tears;
Thou sufferedst here, and didst not fail—Thy bleeding
    feet these paths have trod.
But Thou wert strong, and I am frail; and I am man, and
    Thou art God."—*Lytton.*

IT has been said that "The heart of the world is Britain,
the heart of Britain is London, and the heart of London is
Westminster." The heart of Christianity is the Bible, the
heart of the Bible is the Cross, and the heart of the Cross is
the very heart of God: a heart full of the tenderest compassion for sinful, erring man; a heart that was bruised and
broken while atoning for our guilt. Before we go any
further, shall we silently ask the Holy Spirit to give us a
clearer vision of this wondrous Cross, and a more real and
deeper experience of its transforming power?

The Cross of Christ is at once the most awful and glorious
object ever seen by men or angels outside the gate of
Heaven. In 1 Corinthians 1. 18 we read: "For the Word
of the Cross is to them that are perishing foolishness, but
unto us which are being saved it is the power of God"
(R.V.). The word, or message, of the Cross may not be
heard from any single text of Scripture. If we are to receive
this message in all the fullness of its significance we must
hear the whole Word of God concerning it. The great

---

*In these studies Dr. Weymouth's translation is used.

message of the Cross is much misunderstood, because of the fragmentary fashion in which it is often represented. But no matter how fully the Gospel of the Cross may be preached it will still be to them that are perishing foolishness. How searching this is! It is a sign that you are perishing if you do not see the infinite wisdom and power of God in the Cross of Christ. The word of the Cross is God's Word about the Cross, and His message of love and grace to us through the Cross. What a wonderful Word this is! Let us try to grasp its deep meaning.

I. The Word of the Cross is God's Word **concerning holiness and sin.** I mean the holiness of the Sufferer and the vileness of sin for which He suffered. In John 8. 34 Jesus said: "Whosoever committeth sin is the servant (slave) of sin;" then in verse 46 He says: "Which of you convinceth Me of sin?" According to the teaching of Jesus Christ, sin and slavery are inevitably linked together. There is no true liberty where there has not been the breaking away from sin. "Christ did no sin," if He had, He would have come under its dominion, and thereby forfeit His Messiahship and His fitness to be a sacrifice "without blemish." He was holy, harmless, separate from sinners, yet this Holy One, whose character and words were revelations of the invisible and eternal God, bore our sins in His own body, and was put to death by "wicked hands" (Acts 2. 23). The holiness of God and the sinfulness of man have met in awful conflict in the Cross of our Lord Jesus Christ: that Cross which reveals God at His best, if we might so put it, reveals man at his worst (see Acts 4. 27, 28). As darkness can have no fellowship with the light, neither can the unrenewed spirit of man have fellowship with the Holy Spirit of God. This Word of the Cross then is the word of victory to holiness, the defeat and putting away of sin.

II. The Word of the Cross is God's Word **concerning**

love and sacrifice. When God gave His Son, it was not with any expectation that some way or other He might escape the cursed death of the Cross. God had no hope of saving men but by the death of His Son, so man has no hope of being saved but through the power of His Cross (Acts 4. 12). The Cross stands for the love of God the Father, and the sacrifice of God the Son. "For God so loved the world that He gave His Son" (John 3. 16). Christ also loved us, and gave Himself for us an offering and a sacrifice to God (Eph. 5. 2). Our Lord's own testimony is: "Even the Son of Man came not to be ministered unto, but to minister (not to be served, but to serve) and to give His life as the redemption price of many" (Matt. 20. 28).

The message of the Cross is the message of infinite and undeserved love. Only God could so love a world of sinners as to give His only begotten Son up to the death of the Cross for them. Only God the Son could so love us, while we were yet enemies, as to give His spotless soul a sacrifice for sin. "Herein is love;" herein is sacrifice. The sufferings and sacrifice of Jesus Christ is the proof and expression of the intensity of the love of God.

> "Inscribed upon the Cross we see
> In shining letters, 'God is Love'."

III. The Word of the Cross is God's Word **concerning righteousness and peace.** Some of the early fathers taught that the redemption price offered by Christ was paid to Satan for the liberation of souls. What right had he to the souls of men, who was a "murderer from the beginning?" We are distinctly told that Christ gave Himself a sacrifice to God. The Cross not only stands for infinite love, but also for eternal righteousness, and for peace made, based on righteousness. "He hath made peace by the blood of His Cross." Infinite righteousness is infinitely satisfied with the infinite value of the life and blood of Him who was the Infinite One. Look at Colossians 2. 14. "The bond (law), with its requirements, which was in force against us, and was hostile to us, He cancelled, and cleared it out of the way, nailing it to His Cross." All that was against us in the eyes of a righteous God, and that stood in the way of our reconciliation to Him, was nailed to His Cross: that is, was identified with Him or reckoned His, who suffered and died upon that Cross. So that "now, in Christ Jesus, you who once were so far away, have been brought near through the death of Christ" (Eph. 2. 13). By His Cross righteousness and peace have been made to kiss each other. Now the message of the Cross is: "He is our peace, who has made Jews and Gentiles one, and in His own human nature has broken down the dividing wall, . . . to unite the two sections of humanity in Himself, so as to form one new man, thus effecting peace, and to reconcile Jews and Gentiles in one body to God by means of His Cross" (Eph. 2. 15, 16). Christ knew no other means whereby we could be reconciled to God than the "means of His Cross." Who will dare to say that the means are not amply sufficient for this end? Have you proved them to be so?

IV. The Word of the Cross is God's Word **concerning salvation and power.** Look at the verse with which we began (1 Cor. 1. 18). "The word of the Cross is...unto us which are being saved, the power of God." The Cross is God's symbol of His almighty power to save. All who believe in it, and abide beneath its shadow, are conscious of being in touch with the saving "power of God." As the safety of the Israelite lay in not going out of the blood-sprinkled house till the morning (Exod. 12. 22), so we are safe dwelling under the blood-sprinkled Cross till the eternal day dawns, and the shadows of sin and death flee away. As at the Cross the Lord Jesus Christ lost His life that He might save it in resurrection glory, so here also we must lose our self-life that we might find it anew in Him, to the honour and glory of God the Father.

The Word of the Cross is the Word of the power of God unto salvation to every one that believeth. It is God's unfailing, ever-active instrument, by which any one may instantly, through faith, be lifted out of darkness into light, and be made a new creation. The influence of the Cross is like an endless rope encircling the world and the throne of God. Men, in all their helplessness and need, may catch on anywhere by the hand of faith, and be immediately translated into the Kingdom of God's dear Son. Anywhere and everywhere the Cross is the Power of God. Flee to the Cross of Christ, and you take refuge in the power of God to save.

Romanes was brought to God by discovering that Christ, many centuries ago, said nothing which the growth of knowledge has disproved. The wisdom of men or of angels shall never outrun the wisdom of God, as revealed in the Cross of Christ. "Christ Jesus has become for us a wisdom which is from God, consisting of righteousness, and sanctification, and deliverance" (1 Cor. 1. 30).

No. 2.—THE DEATH OF THE CROSS.

"He humbled Himself, and became obedient unto death, even the death of the Cross" (Phil. 2. 8).

> "Ah, my dear Lord! What couldst Thou spy
> In this impure, rebellious clay
> That made Thee thus resolve to die
> For those who kill Thee every day."—*Vaughan.*

THE death of Christ is directly mentioned in the New Testament 175 times. All the great doctrines of the Bible, like never-withering wreaths, are laid by the Holy Spirit at the foot of the Cross. The Cross and the Christ are represented as One, because they were nailed together. To preach the Cross is to preach Christ and Him crucified. To glory in the Cross is to glory in that grace which, through death, has put away sin and slain the enmity of the human heart (Eph. 2. 16). The death of the Cross is the death of

sin as a barrier in man's way to God, and the death of death
as the wages of sin. Our very voice needs to be sanctified
to speak of such a death as this. It was—

I. A Shameful Death. For robbery or murder, the
Roman slave was stripped naked and crucified. The Holy
One, who was numbered with transgressors, fared no better
than an abject criminal (read John 19. 23-24). "They took
His garments and made four parts, to every soldier a part,
. . . and for His vesture (under-garment) they cast lots."
They stripped Him naked, putting Him to an open shame;
but so deep and strong was His love for sinful men, and
so great was His delight in the will of God, that He "endured the cross, despising the shame" (Heb. 12. 2). To be
hanged on a tree was to be reckoned accursed by earth and
Heaven. It was also written, "Cursed is every one that
hangeth on a tree." He bore the sin and suffered also the
shame, for sin and shame cannot be separated. Are you so
ashamed of your sins that you have ceased putting Him to
an open shame? (Heb. 6. 6). Oh, the shame of being
ashamed of Him who was not ashamed to suffer the painful
and shameful death of the Cross for us, that we might be
saved from the power and guilt of sin, and the agony of an
eternal shame. It would put a deeper meaning into that
little hymn, " I'm not ashamed to own my Lord," if we
would think more deeply into His shameful death on the Cross.

II. A Voluntary Death. The will of God was written
in His heart. In His daily and hourly obedience to that
will, He became obedient unto death, even the death of the
Cross. Hear His own words as recorded in John 10. 17-18:
"For this reason my Father loves Me, because I am laying
down My life in order to receive it back again. No man is
taking it away from Me, but I Myself am laying it down.
I am authorised to lay it down, and I am authorised to
receive it back again. This is the command I received from
my Father." Can this be the death of a martyr in the

ordinary sense? The world has seen not a few who had
the moral power to lay down their lives, but where is the
other who had power to take it again. "Destroy this
temple," said Jesus, referring to His body, "and in three
days I will raise it up." Is that the language of a merely
"good man" about to suffer death for the truth's sake?
The fact that He had power to take His life back again,
gives infinite value to the "laying of it down." His death
could have had no sweet savour unto God as an atonement
for sin had it not been freely and thankfully offered for
this very purpose. Herein lies "the condescending goodness of our Lord Jesus Christ—how for your sakes He
became poor, though He was rich, in order that you, through
His poverty, might grow rich "(2 Cor. 8. 9). His voluntary
death should never be disassociated from His voluntary
life. His obedience was unto death, so that His obedience
and death were one offering—a sacrifice which will have
a sweet-smelling savour unto God through the eternal ages.
Is there any sweet savour in it to your soul?

III. **A Predicted Death.** Better, it was THE predicted
death. The most original thought that has ever entered the
mind of man is connected with the Lamb of God: the
sufferings of the Lord Jesus Christ—"the Lamb who has
been offered in sacrifice ever since the creation of the world"
(Rev. 13. 8). It was no after-thought that led God to give
His Son for the salvation of the world. At the world's
very inception—whenever or however that may have
been—the Son of God was given and slain in the purpose of
God. Peter tells us that Christ "was pre-destined indeed to
this work, even before the creation of the world" (1 Peter
1. 20). His death was the purpose of His incarnation. He
came not to be served, but to serve, and to give His life
a ransom for many. You have but to study "Moses and
the prophets" to find how clearly those holy men, who
spake as they were moved by the Holy Ghost, saw the

sufferings of Christ and the glory that would follow (Gen.
3. 15; 22. 18; Isa. 50. 6; 53. 3-12; Dan. 9. 24-26; Zech.
6. 12, 13; 13. 6, 7; Mal. 3. 1-3).

In Peter's defence at the temple he, as it were, challenges
the Jews, who knew well the teaching of the prophets, to
prove that those things which God before had showed by
the mouth of all His prophets, that Christ should suffer,
had not been perfectly fulfilled (Acts 3. 18).   At that
glorious gathering on the Mount of Transfiguration, the
only subject worthy of their present attention was "THE
DEATH to be accomplished at Jerusalem."   All heaven,
earth, and hell was to be affected by that death.   "O dull-
witted men," said our Lord to those troubled ones He met
on the way to Emmaus, "with minds so slow to believe all
that the prophets have spoken.   Was there not a necessity
for the Christ thus to suffer, and then to enter into His
glory?" (Luke 24. 25, 26).   The death of Christ, with the
glory that is to follow, is the most pre-eminent fact within the
entire compass of revelation.   To lose sight of this is to get
into a false perspective, which may lead to error or confusion,
but which will certainly mar the glory and beauty of the
Word of God, and hinder its influence upon the heart and life.

IV. A Substitutionary Death.   He laid down His life
for the purpose of saving us from guilt and sin, that we
might be brought nigh to God.   What saith the Scriptures?
Surely the Word of God is abundantly clear upon this
most vital point.   Listen to the words of Peter: "The
burden of our sins He Himself brought in His own body to
the Cross, and offered it there" (1 Peter 2. 24).   Hear the
statement of Paul: "Jesus Christ gave Himself for us to
purchase our freedom from all iniquity, and purify for
Himself a people who should be specially His own" (Titus
2. 14).   Isaiah says of Him: "He hath borne our griefs,
carried our sorrows, was wounded for our transgressions,
bruised for our iniquities; the chastisement of our peace

was upon Him." But the innermost heart of the subject is touched when he says: "Yet it pleased Jehovah to bruise Him, He hath put Him to grief. Thou shalt make His soul an offering for sin" (Isa. 53. 4-10). "God made Him, who knew nothing of sin, to be sin for us, in order that in Him we may become the righteousness of God" (2 Cor. 5. 21). "He loved me, and gave Himself for me."

The death of Jesus Christ in the sinner's stead is God's final and irrevocable settlement with sin. The Old Testament sacrifices could never take away sins, in them there was a "remembrance made of sins every year" (Heb. 10. 3, 4). But Christ, by the one offering of Himself, "has for ever completed the blessing for those whom He is setting free from sin" (Heb. 10. 14). That Sacrifice offered on the Cross is God's last remembrance of the sins of His believing people. "Your sins and your iniquities will I remember no more" (Jer. 31. 34). Sin must be an indescribably awful thing in the sight of God, when He could not, and will not, accept any other price for it than the holy, spotless Soul of His own eternally beloved Son. "He (God) made His Soul an offering for sin" (Isa. 53. 10). With this Sacrifice for our sins God is infinitely and everlastingly pleased. Why should not we be? Are you pleased with it?

No. 3.—THE BLOOD OF HIS CROSS.

"God proposed through Him to reconcile the universe to Himself, making peace through His blood, which was shed upon the Cross" (Col. 1. 20).

"Thy love records
That e'en for men like those Thy blood is spilt!
So, to all time, if priests of self and pride,
And scribes—the worldly wise—possess the shrine
Within thy soul, then Pilate's doom is thine—
The awful silence of the Crucified!"

ONE of the most wonderful statements in all the Bible concerning the unique character of our Lord Jesus Christ,

is found in this first chapter of Colossians, in verses fourteen
to twenty, and, if you examine them, you will see that they
begin and close with a reference to the redeeming Blood of
His Cross, as if this was the basis of His glorious
pre-eminence.

Sin and death were linked together as cause and effect
at the very beginning. "In the day thou eatest thereof
thou shalt surely die." When Adam sinned, death at once
appeared in his seeking to bury himself out of God's
sight. The sin of Cain also drove him "out from the
presence of the Lord." The wages of sin is death to all
true fitness for the fellowship and enjoyment of God.
Those who have not been reconciled to Him through the
death of His Son, are represented as dead while they live.
There are two vitally important questions we wish to ask,
and try to answer, in connection with this aspect of the
Cross.

I. What Does the Blood of His Cross Mean? The
Blood of His Cross must be distinguished from the blood
of every other cross. The blood of those who were crucified
with Christ availeth nothing. Although the blood of
all humanity could be spilt upon a cross, it would not
atone for one sin in the sight of God. The emphasis should
not be put on the Cross so much as on the fact that it was
His Cross, and that all that He was in His holy humanity,
in His Divine dignity, glory, and honour, was sacrificed
there. "The life is in the blood," and what a life this
was! All the preciousness and immeasurable worth of the
life of God is here represented in the Blood of Christ. The
pouring out of that Blood on the Cross was the pouring out
of His soul, with all its infinite wealth of purity, love, and
power. He gave Himself for us. This is easily said.
But how can finite minds grasp all that Himself means to
the eye and heart of God. Only the Eternal Father can

understand and fully appreciate the value of the soul of the Eternal Son. The Blood of Christ then, shed for our sins, is that which stands for all that Christ Himself is before God in our behalf. Who will dare to say the price was not enough? It is not a question of the value we may be able to set on the Blood of His Cross, but the value God sets on it. The next question we will ask is—

II. **What has the Blood of His Cross Secured?** It has laid the basis by which God can righteously justify the ungodly. It has opened a channel through which the saving mercy of God can joyfully flow out to the uttermost ends of the earth, and into the uttermost depths of human need. Through the Blood of His Cross there is—

1. PROPITIATION. "He, Himself, is an atoning Sacrifice or Covering for our sins, and not for our sins only, but also for the sins of the whole world" (1 John 2. 2). It was doubtless at the cost of the sacrifice of life that God at first clothed Adam and Eve with "coats of skin." Now, at the cost of the life of His Son, there is a suitable covering offered to every son of Adam. The covering provided by the Blood of Christ is long enough and broad enough to cover the sins of the whole world. He that covereth his own sins shall not prosper. No man-made covering is long enough or strong enough to hide an unforgiven sin from the eye of Him who, as Judge of all the earth, shall sit upon the Great White Throne.

2. REDEMPTION. The Blood of Christ is not only a covering for sin, but it is also a ransom price paid for the sinner. See how Peter puts it: "Knowing as you do, that it was not with a ransom of perishable wealth, such as silver or gold, that you were set free,...but with the precious blood of Christ" (1 Peter 1. 18). "Our great God and Saviour," says Paul, in writing to Titus, "gave Himself for us to purchase our freedom from all iniquity" (chap. 2. 14).

There is no Church of God, apart from the purchasing Blood of the Lord Jesus Christ (Acts 20. 28). To deny the ransoming power of Christ's shed blood, is to deny the very existence of the Church as a people called out for Himself. "Ye are not your own, ye are bought with a price, " is true of every one who is by grace a child of God. Sin is not a debt, it is a crime for which Christ was made a curse. His Blood was poured out, not to pay the debt of sin, but to put it away and to redeem the sinner out of all iniquity. The price was Himself, and it is all-sufficient in the estimation of God for the sins of the whole world. Friend, have you by faith claimed this freedom purchased for you by the Blood of His Cross?

3. FORGIVENESS. The Blood of Christ has not only provided a covering for sin (as the mercy-seat covered the tables of a broken law), and a price sufficient to ransom the sinner, but also the forgiveness of sin. "In Him, and through the shedding of His Blood, we have our deliverance—the forgiveness of our offences" (Eph. 1. 7). He was manifested—approved for the purpose of taking away our sins. He bore our sins in His own body to the tree, and on that cursed tree a death equivalent to sin was died. The wages of the sin of the world was the death of the Son of God. Now that the wages of sin has been paid, sin should have no more dominion over us. "All who believe are justified freely from all things" (Acts 13. 38, 39) The Blood of His Cross is the ground of God's complete and eternal forgiveness. The freeness and fullness of this forgiveness is according to the freeness and fullness of the sacrifice of Christ; not according to any merit or works of our own, but according to His mercy He saves us.

4. CLEANSING. So perfect is this wondrous work of grace on our behalf, that the very defilement, caused by the action of those sins now forgiven, is purged. The blood of goats and bulls, and the ashes of an heifer—those foreshadowings of the Blood of Christ—could only bring about ceremonial purity, but "how much more certainly shall the Blood of Christ (who was strengthened by the Eternal Spirit to offer Himself to God) free from blemish, and purify your consciences from lifeless works" (Heb. 9. 13). This purging is needful, in order that you might "serve the ever-living God." The pure in heart shall see God, and shall so see. Him that they shall gladly serve Him all the days of their lives. We have been redeemed that we might be a purified people unto Himself, zealous of good works. But how are we to be kept clean that we might be continually meet for the Master's use? The answer is given us in 1 John 1. 7: "If we live in the light as He is in the light, we have fellowship one with another, and the Blood of Jesus, His Son, cleanses us from all sin." While we live in the light of His presence, the ever-effectual Blood of Christ keeps continually purging away everything that would mar our fellowship with one another, or hinder our fitness for His service.

5. PEACE. This is not a peace made with God, but a God-made peace. "God hath made peace through His Blood, which was shed upon the Cross" (Col. 1. 20). The long struggle between the sin of man and the righteousness of God has come to an end at the Cross, as far as the redeemed are concerned. This is peace with honour. Eternal honour to the infinite wisdom and love of the Father, and to the infinite condescension and grace of the Son. The Cross of Christ is such an overpowering manifestation of the goodness of God that we have but to see it to have the enmity of the heart slain, and to fall in penitence and glad surrender before it, and so entering into peace—a peace which the world cannot give. "He is our peace."

6. NEARNESS. "But now in Christ Jesus, you who once were so far away have been brought near through the death

of Christ" (Eph. 2. 13). Sin is not only an "uncleanness"
which unfits us for God's presence, but it is "transgression"
and "rebellion" which drives the soul "far away" from
Him. What sin does, the Blood of Christ undoes. The
love of sin leads away from God; love for the Lord Jesus
Christ, as our sacrifice for sin, brings us near to God. Sin
will not lead you afar off if you have nothing to do with it;
neither will the Blood of Christ bring you nigh if you have
nothing to do with it. To have fellowship with sin is to be
afar off from God; to have fellowship with the death of
Christ is to be made nigh. This is the nearness of a child
born into the family of God, and finding its resting-place
in the arms of His everlasting love. As light removes
darkness, so the Blood of Christ removes distance.

7. LIBERTY. "Since our sins and offences are remembered no more, we have free access to the holy place through
the Blood of Jesus by the new and ever-living way which He
opened up for us through the rending of the veil of His
earthly nature" (Heb. 10. 17-20). Liberty to come with
boldness into the Holiest is the greatest of our earthly
privileges. It was the greatest act of which the high priest
was capable on the great Day of Atonement. This liberty
of access into the place of the Presence of Him who is the
Holiest of all is the crowning victory of the Cross. By the
Blood of Jesus the guilt of our sin has been taken away and
the pollution of sin removed from the soul, so that we can
draw near with confidence by faith in Him (Eph. 3. 12).
This liberty of access is the secret and source of liberty in
service. "Therefore, let us come boldly to the Throne of
Grace that we may receive mercy and find grace to help us
in our times of need" (Heb. 4. 16). Those who come
boldly to the Throne of Grace will go boldly to the work of
the Lord. Are we taking full advantage of this Blood-
bought freedom? In the days of slavery "a poor fellow
found his way to Canada. As the train moved into

Toronto, Harriet Tubman, herself an emancipated slave,
found him crouching in a corner, mortally afraid that some
slave catcher might be after him. 'Joe, you fool,' she
said, 'what are you cowering here for? You have shaken
off the lion's paw; you are a free man on free soil. Praise
the Lord, Joe!'" Take the liberty Christ has purchased for
you. You are a free man on free soil. Praise the Lord?

No. 4.—THE PURPOSE OF THE CROSS.

"The Lord Jesus Christ, who gave Himself for our sins, *in order
to rescue us from the present wicked age*, in accordance with the will
of our God and Father" (Gal. 1. 4).

> "Seven times He spake, seven words of love,
> And all three hours His silence cried
> For mercy on the souls of men—
> Jesus, our Lord, the Crucified."—*Faber.*

ON that great day in Israel when the high priest made the
annual atonement, he sprinkled with the blood of the
sacrifice all the vessels of the Tabernacle, signifying that
the way was now opened up for the entering into the enjoyment of all the blessings which they represent. Thus,
through the sprinkling of the blood of atonement, all the
things typically set forth in the Tabernacle were freely
offered to the people. So, we read, "He that spared not
His own Son, but delivered Him up for us all, how shall He
not with Him also freely give us all things?" (Rom. 8. 32).
How shall He not give them, since all those things needed
for life and godliness have been purchased for us by the
death of His Son? It was to His own disciples Jesus said,
"Ask, and ye shall receive; seek, and ye shall find."
What then are those special privileges and blessings that
have been bought by the Blood of His Cross, and left us as
a legacy at His death?

I. Christ died for us to **Purchase our Freedom from
all Iniquity** (Titus 2. 14). "Iniquity" has two aspects—

passive and active; as a state, and as an act. As a state it means inequality; as an act, injustice. Man's natural attitude to God is not right; there is no equality or oneness of purpose, so his works are an injustice to Him. They are called "wicked works." Then, from these works of unrighteousness, and from that crooked and unequal nature that is the author of them, the precious Blood of Christ delivers. To be redeemed from "all iniquity" is to be delivered from everything that hinders the soul from becoming like Him who died for our sins. If we are not freed from all those motives and tempers that mar our equality with the Divine plan, then the purpose of the Cross has not been perfectly fulfilled in us.

II. He died for us, the Just for the unjust, **that He might Bring us to God** (1 Peter 3. 18). The purpose of the death of Christ was not only to deliver us from all guilt and iniquity, but to "bring us to God." "Ye are come," says the writer to the Hebrews, "to Jesus the Mediator, to the blood of sprinkling...and to the city of the living God" (Heb. 12. 22-24). To be brought to God, not as a criminal, but as a Blood-bought Son, is a great triumph for the Cross of Christ. But how can the death of Christ bring us to God. Well, in the first place, it brings us to a knowledge of God. We never could have known the infinite love and mercy of God had His Son not been sent to suffer and die for the ungodly. By the death of His Son, God has given us a new and fuller revelation of Himself. Secondly, the sufferings of Christ brings us into the favour of God. We are reconciled to God through the death of His Son. Thirdly, through this death we are brought by faith into the likeness of God, being made "partakers of the Divine nature." Fourthly, we are brought into the enjoyment of God; and, finally, we shall be brought into the home and immediate presence of God. The purpose of the Cross is not only to bring our souls to God at last, but to bring our daily life in thankful and blissful surrender to His will. Is the power of this Cross bringing you to God?

III. He died for us **that we Might Receive the Adoption of Sons.** "God sent forth His Son... in order to purchase the freedom of all... so that we might receive recognition as sons" (Gal. 4. 5). The privilege of sonship has been purchased by the Blood of His Cross. Before we can call God Father we must be freed from our guilt and from the power of the law. Before God can recognise us as sons we must bear His image, and all the righteous claims of His holy law be fully met. All men, like all creation, are the "offspring of God," but we can only be "the children of God" by faith. To be made a son is to be made an heir; to be made an heir is to be put into possession of all that has been purchased for us by that wondrous death on the Cross. Because we are sons God hath sent forth the Spirit of His Son into our hearts to cry "Abba, our Father" (Gal. 6. 6), so that the Father may hear the cry, and answer in the fullness of His Fatherly wisdom and love.

IV. He died for us **in Order to Rescue us from the Present Wicked Age** (Gal. 1. 4). As long as we are in the body, we shall be exposed to the many influences and crosscurrents of this present evil world. Outside the influence of the Holy Spirit of God all the principles at work in this age are in perfect accord with those "wicked spirits that are now at work in the hearts of the sons of disobedience" (Eph. 2. 2). One of the fruits of Christ's death is to save us from all false principles and unclean motives, and to preserve our souls in health, even in the midst of the poisonous atmosphere of this wicked and perverse age. One of the petitions in our Lord's great priestly prayer was, "I do not ask that Thou wilt remove them out of the world, but that Thou wilt protect them from the Evil One" (John 17. 15). The three Hebrews were not saved from the furnace, but they were saved in it, which was more to the glory of God. The ever-present Cross is an ever-present protection from the evil of this world. We overcome by the Blood of the Lamb. By continually looking to Him, we shall be continually rescued.

V. He died for us **in Order that we May no Longer Live to Ourselves, but to Him who Died for Us** (2 Cor. 5. 15). He died for us that we might be rescued from the deadly condition of being self-centred, and that we might find a new life centre in Himself. To live to ourselves is to be, in the sight of God, dead while we live. The soul that has not been drawn by the power of His Cross to find its centre of life and work in Him, cannot be said to have found its true rest. The most subtle temptations with which we have to do are those which seek to lure us into "living to ourselves." All self-energy, in some form or another, seeks the glory of self. The waters that spring out of the selfish heart will not rise above the level of selfish honour. When the heart becomes the channel of divine energy, instead of the fountain of self-effort, the issues of life will rise above the human agent to Him who is the source of life and salvation. Christ suffered for us, leaving us an example that we should follow His steps. "He pleased not Himself." Ye have been redeemed with a price, therefore glorify God in your body and your spirit, which are His. The language of the redeemed soul is: "Not I, but Christ."

VI. He died for us **in Order that we may Receive the Promised Spirit** (Gal. 3. 13, 14). He has purchased our freedom from the curse of the law, that we might receive the gift of the Holy Spirit. Pentecost was in Calvary. The power of the Spirit has been secured for us through the power of His death and resurrection. We are taught here that no one can receive the promise of the Spirit unless they have been redeemed from the curse by Him who was made a curse for us. The Blood of Christ must first cleanse the heart before the blessed Holy Spirit can take up His abode there. The blood of Christ provides every spiritual blessing for us: the Holy Spirit comes to help us into the experimental enjoyment of those blessings, and to work in and through us that which is pleasing in the sight of God. He died to save us from our sins, not only that we might escape the wrath to come, but that we might become temples of the Holy Ghost, and thereby witnesses for Him (Acts 1. 8). The Father's promise of the Spirit, like the promise of salvation, is received by faith.

VII. He died for us **that He might be Lord both of the Dead and of the Living.** "For this was the purpose of Christ's dying and coming to life, namely, that He might be Lord both of the dead and the living" (Rom. 14. 9). He humbled Himself to the lowest, and God exalted Him to the highest. He who made Himself of no reputation is now crowned Lord of all. He redeemed us by His Blood that He might be Lord of our lives. "Ye are not your own." He has bought us that we might be His own peculiar treasure, freely given, and wholly at His disposal. What a blissful privilege to belong to Him, who, through suffering and death, is exalted "far above all," having all power in Heaven and on earth, and who desires and claims the right to relieve us of all undue anxiety and carefulness, to protect and govern our lives for our own eternal good, and His own eternal glory. If Christ is your Redeemer, then He also is your Lord. Through death He has become Lord both of the dead and of the living. Only those alive unto God will own Him as their Lord; those who die in their sins will confess Him Lord when they meet Him at the throne of judgment. Let the government of your life be upon His shoulders now. Let the Lord, your Redeemer and God, take His rightful place upon the throne of the heart, and His kingdom will come in you, and His will be done in

your earthly life, as it is done in Heaven. For this purpose
"our Lord Jesus Christ died on our behalf, so that whether
we are awake or are sleeping we may share His life"
(1 Thess. 5. 10).

No. 5.—THE TRIUMPHS OF THE CROSS.

"The hostile princes and rulers He shook off from Himself, and
boldly displayed them as His conquests, when by the Cross He
triumphed over them" (Col. 2. 15).

"Through the shadow of an agony
Cometh redemption."

OF all the lives that have suddenly closed on the face of the
earth, no one seemed more like failure and defeat than did
the life of our Lord Jesus Christ. To be "hanged on a
tree" was, in the estimation of men, to have the memory of
your name blotted out of earth and Heaven. But His Cross,
the symbol of the curse, becomes the symbol of eternal
triumph. Here His enemies, seen and unseen, put Him to
an open shame; here, also, He made a show of them openly.
The first trophy of the Cross was seen in that poor, penitent
fellow-sufferer on the tree. The next man whose enmity
was slain by the Cross was the centurion, who is compelled
to confess that "Truly this was the Son of God." The
death of Christ was the greatest achievement that ever
was accomplished in this world. Its influence and results
are as far-reaching as the uttermost parts of heaven, earth,
and hell. As the climax of man's sin and failure is seen
at the Cross in the crucifying of the Lord of Glory, so
Christ's greatest triumph has come by His Cross. In what
does this great victory consist? It is—

I. A Triumph Over the Law. "The bond, with its
requirements, which was in force against us and was hostile
to us, He cancelled, and cleared it out of the way, nailing it
to His Cross" (Col. 2. 14). Whatever was nailed to His
Cross was identified with Him in His death. The law, with

its righteousness and incessant requirements, which was in full force against us because of our transgression and sin, He, by taking our sins in His own body, and nailing the law to His Cross, has made reconciliation by the sacrifice of Himself, clearing away both sin and the law, as obstacles in the way of our approach unto God. The moral law as a way of life has been cancelled by the death of Christ. There is now no road to Heaven that way, "for on the ground of obedience to law no man living will be declared righteous before Him" (Rom. 3. 20). "I am the way, no man can come unto the Father, but by Me." The death of Christ is His triumph for us over the broken law.

II. **A Triumph Over Sin.** "Christ has appeared once for all, at the Close of the Ages, in order to do away with sin by the sacrifice of Himself" (Heb. 9. 26). Our sins, as well as the law, were nailed to His Cross, in order that they might be put away as dead things. "Now sin is the sting of death, and sin derives its power from the law; but God be thanked who gives us the victory through our Lord Jesus Christ" (1 Cor. 15. 56, 57). We are not to think of that sin, for which Christ died, as something outside of, and far away from, ourselves. It is that abominable thing in your heart and mine that unfits us for the fellowship of God, and makes Christ Himself so far away and unreal to the soul. He died for our sins that we might daily triumph over sin's power. If sin is in any form having dominion over us, it is proof positive that the Cross of Christ has not its due place in our lives, for the presence of this means the defeat of sin.

III. **A Triumph Over Death.** "He Himself took on Him a share of human nature, in order that...He might set at liberty all those who, through fear of death, had been subject to lifelong slavery" (Heb. 2. 15, 15). Sin earns death, and the fear of death shackles a man's liberty for life. Death always means separation. Spiritual death is spiritual separation from God, the Author and Giver of all spiritual life. The death of Christ is the death of the fear of death to all who are believing in Him. Paul, writing to Timothy, says: "Our Saviour, Christ Jesus, has put an end to death, and has brought life and immortality to light through the good news" of His death and resurrection (2 Tim. 1. 10). Those who by faith have seen the Christ tasting death for them, have His promise that they shall never "taste death"—"never see death." They can shout triumphantly, "Where, O death, is thy victory? Where, O death, is thy sting? Sin is the sting of death, but God be thanked who gives us the victory, through our Lord Jesus Christ." Death was swallowed up in the victory of His Cross (Isa. 25. 8).

IV. **A Triumph Over the Work of the Devil.** We are distinctly told that "the Son of God appeared for the purpose of undoing the work of the devil" (1 John 3. 8). What is the work of the devil? He is a deceiver and liar from the beginning. His chief business is to deceive men by blinding their minds to the things of God and His Christ. The work of Christ is to undeceive men by giving them the true light and knowledge of the true God. The Cross of Christ is the undoing of that lie of the devil that "Ye shall not surely die." For the wages of sin is death, and Christ "must suffer" if sin is to be put away. If God will not punish sin, it is because He has punished it in the Person of His Son. All who believe in the Lord Jesus Christ, trusting in the efficacy of His redeeming Blood, have been delivered from the deluding spell and thraldom of the devil, and are now freed ones in the Kingdom of God's dear Son. The work of the devil will be utterly abortive in the case of those who "glory in the Cross." It is the great weapon, against which neither the devil nor his works shall ever be able to stand.

V. **A Triumph Over Satan Himself.** John tells us

that he heard "a loud voice in Heaven which said, The accuser of our brethren has been hurled down... they have gained the victory over Him, because of the Blood of the Lamb" (Rev. 12. 10, 11). The Blood of the Lamb triumphs over all the accusations of the devil, and has power to hurl him down from his vantage ground to where he is utterly powerless to tempt. By the Blood of the Lamb the devil and all his accusations may be hurled out of that soul for which Christ did die. The bruising of Christ's heel by Satan was the earnest of the bruising of Satan's head by Christ (Gen. 3. 15). The bruising of Christ's heel may seem to have cut short His walk on earth amongst men, but the bruising of Satan's head was the crushing of the seat of his government and power   Resist the devil with the Blood of the Cross, and he will flee from you.

> "Satan trembles when he sees
> The weakest saint upon his knees. "

Another couplet may be added:

> "Satan rejoices when he sees
> Lukewarm Christians all at ease. "

VI. A Triumph Over All. All the representatives of the forces of evil were cast off and put to shame by His dying on the Cross. "The hostile princes and rulers He shook off from Himself, and boldly displayed them as His conquests, when by the Cross He triumphed over them" (Col. 2. 15). The strong and mighty Prince of Darkness held His goods in peace till Christ, the stronger than he, overcame him by the power of His Cross, and took from him every weapon wherein he trusted. The death and resurrection of Jesus Christ was not only the frustration of the purposes of those organised powers of evil, manifested in those priestly rulers and Roman princes, but it was also a triumph over all humanity. Hear Christ's own solemn words in this matter. He had just been confessing that

"Now is My soul full of trouble." The agony of that awful
death upon the tree was already coming upon Him. "But,"
He says, "for this purpose I have come to this hour."
Then, after the heavenly voice has spoken a word of comfort to Him, He said, "Now is the judgment of this world;
now will the prince of this world be driven out, and I, if
I am lifted up from the earth, crucified upon a Cross—will
draw all men to Me" (John 12. 27-32). "This He said to
indicate the kind of death He would die" (v. 33). This
"kind of death" was to be so wonderfully unique and
powerful that it would affect, in one way or another, all
men, as well as all devils and holy angels. All men must
be drawn to Him, either for grace or judgment, because,
by virtue of Christ's dying for the sin of the world, and
being raised again, God hath appointed Him as Judge of
the world (Acts 17. 31). Because He was lifted up on the
Cross, He is now lifted up on the Throne. All men must
appear before Him, either at the Throne of Reward (2 Cor.
5. 10), or at the Great White Throne of Eternal Judgment
(Rev. 20. 11-15): either as sinners saved by His blood,
or as sinners who have deliberately rejected His sacrifice,
or died in ignorance of it. The fact that all men will be
drawn to Him can in no wise prove that all men will be
saved; but it proves that because Christ died to make reconciliation for a¹¹, all are accountable to Him who is to
"judge the quick and the dead." The ungodly will see
the power of the Cross of Christ in a new light when they
see the nail-pierced Saviour seated as Judge of all the earth
upon His throne of whiteness. Surely the Judge of all
the earth shall do right after having given Himself for the
redemption of the world.

The victory of the Cross is seen also in Heaven. While
John was weeping because no one was found worthy to
open the book, one said to him, "Do not weep: the Lion
which belongs to the tribe of Judah . . . has triumphed,

and will open the book. " Then he heard this new song,
"Thou shouldst be the One to take the book, and break its
seals, because Thou hast been offered in sacrifice, and hast
purchased for God with Thine own blood some out of every
tribe . . . and nation" (Rev. 5. 4-10). The worthiness of
the Lamb to open this book lay in the fact that "He had
been slain. " That book very fitly represents the human
soul, taken by Him and opened up for the honour and glory
of His Name. None but He is able to break those seals
which hinder the souls of men from serving the living God,
because He alone has died to purchase our freedom with
His own blood. Yield thyself to Him, and His triumph
will be yours. "We are more than conquerors through
Him who has loved us. " The forcible words of Dr. Forsyth
may be added here. He says that "When he read, 'He
loved me and gave Himself for me,' the Gospel of the
Atonement leapt out of the Book and clasped him. 'Who,'
he asked, 'shall separate me, with all my wretched schism,
from Christ's love?' 'Who shall dislodge me from the
security of God's love in Christ?' I am secure, not because
it is written, but because the writing becomes luminous
with the passage through it of the Holy Ghost. The wire
glows with current. The whole soul of the Bible searches
me, and settles and stills me with the grace of God. " Has
it so triumphed over you?

No. 6.—THE OFFENCE OF THE CROSS.

"The Jews demand miracles, and Greeks go in search of wisdom,
while we proclaim a Christ who has been crucified—to Jews a
stumbling-block, to Gentiles foolishness, but to those who have
received the call,...Christ the power of God, and the wisdom of
God" (1 Cor. 1. 22-24).

"As for me, " says the Apostle in writing to the Galatians,
"If I am still a preacher of circumcision"—as a condition of
salvation, to please those Judaizing teachers—"how is it

that I am still suffering persecution?" How is it that those who teach that we must obey the whole law of Moses to be saved still persecute me? "In that case the Cross has ceased to be a stumbling-block " (Gal. 5. 11). The inference is clearly this: that if we are faithful to the truth of God as revealed in the Cross of Christ, it will be an offence and a stumbling-block to those who are trying to be saved by their works. The Cross proclaims liberty, without the deeds of the law; the law is a task-master, whose service is the yoke of slavery (Gal. 5. 1). But the Cross of Christ can never be anything else than a stumbling-stone in the way of those who refuse to be saved by grace alone. It will be a fearful fall to stumble over His Cross into hell. In looking at this aspect of the Cross we shall try and answer two questions. The first is—

I. **Why is the Cross of Christ a Stumbling-Block?** Was it not meant to take the stumbling-block of sin out of our way? Then, why should the Cross itself become a stumbling-block?

Death can seldom ever be said to be attractive, but the death of the Cross was the most ignominious of all. That the holiest of men should suffer the most shameful of deaths is in itself a staggering thought to those who believe in the over-ruling providence of a Personal God. The Cross was the death-blow to human pride and worldly honour and glory, and to be identified with one who suffered on a cross was also to suffer loss.

When the divine mystery of the Cross of Christ is not understood, it is looked upon as a shame, a misfortune, or a martyrdom—one who suffered because of his principles. The fact is, some can be very religious and see nothing attractive in the Cross of our Lord and Saviour. They rather shun it, its every shadow is offensive to them, because there is no place for it in their heart and life. The high priests, with the Scribes and elders of old, cried out, "Let Him come down from the Cross and we will believe on Him." Like many to-day, they would have a Christ without the Cross, but the Cross and the Christ, in the gracious purpose of God, have been eternally nailed together. There is now no Christ but the Christ who was crucified; even in Heaven He is known as "the Lamb that was slain." When the Lord Jesus came within sight of His Cross, some of His own disciples "forsook Him and fled." The Cross of Christ is a stumbling-block to those who are satisfied with a religious self-life, because if we would follow Him fully, we must be willing to be crucified with Him. Ah! this is the rock of offence. We do not wish these little self-governed barques of ours to make shipwreck by dashing themselves to pieces against the riven Rock of Ages. But he that loseth his life here shall save it. The next question is—

II. **To whom is the Cross of Christ a Stumbling-Block?** Paul preached Christ crucified—"to the Jews a stumbling-block, and to the Greeks foolishness." The Jews and Greeks may be looked upon as typical and representative classes. The first stands for religious works, the second for worldly wisdom. To the one the Cross of Christ is a stumbling-block, to the other a laughing-stock. Neither the proud religionist nor the worldly wise can possibly pass the Cross without being affected in some way by it. It knocks the feet from the legalist, and pricks the gaudy bubble of fleshly wisdom.

1. WHO IS THE JEW? Whom does he represent? He is the man who has been brought up religiously he is quite in the habit of saying prayers; he regularly attends public worship; he gives of his means for the upkeep of the church; he is quite orthodox in his beliefs; he has no fellowship with drunkards or gamblers; he is a son of the church, and bears a blameless name among his fellows; he is a very righteous and religious man, but the Cross of

Christ to him is of none effect: he may hear about it, and wonder at it, but he cannot see any need for it—to him it is a stumbling-block. He has no sense of sin, no felt need of atoning Blood. It is nothing to him. The Cross is a manifestation of the mercy of God, but he does not need mercy. It is a declaration of the righteousness of God, but he is righteous, and has no need of God's righteousness. It is an offer of the riches of God, but he has need of nothing. When the meaning of the Cross is pressed upon Him, he is stumbled, for it makes his own righteousness as filthy rags, and sets no value at all upon his prayers and performances. For him to accept the Cross, would mean the crucifixion of his own goodness. There is no self that dies so hard as religious self. To the self-religious man the Cross of Christ is a stumbling-block.

2. WHO IS THE GREEK, to whom the Cross of Christ is foolishness? The Greek represents those who give themselves to art, philosophy,. and physical culture. All good in themselves, but when these things become the objects of life and the hope of all future good, then the Cross of Christ is foolishness. In the days of Paul, Athens was the "City of Schools, " even Roman youths, who sought to distinguish themselves, came here to study. "All the Athenians and their foreign visitors used to devote their whole leisure to telling or hearing about something new" (Acts 17. 21). But all human culture and philosophy are of themselves utterly incompetent to appreciate the Cross of Christ, because no flesh can glory in its presence. Every product and achievement of the unspiritual man withers and fails as soon as they come within reach of the power of the Cross. To all materialists and rationalists the Cross is foolishness, because to them it is incomprehensible. But this thing, which is foolishness in the eyes of the worldly wise, who walk in the light of the sparks of their own kindling, is, in deed and truth, "the wisdom of God. " For the preaching

of Christ crucified is to them who obey the call, "Christ
the power of God and the wisdom of God" (1 Cor. 1. 24).
Think now of—

III. **What the Cross Really Is.** Not the Cross apart
from Christ, but as representing Him who was crucified.

1. IT IS THE POWER OF GOD. It is not the preaching
that is the power of God, but the "Christ crucified" who is
preached. The Cross of Christ is God's dynamic (power)
in operation for the salvation of the world. All the force
that God can bring to bear upon the redemption of men
from sin and death is here in the Cross of Christ.

2. IT IS "THE EXCEEDING GREATNESS of His power to
us-ward who believe" (Eph. 1. 19). It takes the power
of God to save, and this almighty power can only work
through the death of His Son. To believe in that death is
to put yourself in touch with the power of God, that
delivers from all iniquity and saves with an everlasting
salvation.

3. IT IS ALSO THE WISDOM OF GOD. It is only after we
have experienced the saving power of God through the
Cross that we can really see it to be "the wisdom of God"—
the manifestation of infinite skill. The planning of man's
redemption by the gift of His Son and Blood of His Cross,
was a revelation of the wisdom of God as well as the love of
God. When we get a true vision of the Crucified One we
are constrained to say, "O the depth of the riches, both of
the wisdom and the knowledge of God." To flee to that
Cross is to put your helplessness and weakness into His
power—your foolishness and ignorance into His wisdom.
"Then shall you be strong, and wise, and safe in Christ
Jesus your Lord."

> "The Cross, it takes our guilt away,
> It holds the fainting spirit up;
> It cheers with hope the gloomy day,
> And sweetens every bitter cup.

It makes the coward spirit brave,
    And nerves the feeble arm for fight
It takes the terror from the grave.
    And gilds the bed of death with light.

The balm of life, the cure of woe,
    The measure and the pledge of love;
The sinner's refuge here below,
    The angels' theme in Heaven above. "

"God forbid that I should glory in anything except the
Cross of our Lord Jesus Christ" (Gal. 6. 14).

No. 7.—THE ENEMIES OF THE CROSS.

"There are many whom I have often described to you, and I now
with tears describe them, as being enemies of the Cross of Christ"
(Phil. 3. 18, 19).

"Is it nothing to you, all ye that pass by?" (Lam. 1. 12).

PAUL had such a clear vision of the grace and glory of the
Cross of Christ, and such a sight of the guilt and danger of
those who are its enemies, that he could not speak of them
without the tears starting in his eyes.   It is a fearful thing
to be an enemy to that greatest of all manifestations of the
love and wisdom of God.   To be an enemy of the Cross of
Christ is to be an enemy of God, a rebel against His merciful will to save men from their sins by the death of His Son.
There are many who honour the Lord as a babe in the
manger, who deny Him on the Cross.   They love the songs
of the nativity, but they don't care for the songs of redemption.   They may not be the pronounced enemies of the
Cross, but they are ashamed of it.   Why should anyone be
an enemy of the death of Christ, who is not an enemy of His
birth?   He was born that He might die.   He came for the
very purpose of giving Himself a sacrifice for sin.

The enemies the apostle here refers to were those in
Philippi, who had come under the power of the Antinomian
heresy.   They professed to believe in Christ, yet lived lives

of sin and uncleanness. They loved sin and so proved themselves the enemies of the Cross, for the Cross of Christ is the enemy of sin. To love sin is to kiss the sword that pierced the soul of Jesus. "If I believed that the Blood of Christ put away sin, " said one man to another, "then I would take my fill of sin. " Then said the other, "And how much sin will it take to fill a Christian?" How much poison would it take to satisfy a man who hates it? We shall now look a little more closely at the object of this enmity. They are the enemies of the Cross of Christ. What does the Cross of Christ mean, and how can they be its enemies? The Cross of Christ stands for—

I. **Divine Sacrifice.** "God's love for us has been manifested in that He has sent His only Son into the world so that we may have life through Him. This is love indeed. We did not love God, but He loved us and sent His Son to be an atoning sacrifice for our sins" (1 John 4. 9, 10). The coming, and the dying of Jesus Christ upon the tree, was God's divinely expressive way of revealing His own heart— a heart moved to infinite sacrifice through the agony of love. Men, for the love of gain, will sometimes sink their all in a business speculation. God, through love to sinful men, has sunk His all in the transaction of the Cross. This was no mere speculation, but a merciful expenditure of almighty grace for a definite, infallible purpose. To be an enemy of the Cross of Christ is to be an enemy of the love and purpose of God as revealed in the Cross.

Those opposers of the Cross whom Paul refers to, showed their enmity by their self-indulgent lives, "Whose God is their belly, " he says. Self-indulgence cannot but be opposed to the self-sacrificing spirit of the Cross. The Cross of Christ is the highest exhibition of self-denial—to live a mere sensual life is a denial of the Cross. The carnal mind—the mind that is set on earthly things—is enmity against the Mind and Spirit of God. The Mind of Christ

as revealed in the Cross is that of self-abandonment for the
glory of God and the salvation of men.   Therefore those who
live for themselves are living in rebellion against the spirit
and purpose of the Cross.   To be more concerned about the
body than the spirit, is like being more concerned about the
wood of the Cross than the Christ.   A wealthy gentleman
who had built a little chapel close to his house was showing
it to a friend one day, when he remarked that it would
make a good kitchen.   The reply was, "Yes, I will make
a kitchen of it when I make a god of my belly."   Human
selfishness is essentially opposed to the divine sacrifice offered
upon the Cross.   Such carnal-mindedness is an evidence
of death (Rom. 8. 6).   The Cross of Christ stands for—

II. **Divine Holiness.**   The intensity of God's hatred to
sin could not be more emphatically expressed than by the
death of His Son on the Cross.   The greatness of the
sacrifice God made, in giving His Son, shows the greatness
of the need.   The need was great on man's side, because of
sin; the need was great on God's side, because of holiness.
To come between the fires of human sinfulness and divine
holiness required human sinlessness and divine fullness,
qualifications that could only be found in the Man Christ
Jesus.   Think ye not, if it had been possible for a Holy God
to save sinners without the death of the Cross, would He not
have answered that agonizing prayer of His Son, accompanied with tears of blood, in the garden, when He cried,
"Father, if it be possible, let this cup pass from Me"
(Matt. 26. 39).   It was the love of God to a perishing
world that offered Him this awful cup; it was the holiness
of God that could not let it pass from Him if an end was to
be made of sin; and even when that blessed One was hanging
on the accursed tree He had to cry out, "My God! My God!
why hast Thou forsaken Me?" (Psa. 22. 1).   The holy
Father had to hide His face from His holy Son, because the
curse of imputed sin was upon Him.

Now to be an enemy of the Cross of Christ is to be an enemy to that holiness which is the character of God Another characteristic of those enemies referred to by the Apostle was that they "gloried in their shame" (Phil 3 19). To glory in things that are shameful is devilish To glory in anything that the Cross of Christ was meant to put away is to be an enemy of the Cross. The drunkard, the glutton, and the gambler, glories in how much they can appropriate for their own selfish ends The prosperous "man of the world" and the self-righteous bigot, who glory in the portion which they have in this life, are the enemies of the Cross of Christ To love sin is to hate the Cross. Sin is of the devil, holiness is of God Ye cannot serve these two masters Choose this day whom ye will serve The Cross of Christ stands for—

III **Divine Riches**   "He who did not withhold even His own Son but gave Him up for all of us, will He not also with Him freely give us all things" (Rom 8 32) The death of Christ is the divine pledge to all believers that every needful blessing is within their reach   "The condescending goodness of our Lord Jesus Christ was seen in that though He was rich he became poor, in order that we through His poverty might grow rich" (2 Cor 8. 9)   The treasure house of the unsearchable riches of Christ has been opened for us by the Blood of His Cross   When Christ gave Himself for us, He gave His all to us   These spiritual and eternal riches consist not only of what God has, but of what He is He not only gives gifts unto men, but He makes us, through faith, partakers of His own nature. These words of our Lord will surely have a deeper meaning for us when read in the light of His Cross. "Take no thought for your life, what ye shall eat, or what ye shall put on...your heavenly Father knoweth that ye have need of these things" (Luke 12. 22-31) Make the kingdom of God the object of your pursuit, and these things shall be

given you in addition. All is promised in the Cross, and
all may be claimed there. Every temporal and spiritual
blessing, every Pentecostal baptism, with all its joy and
power and fruitfulness, was potentially in the Cross of
Christ. Every conversion to God, every revival through
the Spirit of God, every outburst of missionary zeal for the
heathen, have all had their motive power from the Cross
of our Lord Jesus Christ.

Yet there are those who are the enemies of the Cross of
Christ, although that Cross is the symbol and pledge of
heavenly and eternal riches. The third characteristic Paul
mentions of those who are its enemies is that "they mind
earthly things." That is, their minds are wholly devoted to
the things of earth, they reject, or ignore, those heavenly
things provided for them by the death of Christ, and so
become the enemies of His Cross. The man whose heart is
set on earthly things has no portion in the Cross of Christ.
He died for us that we might set our affections on things
above. It may seem but a small offence to "mind earthly
things," but it is an offence against the spirit and purpose
of that Cross of which the Apostle Paul said, "The world is
crucified unto me, and I unto the world." If any man love
the world, the love of the Father, as manifested at Calvary,
is "not in him." The Cross of Christ also stands for—

IV. Divine Ultimatum. It is God's final offer as to
terms of peace. Regarding those enemies of the Cross,
Paul tells us "Their end is destruction." In rejecting the
sacrifice of Christ on the Cross, they rejected God's conditions of peace, and so went on to their doom. The wages
of sin is death. To live in opposition to the message and
claims of the Cross is to live in actual rebellion against the
last and greatest proposals of infinite love. How shall we
escape if we neglect so great salvation? God's terms
cannot be altered; the treaty of the Cross shall never be

broken. We are shut up to faith in Christ, or die in our sins and suffer the eternal judgment. Acquaint now thyself with God and be at peace. As many as receive Christ, receive the right to become the children of God, even as many as believe on His Name (John 1 12).

No 8.—THE FELLOWSHIP OF THE CROSS

"I have been crucified with Christ, and it is no longer I that live but Christ that lives in me and the life which I now live in the body I live through faith in the Son of God, who loved me and gave Himself up to death on my behalf" (Gal. 2. 20)

> "From pain to pain, from woe to woe,
> With loving heart and footsteps slow
> To Calvary with Christ we go
> Was ever grief like His? Was ever sin like ours?"

"I HAVE been crucified with Christ " The crucifixion of Jesus Christ, the second Adam, was potentially the cruci fixion of humanity All are represented in Him. It is a great discovery to make, that I have been crucified for my sins on the Cross of Christ. This is the discovery faith makes when the Gospel of Christ is believed. Have you seen it and received it; how that God has accepted the death of His only Son as your death for your own sins, that you might no longer live in sin, but in that newness of life which is yours in Him? The Lord was crucified about twelve months before Paul was converted, yet he says, "I have been crucified with Christ " It was a thing done before he was born of God. He had found out that the Lord Jesus Christ had so identified Himself with him and his sins that he (Paul) had been put to death for them with Christ on the Cross Now, he says, "It is no longer I that live, but Christ that lives in me. " The old self-confident life is dead, and now "I live through faith in the Son of God, who loved me and gave Himself up to death on my behalf. "

The Apostle does not speak of crucifying Himself. Self-crucifixion is impossible. No man could drive the nails into his own hands and feet. We are commanded to crucify the flesh with its passions and lusts, but who shall crucify that spirit that would exalt itself against God? that carnal mind which is enmity against God; who shall crucify it? "O wretched man that I am! Who shall rescue me from this death-burdened body? Thanks be to God through Jesus Christ our Lord" (Rom. 7. 24, 25). By the death which Christ died he became, once for all, dead in relation to sin. Likewise reckon or regard yourselves as dead in relation to sin (Rom. 6. 10, 11). Not our sins only, but our sinful selves have been, in the great redeeming purpose of God, nailed to His Cross. It is now, "Not I, but Christ who lives in me." I have been crucified with Christ, therefore I must reckon my sinful self as judged by God in His own Son on the accursed tree, and put in the place of death. Ye are dead, and your life is now hid with Christ in God. Blessed paradox—dead, yet alive! Wonderful mystery—Christ living in me!

All who have believed in the Lord Jesus Christ as their atoning sacrifice before God, have been by the Holy Spirit baptised into His death, that they might be sharers in His resurrection (Rom. 6. 3-5). There is no possibility of knowing the power of His resurrection in our souls, if we have not first been made conformable unto His death (Phil. 3. 10).

When the mother of Jesus saw her Son dying upon the Cross, and when the soldier "pierced His side with a spear," then were the prophetic words of old Simeon to Mary fulfilled, "Yea, a sword shall pierce through thine own soul also." She was pierced with Christ on the Cross. Had it not been for the faith and love that Mary had in and for her Lord and Saviour, the spear that cut the heart of Christ asunder would never have touched her soul. So it is

with us. If we believe that that awful death of the Cross
was voluntarily chosen and endured by Christ in love to our
sin-ruined souls, with that belief their springs up within the
soul a new affection for the suffering Son of God, a love so
pure and tender that the pangs of Christ's Cross pierce our
own souls, then hard-hearted, cold-hearted, sinful self is
crucified with Christ. We have never seen Christ pierced
for us to any advantage, unless we have felt the spear-
thrust of conviction in our own souls. Has the fact that
Christ was wounded and bruised for your iniquities ever
made any wound or bruise in your soul? If, through
unbelief or hardness of heart we refuse to "die as He died,"
then we can have no "share in His sufferings," and so
cannot "know the power which is in His resurrection."
Seeing that the crucifixion of self is such a definite and
painful experience, surely the effects of it will be marked
and well-defined. We shall try and point out a few of
them.

I. **The Crucifixion of the World.** In his letter to the
Galatians, Paul says, "But as for me, God forbid that I
should glory in anything except the Cross of our Lord
Jesus Christ, upon which the world is crucified to me"
(chap. 6. 14). To Paul the world had been stripped naked
of all its glory and power, and nailed as a helpless, shameful
thing on the Cross with Christ. To him it was a dead or a
dying thing, without power to tempt or tantalise his soul.
The glory of the grace of the crucified Christ had come
between him and the world, and so blinded his eyes with
the vision of heavenly things, that the things of this world
became to him as so many corpses. "If any man love the
world, the love of the Father is not in him." The workings
of the principles of this world found, as it were, their climax
in the crucifixion of the Son of God. The world by wisdom
could not find out God, it could only crucify Him, therefore
its ungodly spirit should be as a crucified thing to us.

II. **The Crucifixion of Self.** Not only is the world crucified to me, but "I am crucified to the world," adds the Apostle. The death of Christ has not only separated the world from me, but it has also separated me from the world. The Cross of Christ has come between me and the world, and has crucified it to me, and me to it. That "old self," which loved the world, and sought a share of its honour and glory, "was nailed to the Cross with Him, in order that our sinful nature might be deprived of its power, so that we should no longer be the slaves of sin" (Rom. 6. 6). He who has paid the penalty of death stands free from his sin (v. 7). The first act of self in Adam was to long for a forbidden thing. This is the self that was crucified with Christ—the self that would long for anything outside the good will of God. Although the self in Christ was perfectly human and perfectly sinless, yet "He pleased not Himself." He delighted to do the will of His Father. The demands of self are many and urgent, and usually put in the most plausible way, but every time self is pleased and honoured, the Cross of Christ is denied. One of the messages that comes through the Crucified One to us is, "I have died for you, in order that that self-life of yours might die in Me." "Except a corn of wheat die, it abideth alone." That self-life of yours will abide alone in barrenness and fruitlessness, unless it die, and is buried in the grave of Christ. But if it die—comes to an utter end of itself—it will bring forth the fruits of a new life in Christ Jesus. To be dead to the world is to be alive unto God, and abundantly fruitful in the world. To be crucified with Christ implies further—

III. **A New Life for Service.** "It is no longer I that live, but Christ that lives in me" (Gal. 2. 20). "Having become one with Him by sharing in His death, we shall also be one with Him by sharing in His resurrection" (Rom. 6. 5). If I reckon my self-life crucified with Christ, then I may reckon on Him living in me in the power of His resurrection. If self has died, then there is no hindrance to the life of Jesus being manifested in our mortal bodies (2 Cor. 4. 10) One of the clearest proofs that we have died to self and sin is that we are wholly "alive unto God." The measure of our life and liberty for God is the measure of our freedom from the power of self and sin. Self spells bondage in the service of the Lord. There is no room for it if Christ is to be glorified in us. If Christ lives in me, then He has taken this *me* that He might sanctify it, fill it, and use it for the glory of His own Name. To seek our own praise and honour is to deny Him who lives within. If Christ lives in me, then all the wealth of His unsearchable riches is within my reach for His service among men. "The Cross, as a moral event, belongs to all time," said Dr Gordon, therefore its power to crucify self, and prepare the way for resurrection life, is ever present with us. The life of the unregenerate man is, "I, not Christ;" the life of the regenerate man is, "Not I, but Christ." The Cross of Christ is a dreadful place, but is the gate of Heaven.

No. 9.—GLORYING IN THE CROSS.

"But as for me, God forbid that I should glory in anything except the Cross of our Lord Jesus Christ" (Gal. 6. 14).

> "On the Mount of Crucifixion
> Fountains opened deep and wide,
> Through the flood-gates of God's mercy
> Flowed a vast and gracious tide.
> Grace and love, like mighty rivers,
> Poured incessant from above,
> And Heaven's peace and perfect justice
> Kissed a guilty world in love."

C. H. SPURGEON said, "The heart of the Gospel is redemption, and the essence of redemption is the substitutionary Sacrifice of Christ. I have found by long experience that nothing touches the heart like the Cross of Christ." As it took the eyes of a Michael Angelo to see an angel in a rough slab of marble, so it takes the eyes of a Spirit-inspired man to see the glory of the Cross of Christ. What is a stumbling-stone to some is the wisdom of God to others.

There were several things in which the Apostle might have gloried, if the glory of the Cross had not blinded his eyes to the glory of everything else. Even as a Christian he might have gloried in his unique conversion, although he greatly rejoiced in it, and did not fail to speak of it as opportunity occurred. Yet he did not glory in being saved so much as in the fact that the Lord Jesus Christ had so loved him that He gave Himself to the death of the Cross on his behalf. "Hallelujah! I am saved," is not quite the same as "Hallelujah! Jesus Christ has saved me." It is better to be taken up with the glories of the Saviour than the comforts of salvation. He might have gloried in his unique position as an apostle to the Gentiles. But even the glory of his high calling was overshadowed with the glory of the Cross. Or, he might have gloried in his success as a minister of the Gospel and a servant of Jesus Christ. But no; he would glory in nothing else, because that "Christ and Him crucified" was the Source and Giver of all. The glory of His Cross can never be left behind as a "beggarly element" or a "first principle." It is everlastingly present in its eternal efficacy. Even in the heaven of glory, Jesus Christ is known as "the Lamb that was slain."

The preacher who has ceased glorying in the Cross of Christ has ceased preaching in the power of the Holy Spirit. The whole Counsel of God finds its centre in the Crucified One, therefore to glory in the Cross of Christ is to glory in the wisdom and power of God. "Let not the wise man glory in his wisdom, neither let the mighty man glory in his might, let not the rich man glory in his riches: but let

him that glorieth glory in this, that he understandeth and
knoweth Me" (Jer. 9. 23, 24). To know the meaning of the
Cross of Jesus Christ is to understand and know God, and to
glory in Him. To glory in any earthly thing is to deny the
Cross of Christ, and to rob God of His glory. "He that
glorieth, let him glory in the Lord." In these days few
seem to have the determination that Paul had: "Not to
know anything among you, save Jesus Christ, and Him
crucified" (1 Cor. 2. 2). Here are some good reasons why
we should glory in the Cross of our Lord Jesus Christ.

I. **By It the Love of the Father is Seen.** "God's love
for us has been manifested, in that He sent His only Son
into the world, so that we may have life through Him"
(1 John 4. 9). "For God so loved the world that He gave His
only begotten Son." His love for the world must have been
great to send His only Son even into a world like this; but
the depth and intensity of that love can only be realised
when we think of the infinite humiliation of the death of
the Cross. "This is love indeed; we did not love God, but
He loved us, and sent His Son to be an atoning sacrifice for
our sins" (1 John 4. 10). By giving His Son up to the
world for us is God's way of commending His love to us
(Rom. 5. 8). Even the wisdom of God could devise no
more impressive and powerful a way of manifesting His
love than this. We glory in the Cross, because herein is
the glory of His love.

II. **By It the Love of the Son is Declared.** "He loved
me, and gave Himself for me." "The Good Shepherd
giveth His life for the sheep" (John 10. 11). The greatest
manifestation of human love is "that a man should lay
down his life for his friend; but, while we were yet sinners,
Christ died for us." The many deep waters of human
indifference, ingratitude, mockery, and hate did not quench
or check the outflow of His love, for His was a love that

was stronger than death.   Those nail-prints in the hands
and feet, even of the glorified body of Jesus Christ, are the
everlasting monuments of that love that led Him to the
sacrifice of Himself upon Calvary's tree, as a ransom for the
sinful souls of men.   The warmth of Christ's love is only
equalled by the preciousness of His Blood.   Do we not hear
those searching words spoken to Peter coming home to our
own hearts, as from His dying lips on the Cross: "Lovest
thou Me?"   Think of all He has done for thee.

III. **By It Sinners are Reconciled to God.** "While we
were hostile to God we were reconciled to Him through the
death of His Son" (Rom. 5. 10).   The only way to the
enjoyment of the presence of God is through reconciliation;
the only way to reconciliation is through the death of His
Son.   The moment that the soul, which has hitherto been
hostile to God, takes hold by faith on that atoning Sacrifice
on the Cross, that moment the hand of God's power takes
hold of that soul, and instantly there is reconciliation and
salvation.   The Cross of Christ, like Jacob's ladder, was set
up on the earth as the way to God.   Here the angels of
grace, mercy, and peace ascend and descend upon the Son
of Man.   This is a dreadful place, but this the gate of
Heaven.   "Dreadful," as the place of judgment; "beautiful," as the gate of Heaven.   "I am the Way, the Truth,
and the Life, no man cometh unto the Father but by Me."
Acquaint now thyself with Him, and be at peace.   We
glory in the Cross, because that—

IV. **By It Believers are Separated from the World.**
This is the chief reason, given by the Apostle in Galatians
6. 14, why he gloried in nothing save the Cross of Christ,
"for," he says, "by it, or upon it, the world is crucified to
me, and I am crucified to the world."   To many this appears
more like a calamity than a victory.   To have the agonies
of Christ's Cross come between them and the pleasures and

false principles of this world is to them like being disin
herited. They wish to honour Jesus Christ as a teacher
come from God, but they don't wish His Cross to come in
and mar their fellowship with the world. Such cannot
glory in the Cross, because they are glorying in those things
which the Cross of Christ was meant to put away Paul
counted deliverance from this present evil world such a
great blessing that he gloried in that Cross by which this
marvellous achievement had been accomplished. A complete and final separation had been made, for, by the Cross,
both He and the world were crucified, the one to the other.
The sinful pleasures of the world are so subtle, powerful,
and treacherous that only by the power of His Cross can the
soul escape from their snares and illusions. Christ came
not to condemn the world, and the world in condemning
Christ, by casting Him out, has condemned itself, but out
of this condemnation, we who believe in Jesus have been
delivered. "Wherefore, come out from among them, and be
ye separate, saith the Lord." We glory in the Cross
because that—

V. By It Every Needful Blessing is Pledged. "He
who did not withhold even His own Son, but gave Him up
for all of us, will He not also with Him freely give us all
things" (Rom. 8. 32). He who delights to give golden gifts
will not grudge copper ones. God, in giving us the sunshine
has also with it freely given us all the colours with which
the eye is familiar. In giving us the sea, God has freely
given us all that is in it. In giving us His Son, all that
Christ was and has is, as it were, made over to us for life
and godliness. "Everything belongs to you, since you
belong to Christ, and Christ belongs to God" (1 Cor. 3.
21-23). Having overcome by the Blood of the Lamb, we
are made heirs of all things (Rev. 21. 7; Rom. 8. 17).
All the promises of God are in Christ, yea, and amen!
Being in Him, we become sharers with Him. To receive

Jesus Christ—the gift of God—as our Sacrifice, our Saviour, and our Lord, is to receive with Him God's unfailing promise that all things needful for time and eternity will be given freely. Surely this is a good reason for glorying in the Cross, but there is another—

VI. **In It Lies God's Remedy for all the Woes of the World.** "For so greatly did God love the world that He gave His only son" (John 3. 16). God so loved the world, that He gave to the world One who was abundantly able and willing to save it from all its sins, and to heal all its diseases. God's plaster is big enough to cover the world-wide sore of sin. God has no other remedy for the world's diseases than the Blood of His Son. Man-made mixtures are often substituted for the gift of God, and so often do they end in failure and disappointment. The health of the people is not recovered. There is no power like the Cross of Christ for healing the moral, social, and political plagues of the world. Every spiritual revival is a proof of this. Fresh, wholesome blood is infused into the man or the nation that bows believingly to the Son of God. As many as so touch Him are made whole. The world is an hospital, full of incurables, apart from the Divine remedy. There is none other Name under Heaven, given among men, whereby we can be saved. Over the portals of this world-wide gate the hand of inspiration has written: "JEHOVAH-ROPHECA" (The Lord that healeth thee). He, in His infinite wisdom, has made a special study of every individual case. His healing word never fails when it is trusted. God is able to save them to the uttermost that come to Him through His Son. "By His stripes we are healed."

Have you realised this vital fact, that God's provision for the sins and sorrows of your own soul is here for you in the death of His own Son! The hand that lays hold on it may be feeble, but the blessing grasped is the all-sufficient

mercy and power of God   All the virtue that is in Jesus
Christ is yours for a touch (Matt. 11. 21).

> "She only touched the hem of His garment,
>   As to His side she stole
> Amid the crowd that gathered around Him,
>   And straightway she was whole.
>
>   Oh, touch the hem of His garment!
>   And thou, too, shalt be free.
>   His saving power this very hour
>   Shall give new life to thee."

Can you now say· "As for me, God forbid that I should
glory in anything except the Cross of our Lord Jesus
Christ?" (Gal. 6. 14).

OUR CITIZENSHIP.

A CITIZEN is one entitled to all the privileges of a city,
and who trades with the goods of that city for his own
benefit and that of his fellow-men. "Our citizenship is in
Heaven." Are we claiming all the privileges of the
heavenly city? Are we trading with the things which
belong to that city, for the enriching of our own souls and
the profiting of others? The Great Lord Mayor of this
heavenly city will take pleasure in every such true and
honourable citizen.

THE LIGHT OF THE GOSPEL.

WHEN the sun shines in at our window it does not light
only that part which is directly accessible to its rays, but
every part of the room is illumined, and everything in it is
manifested by the light. When the word of the Gospel of
Christ is believed it will be as the shining of the sun into
the heart, bringing the light of life to the soul, and lighting
up all the dark places within the chamber of the heart
Thus our true relationships and responsibilities to God
and men are clearly revealed. "In Thy light shall we see
light clearly."

SEED THOUGHTS.

CHEER FOR THE TROUBLED.
JOHN 16. 33.

1. The Place of **Trial**, ... "In the world."
2. The Secret of **Victory**, .. "I have overcome."
3. A Word of **Comfort**, ... "Be of good cheer."

DIVINE CLEANSING.
1 JOHN 1. 7.

1. The **Disease**, ... "Sin."
2. The **Remedy**, ... "The Blood of Jesus."
3. The **Result**, ... "Cleansing."

DIVINE KEEPING.
ISAIAH 26. 3.

1. The **Keeper**, ... "Thou wilt keep him."
2. The **Keeping**, ... "In perfect peace."
3. The **Kept**, .. "Whose mind is stayed on Thee."

BLESSED SERVICE.
MATTHEW 11. 29.

1. The **Yoke**, ... "My yoke upon you."
2. The **Example**, ... "Learn of Me."
3. The **Reason**, ... "For I am meek."
4. The **Promise**, ... "Ye shall find rest."

BEWARE.
GALATIANS 6. 7.

1. A Great **Responsibility**, "Whatsoever a man soweth."
2. An **Unchanging Law**, .. "That shall he also reap."
3. An **Unalterable Fact**, .. "God is not mocked."
4. A **Solemn Warning**, ... "Be not deceived."

MIGHTY TO SAVE.
MATTHEW 9. 35.

JESUS CHRIST is—
1. A Wise Saviour, ... "Teaching."
2. A Gracious Saviour, .. "Preaching the Gospel."
3. A Mighty Saviour, .. "Healing every disease."
4. A Willing Saviour, ... "He went about."

GOOD CHEER FOR WORKERS.
ACTS 18. 9, 10.

1. The **Work**, . "Speak and hold not thy peace."
2. The **Assurance**, "Be not afraid, I am with thee."
3. The **Promise**, .. "No man shall hurt thee."
4. The **Prospect**, .. "I have much people in this city."

TO-DAY
HEBREWS 3. 15.

1. A Precious **Privilege**, .. "Hear His voice."
2. A Possible **Danger**, "Harden...your hearts."
3. A Present **Opportunity**, ... "To-day"

RAHAB'S SALVATION.
HEBREWS 11. 31.

1. Her **Character**, ... "Harlot."
2. Her **Danger**, .. Living among them that perished.
3. Her **Deliverance**, .. "She perished not."
4. Her **Faith**, .. "By faith she perished not."
5. Her **Works**, .. . "She received the spies."
FAITH WITHOUT WORKS IS DEAD.

WHOSOEVER WILL.
JOHN 6. 37.

1. A Great **Opportunity**, ... "Come to Me."
2. A World-Wide **Offer**, ... "Him that."
3. A Simple **Condition**, ... "Cometh."
4. A Precious **Promise**, "I will in no wise cast out."

FOUR THINGS JESUS WILL DO.
MATTHEW 3. 11, 12.
HE will—

1. "Baptise you."   3. "Gather His wheat."
2. "Purge His floor."   4. "Burn the chaff."

LIFE FOR A LOOK.
JOHN 6. 40.

1. The **Promise,** .. .. .. "Everlasting life."
2. The **Person,** .. .. "The Son."
3. The **Purpose,** .. .. .. "Him that sent Me."
4. The **Condition,** .. .. .. "Seeth...believeth."
5. The **Offer,** .. .. "Every one."
6. The **Encouragement,** .. "This is the will of Him."

THE SAVIOUR.
MATTHEW 1. 21.

1. Who He is. "Thou shalt call His name Jesus," not Moses.

2. What He does. "He shall save," He does not try to save, He does it.

3. Whom He saves. "His people." All who receive Him (John 1. 12).

4. How He saves. "From their sins." Sin brings death (Rom. 6. 23).

A PRECIOUS PROMISE.
MATT. 28. 18-20.

1. Who is the Promiser? Jesus, He who has all power given unto Him in Heaven and in earth.

2. What is the Promise? It is the promise of His presence. "Lo, I am with you alway."

3. Why is it Precious? It is precious (1) Because it is true. "He is faithful who has promised." (2) Because it implies all-sufficiency, both for earth and Heaven. He has all power.

FULL ASSURANCE.
2 TIMOTHY 1. 12.

To have this full assurance implies—

1. A personal **Knowledge** of His character. "For I know WHOM."

2. A personal **Faith** in His Word. "I know whom I have believed."

3. A personal **Committal** to His keeping. "That which I have committed unto Him."

4. A personal **Conviction** of His ability. "And am persuaded that He is able to keep."

HEREIN IS LOVE.
LUKE 15. 20.

1. A love that is **paternal**. "His father saw him."

2. A love that is **quick-sighted**. "He saw him a long way off."

3. A love that is **sympathetic**. "He had compassion."

4. A love that is **eager to help**. "He ran."

5. A love that **yields its all**. "He fell on his neck." In giving himself he gave his all.

6. A love that **delights to forgive**. "He kissed him."

THE SAVING NAME.
PSALM 9. 10.

1. **A Needful Knowledge.** They that know Thy name. All the significance of God's character is in His Name (Exod. 33. 19). Christ is the revelation of this Name in its eternal fullness.

2. **A Blessed Result.** "Shall put their trust in Thee." To know His Name is to know Him, whom to know is life eternal. To know Him is to love, trust, and obey Him.

3. **A Universal Encouragement.** "Thou, Lord, hast not forsaken them that seek Thee." Seek and ye shall find. His Name is the guarantee of this.

ILLUSTRATIONS.

GIFTS NEGLECTED.

It is a well known fact that "cave fishes" are blind. The reason for this, we are told, is "that the continuous disuse of the organs does, in time, react on the nutrition of the parts affected, and, finally, atrophy or disappearance is the result. " Darwin confessed that since "his mind seemed to have become a kind of machine for grinding general laws out of large collections of facts, he had lost all taste for poetry or music. " This is a law in the spiritual world, as well as in the natural. Stir up the gift that is in thee. If faith is to be nourished and strengthened, and saved from atrophy, it must be exercised.

SPIRITUAL INFLUENCE.

Park Benjamin, in his "Age of Electricity, " explains to us how that "around the pole of a magnet there exists a strange atmosphere, a so-called 'field of force,' in which exists strains, and pulls, and pushes, as if a host of infinitesimal beings were at work. " This mysterious but real and potent influence of the magnet is a true symbol of that spiritual power which is always associated with that soul which is filled with the mighty Holy Spirit of God.

DWELL DEEP.

Geologists assure us that there still exists in the deep sea "living species of animals which, in former geologic periods dwelt in the coastal districts of the ocean. " Here they seemed to have found an asylum from the dangers which seemed to threaten their very existence. Our safety, like theirs, depends upon our dwelling deep in the eternal God, who is a refuge for us (Psa. 46. 1).

WORKERS.

THERE is a great difference between the ant and the jackdaw as workers. The ant takes advantage of accidental circumstances, while the jackdaw fails. If it cannot enter the narrow aperture leading to the nest, with the little branch in its bill crosswise, will drop it. If you have a work to do and cannot succeed in the way you expected. don't drop it. If your purpose will not work crosswise, try it longwise. If the word of the Gospel will not enter broadwise, try it edgewise; but, in anywise, don't play the jackdaw by dropping it.

UNION.

SOME pieces of matter have a marvellous power of attraction when they are brought into close contact with one another. How difficult, for instance, it is to separate two equal bits of polished glass when they have been placed against each other! The secret of this inseparable union lies in the fact that there is nothing on either side of the pieces to hinder the adhesion. If our union with Christ, or with one another, is to be close and abiding, there must be nothing between. No grit of unconfessed sin or uncharitableness. On Christ's side there is a perfect plane, on our side there may be much unevenness, but the plane of the Holy Spirit is equal to the plane of the Holy Son, so that in the Spirit there may be perfect oneness.

BENEFITS OF ADVERSITY.

IT is an acknowledged fact that the "dim evening twilight" is much more favourable for profitable reflection, as "much light stimulates the optic nerve to a degree that distracts the attention." The "much light" of prosperity has often the effect of distracting the attention from the more enduring things; while the dimness of adversity proves more suitable for spiritual reflection.

IMMORTALITY.

IT is a well-authenticated fact that migratory birds (quails) although born in captivity and well domesticated, will, at the time of migration, dash themselves against their cages in their eagerness for liberty and change. This instinct is part of their nature, and no matter where they have been born, or how they have been brought up, it shows itself at certain times. So is it with man in regard to his desire for immortality. No matter where he has been born, or in what circumstances he has been reared, like migratory birds, this instinct does in some way or other assert itself. This instinct in the bird would not be there if there were not a corresponding something somewhere to meet that inborn desire.

CREATED ANEW.

EVERY seven years the whole structure of the body is said to be renewed. Every moment of our lives we are throwing off the old and putting on the new. This is the law of a healthy physical life. It is also the law of a healthy spiritual life. Put off the old man (self) with his deeds, and put on the new man (Christ). Abiding in Christ we are created anew unto good works. Although the body is constantly changing, the individuality remains the same. Regeneration by the Holy Spirit does not destroy individual responsibility.

TEMPTATIONS.

TEMPTATIONS may be evidences of spiritual life and wealth. Why is it that the Dead Sea has never the "deep-sounding roar" of the ocean? Because it is dead. Why is it that it is never visited by the flight of gulls, or pelicans, or sea-mews? Why is it that all "migratory birds sweep over it without even a pause to seek for prey?" Because it is dead. Why is it that the unconverted are not visited with the temptations of the Christian? Because of the same reason.

HOW TO BE BLESSED.

SOMETHING akin to the laws of nature are often seen at work in the spiritual world. Why do the refreshing showers of Heaven never fall upon the great sandy desert? Humboldt explains that "the more barren the surface and the greater the degree of heat acquired by the sand, the higher will be the ascent of the clouds, and the less readily will the vapours be precipitated." The life that is destitute of the moist of the grace of God and warm with the enthusiasm of self-confidence can never become a fruitful garden unto the Lord. The more intensely we pour forth the warmth of our fleshly energy, the farther off must the cloud of spiritual blessing go.

THE DOOM OF THE UNFIT.

IT is a universal fact that any living thing not properly equipped for all the circumstances of that life into which it may be brought is doomed to die. For every sphere of existence a corresponding fitness is needed. For the spiritual sphere of the kingdom of God a spiritual fitness is needed. Without this inward adjustment of character to the circumstances of the heavenly and eternal life there is the sentence of death. Except a man be born again he cannot see the Kingdom of God.

REALITY OR SHAM?

THERE is a great difference between mother-of-pearl and soap bubbles. Yet the same variety and richness of colour characterise both; but the value and enduring power of the one is infinitely greater than the other. It is quite possible to have many points of resemblance to the true Christian life and yet be as destitute of the real virtue—in the sight of God—as the soap bubble is of the worth of mother-of-pearl. Soap-bubble Christians will never stand the test of the fiery trial.

POWER AND SERVICE.

ALL light and power depend upon having their own proper condition. A red-hot chip of wood bursts into flame when plunged into a jar of oxygen. A soul red-hot with heavenly zeal, when baptised into the atmosphere of the Holy Ghost, will burst into a flame of mighty power for God, a flame that all the storms and opposing forces of earth and hell will not be able to extinguish. But, as a successful burning depends upon the constant presence of the oxygen, so a continual and successful burning testimony for God depends upon our abiding in the power of the presence of the Holy Ghost. "I am full of power by the Spirit of the Lord" (Micah 3. 8). Be filled with the Spirit.

NEGLECT.

SHELLEY, the poet, would sometimes ask his wife, "Mary, have I dined?" after having left his plate upon his book-shelf for hours untouched. A dinner on the shelf could not satisfy his hunger any more than a Bible on the shelf will satisfy yours. Take it and use it, then you will not be in any doubt as to whether you have profited by it or not.

THE DECEITFULNESS OF SIN.

THE fishing frog, as described by Professor Forbes, is a most deceitful creature. This artful dodger lives to deceive and to destroy. On the top of its head it has two long, moveable, bony filaments, one of which has a silvery lustre; this is waved to and fro to tempt the little fish, which is attracted by it, expecting something to eat, while the monster, with its horrible mouth, lies half buried in the sand or mud beneath. Beneath every sin lies the hungry jaws of death. Sin has often the appearance of a silvery delight, and there may be a momentary pleasure in it, but "sin, when it is finished, bringeth forth death."

RESPONSIBILITY.

PLANTS shut themselves up at the approach of night, and open to the dawn of morning. Consider the plants how they grow. The darkness of sin and doubt cannot add to the beauty of the Christian life. We cannot avoid coming into contact with such darkness, but, like the plants, we can close up our being to its hurtful influence.

SUBTLE, SINFUL SELF.

A TRAVELLER in South Africa says: "It is remarkable how the vultures seem to escape from a cavern in the sky when a carcase is left exposed for a few minutes. A little while ago not one was visible, now they feed on the putrid body." How like this is to the workings of sinful self. We imagined that the world-loving, self-seeking spirit within was dead and buried out of sight. And it may be for a time no trace of its movements have been detected, but some temptation comes suddenly, some opportunity for self-honour or worldly applause. Then how quickly, like a vulture from the fathomless blue, does the old proud spirit show itself, ready and hungry for the carrion of self-exaltation.

EATING AND WORKING.

PALLAS, in his travels, has pointed out that those herbivorous animals which get their food easily are usually indolent and possess little mental activity, while the carnivorous are more lively and prompt; their sensations are more intense. These two classes of animals seem to represent two classes of Christians. The first find what they eat without any difficulty at all; there is no eager searching of the Word, and there is always a dullness about their spiritual sensibilities. The other class search the Scriptures as for hidden spoil; they make it their business to discover fresh food for the new life, and so they keep wide awake and active in the work of the Lord.

PRIVILEGE NOT ENOUGH.

MODERN scientists teach us that it is quite possible that
the distant Saturn may be a very warm world, while
Mercury, so very near the sun, may be a cold one. This
depends on the character of the atmosphere of each. The
atmosphere is a world's capacity for receiving and retaining
that heat which is the gift of the sun. Every man is a
miniature world in the universe of God. His faith, or his
unbelief, determines his capacity for receiving, or not
receiving, those things freely given him of God. He may
be near in point of privilege, and yet afar off in point of
experience.

INVISIBLE THINGS.

SPIRITUAL things cannot be seen by the carnally-minded,
any more than those atom creatures, which find a world of
space in a drop of water, can be seen by the unaided eye.
But how foolish it would be to say that no such creatures
exist because they cannot be discerned without the help of a
powerful microscope. The powerful lens of a living faith
is needed to see spiritual and eternal things. To those
whose eyes are opened by the Spirit of God a new world of
life and beauty appears in every drop of water in that ocean
of God's revealed truth. The unaided eye hath not seen,
nor hath the unaided ear even heard the things which God
hath prepared for them that love Him

"The weightiest and highest truths, which most quicken
and comfort the faithful, confound the ungodly."

—Gossner.